THE ILLEGAL CITY

Gender, Space and Society

Series Editors: Peter Hopkins, University of Newcastle, UK and Dr Rachel Pain, Durham University, UK

The series on Gender, Space and Society aims to publish innovative feminist work that analyses men's and women's lives from a perspective that exposes and is committed to challenging social inequalities and injustices. The series reflects the ongoing significance and changing forms of gender, and of feminist ideas, in diverse social, geographical and political settings.

The themes it covers include, but are not restricted to:

- The constitution and transformation of gender in different political and economic regimes around the world.
- Men's and women's lived experiences of femininities and masculinities in diverse spaces and environments.
- The ways in which gender is co-constituted and intersects with a range of other social identities, such as race, ethnicity, nationality, class, age, generation, religion, (dis)ability, sexual orientation, body size and health status in different places and times.
- Challenging distinctions and offering new understandings of the relationships between public/private, economic/social (re)production, geopolitical/intimate and so on.
- Destabilising the binary man/woman, and developing more complex ways of understanding gendered social and spatial relations.
- Developing theoretical perspectives that shed light on the changing nature of gender relations, such as indigenous, postcolonial, queer, Marxist, poststructuralist and non-representational feminist theories.
- Exploring innovation in methodology, praxis, knowledge co-production and activism as means of challenging social injustices.

The Illegal City
Space, Law and Gender in a Delhi Squatter Settlement

AYONA DATTA
University of Leeds, UK

ASHGATE

Published by
Ashgate Publishing Limited
Wey Court East
Union Road
Farnham
Surrey, GU9 7PT
England

Ashgate Publishing Company
Suite 420
101 Cherry Street
Burlington
VT 05401-4405
USA

www.ashgate.com

British Library Cataloguing in Publication Data
Datta, Ayona.
  The illegal city : space, law and gender in a Delhi squatter settlement. – (Gender, space and society)
  1. Squatter settlements–Government policy–India–Delhi. 2. Squatters–Legal status, laws, etc.–India–Delhi. 3. Squatters–India–Delhi–Attitudes. 4. Sociology, Urban–India–Delhi.
  I. Title II. Series
  307.3'364'095456-dc23

Library of Congress Cataloging-in-Publication Data
Datta, Ayona.
  The illegal city : space, law and gender in a Delhi squatter settlement / by Ayona Datta.
    p. cm. – (Gender, space and society)
  Includes bibliographical references and index.
  ISBN 978-1-4094-4554-8 (hbk. : alk. paper) – ISBN 978-1-4094-4555-5 (ebook) 1. Squatter settlements–India–Delhi. 2. Slums–Government policy–India–Delhi. 3. Squatters–Legal status, Laws, etc.–India–Delhi. 4. Urban poor–India–Delhi–Social conditions. 5. City planning–India–Delhi. 6. Urban policy–India–Delhi. I. Title.
  HD7287.96.I42D454 2012
  307.3'364095456–dc23

2012022751

ISBN 9781409445548 (hbk)
ISBN 9781409445555 (ebk)

Printed and bound in Great Britain by the MPG Books Group, UK

To

My grandmother who encouraged me to write this book
My mother who gave me my first feminist vocabulary
and
Riddhima who made me question that vocabulary

Contents

List of Figures

Acknowledgements

This book would not have been possible without the support, cooperation and assistance of Lakshmipuri Camp (name changed) residents at every step of my fieldwork. They watched out for me, gave me and my research assistant innumerable cups of tea and coffee and were extremely generous in giving their time answering questions and giving us an insight into their everyday lives. For that and much more, I will remain forever grateful.

My gratitude also goes to my research assistant Ritu Mishra, who worked tirelessly everyday in collecting data, recruiting participants, building trust among participants and keeping a meticulous journal account of his interactions. The timely completion of my fieldwork is due largely to his initiative and hard work.

The participant interviews were transcribed and translated by a number of freelancers. Of them, Asha Achuthan worked on the bulk of the files and despite the huge time pressures, was a star and delivered them all on time. Sreerupa Mitra Sen, Shibani Bose and employees of Transworx worked on the rest of the interviews files and produced professional results. To them all I am grateful.

The research in this book was funded by the British Academy Small Research Grants (Award no SG-39255) in 2005–2006. I remain grateful for these funds which paid for my fieldwork, recruiting of research assistant, remuneration to participants and transcription/translation of interviews. I began analyzing the data and writing this book in 2009 during my three month sabbatical in the London School of Economics. I am grateful for the time away from my teaching duties which allowed me to focus on a book idea.

The discussions in this book have benefitted from feedback during a number of invited lectures/seminars in – Centre for Research in the Social Sciences and Humanities, University of Cambridge; Department of Geography, University College London; Centre for Study of Regional Development and Women's Studies Programme, Jawaharlal Nehru University (JNU), Delhi; National Institute of Urban Affairs, Delhi; Ben Gurion University of the Negev, Israel; Department of Geography, University of Bristol; Department of Geography, King's College London; Cities Programme, London School of Economics. I am particularly grateful to the audience in these venues, and to discussant feedbacks from Kalyani Menon-Sen and Amita Baviskar in JNU, Abdou Maliq Simone in King's College, and Oren Yiftachel in Ben Gurion University. Different aspects of this book's ideas have also been presented in a number of conferences in – Association of American Geographers Annual Meeting in Chicago, 2006; World Historical Association Annual Conference in London, 2008; Women's Worlds Conference in Madrid, Spain, 2008; The Right to the City: New Challenges, New Issues in Vadstena, Sweden, 2008. A note of appreciation also to Katherine Brickell for providing feedback on the Introduction to this book. Lastly, I am grateful for critical comments from Jenny Robinson and John Sidel on earlier drafts, which helped me become more postcolonial in my approach.

I am grateful to the Ashgate editorial team, particularly Katy Crossan for her professionalism and promptness in answering queries on various issues relating to publication. I am also grateful to the series editors Rachel Pain and Peter Hopkins for reading my manuscript and supporting the book idea.

Finally, I am grateful to my family for constant moral and emotional support throughout the years of research and writing. Most importantly, words cannot express my gratitude to my life partner, friend and critic Rohit Madan who encouraged me to keep going, especially when I myself could not see the end of this journey. I am grateful to him for proofreading the entire manuscript as well as for tirelessly providing childcare and housekeeping while I finished this book. This book could not have been completed without him.

Introduction

In 2002, on a late winter morning, a municipal bulldozer rumbled into a squatter settlement in Delhi and randomly demolished a few houses along the main road. The family members were inside but managed to rush out just before the roof collapsed. When challenged by residents, the municipal officers said that they had warrants to demolish the unauthorized construction on the main road and that they would be back to demolish more houses in a few days.

When I came into the settlement later that day, I was given graphic descriptions by other residents of the injustice of this action taken by the municipality. The crowd that had gathered around the broken houses argued that it was unjust to demolish a 'poor man's hut'; that it was illegal to do this without giving any formal notice to those affected; and that this was above all an 'act of cowardice' by the municipality to demolish a poor squatter home, which at the time was inhabited by women and children. I hung around till the evening that day because I was told that there would be a public meeting organized by the women's collective. As it started to get dark, I saw people gathering around near the tree on the main road. Very soon I recognized a couple of women walking in who were from a feminist NGO and worked with the resident women's organization. When everyone settled down, the *panchayat*[1] leader picked up the microphone and began denouncing the demolition. Soon, a few more men picked up the microphone to denounce the government for criminalizing the poor. They challenged the procedures of law, calling this the arm of the state, and its enforcement as violations of the state's legal duty of care towards those most vulnerable (women and children). Residents deliberated upon valid forms of social and political action that would deliver desirable outcomes, decided to visit the local MP's office to protest against this incident and to demand to see concrete plans for their future. The next day, they returned with assurances that they would be provided resettlement but that the terms (or location) of this has not yet been finalized. In the next few days, the families rebuilt their demolished houses and moved back in.

Such demolitions of 'illegal' settlements are common in Delhi and other parts of the global south. I begin with this incident because it occurred in the aftermath of a series of court rulings in India since 2000, when across Delhi and in other Indian cities, a wave of demolitions of 'unauthorized' structures were not just judicially sanctioned, but the municipality and local authorities were warned of severe consequences by the Supreme Court if they failed to comply with these

---

1 Panchayat is a form of traditional rural local governance and is derived from the oldest judicial systems in India where decisions were taken by a group of five (usually male) elderly members of a collective.

Figure I.1   Demolished house on the main road in a Delhi squatter settlement. Photo: Author 2002

Figure I.2   Public meeting under the tree on the main road in a Delhi squatter settlement. Photo: Author 2002

orders. In this context, the legal status of squatter settlements suddenly acquired immense significance. The judicial rulings radically reordered Delhi's urban spaces to remove squatter settlements and to make way for an extended and contested process of resettlement of its residents to the peripheries of the city. During this process, a judicial interpretation of a law that labelled squatters as 'pickpockets' of public land and hence illegal urban citizens produced a 'violence of law' (Benjamin 1978) in the lives of squatters.

In Delhi's Masterplan, the settlement I was studying was classified as a *jhuggi jhopri* (JJ) colony, which meant that they were living on land which they did not legally own. Most of the residents were eligible (in principle) for resettlement since they had settled on this land during the late 1970s to the early 1980s, before the cut-off date of 1989 fixed by the courts for providing resettlement (I will discuss this issue in more detail in Chapter 4). This had however, been the case with many other squatter settlements in the city which since 2001 were demolished but their residents were not always resettled. Since 2002, residents in this settlement had been assured by a variety of 'official' sources (including slum officials and local MPs) that their homes would be demolished and 'eligible' residents resettled. They did not know its terms because the terms kept changing every time there was a new MP or a new ruling party. Once they were told that they would be moved to the resettlement colonies being developed on Delhi's urban peripheries, another time that they would be re-housed on the same land on high-rise blocks. They did not desire high-rise living, nor did they want to move outside the city, but they perceived that demolition of their homes was their inevitable future.

Waiting for resettlement

In his critique of violence, Walter Benjamin wrote – 'law-preserving violence is a threatening violence. Its threat is not intended as the deterrent … This makes it all the more threatening, like fate' (Benjamin 1978: 285). (Benjamin 1978)Benjamin gave the example of criminal punishments, but this is relevant for those squatter settlements awaiting resettlement by the state. Law-preserving violence is the violence that ensures the enforceability of a rule of law, which Derrida (1992) calls the 'force of law'. In the case of squatters, the force of law by order of court, threatens them with demolitions of their 'illegal' homes in squatter settlements. Their only hope then remains in receiving state sponsored resettlement.

Waiting occupies the space between a rule of law and its enforcement. Waiting is an unsettling experience because it is lived as a threat. It means that one is never certain when this wait will end and what will be the outcome of this waiting. It means that one is continually living in a sense of transience. And it means that even if there was previously a sense of security about their homes, in the process of waiting, this has given way to a sense of impatience and anxiety about future. These anxieties are related to the perceived erasure of the family through the demolition of their homes and to the desire for a permanent and secure home in the city. I found that while these anxieties provoked a need to be seen as 'legal' they also shaped participation in local politics, a desire to seize control of particular spaces and places of social power, and a need to reinforce ideological notions of home and family in everyday life.

Demolition is not a condition that squatters desire. They have accepted it as the only route to a legitimate status in the city, because if demolished, they might receive resettlement from the state. The men and women, whom I interviewed, were often disparaging or cynical about any connection between law and justice. Yet in 2005, as a 'culture of legality' (Comaroff and Comaroff 2006) began to pervade urban life and led to a spate of demolitions of squatter settlements across Delhi and other Indian metropolitan cities, residents were anxious about aspects of law that would shape their future in the city. They were certain that in the future there would be no place in Delhi for the type of illegality vested in squatter settlements. They attempted to present themselves as 'legal' at all costs, while also at the same time maintaining a disdainful attitude towards the rule of law, its agents through which law was enforced, and the possibilities of a fair deal for them within procedural justice. As the desire for legalization began to surface repeatedly in interviews with participants, so did the simultaneous acceptance of demolition as a route towards the legal city.

This book is set in this context of transience. It is about the fears, uncertainties, anxieties and manipulations that people engage in when threatened simultaneously by a violence of law and its judicial interpretation. In the case of the settlement under study, this transience has extended over a long period – since 2000 when the judiciary decided that all illegal slums were to be removed from the city. Since then, the anxieties, uncertainties and speculations increased around their future location in the city. But none of them expected this moment to last very long – Delhi's aspirations to become a world city through the 2010 Commonwealth Games (which spurred the removal of illegal slums from the city) had ironically produced hopes of resettlement for all 'eligible' squatters. Yet, beyond the Games, this and many other squatter settlements are still awaiting resettlement. This book then captures a temporal moment in the everyday life of squatters in contemporary Delhi when they encountered law within their everyday spaces and consequently transformed their social relationships with the city and with each other.

In this book, I focus on the particular kinds of politics around space, law and gender, which are produced from within this temporality of waiting. I saw this in the public meeting in 2002 where the men were most vocal – they made announcements over the microphone, they called other residents to attend the meeting and they spread the carpets under the tree on the main road for everyone to sit on. The men suggested different options and then took hand-counts of residents to decide upon the course of action with respect to the demolition. When the residents decided to march to the local MP's house in protest, the men agreed to organize this action and raise money to hire the van to take the residents there. When I asked the women's collective members why they were not more vocal, they said that they would prefer the men to take some responsibility because women 'already had enough on their hands'. The men, who I asked the same question on the other hand, said that it was because they were more capable of dealing with political parties and municipality, who in turn preferred to deal with men rather than women. It seemed then that it was not just the dialectics of law and illegality that had transformed squatters' relationship with the state; rather this dialectic had led to a fundamental transformation in the nature of gendered power relationships amongst themselves.

The informal city and the illegal city

> The urban poor are trapped in an informal and 'illegal' world – in slums that are not reflected on maps, where waste is not collected, where taxes are not paid and where public services are not provided. Officially, they do not exist. As illegal or unrecognized residents, many of these slum dwellers have no property rights, nor security of tenure, but instead make whatever arrangements they can in an informal, unregulated and, in some respects, expensive parallel market. (UN-Habitat 2003: 6)

> The *informal city and the city of illegality* comprises the slums of the developing megacities and where the informal sector has its base; where services are poor or non-existent; where residents are invisible to legal status systems; and where harassment by authorities is commonplace. (UN-Habitat 2003: 23) [My emphasis]

In 2003, the UN report *Challenge of the Slums* (UN-Habitat 2003) highlighted what they considered to be an alarming trend in the growth of slums worldwide. Characterized by overcrowding, substandard and/or informal housing, inadequate access to clean water and sanitation, and insecure tenure, the megacities of Asia, Africa and Latin America were seen as leading the growth in slums. The report suggested that informal *and* illegal settlements occupied land that did not belong to them, and hence were most vulnerable and marginalized when it came to accessing urban basic services. These 'illegal cities' constituted the official image of the slum – as places of informality, crime and disease.

The 'informal city' and the 'illegal city' are often tied together as one and the same thing in urban development – as places of urban poor, of non-existent services, of marginalization and largely located in the rapidly globalizing megalopolises of the south (UN-Habitat 2003). There are however, huge divergences in the degrees of 'illegality' associated with slums in different contexts. UN classifies slum typologies based on their morphologies as inner-city slums, slum estates, squatter settlements, illegal settlements and subdivisions (UN-Habitat 2003). But it is in fact squatter settlements that occupy land without legal rights, which are considered illegal. Since urban development is regulated through zoning and land use laws, the absence of land rights often results in forced evictions of squatters from public land.

Let us take the example of Delhi in Table I.1. The different typologies of settlements have different relationships with informality and illegality within Delhi's Masterplan (I will discuss this at length in Chapter 2). Squatter settlements are denoted by *jhuggi jhopri* or 'JJ clusters' which are largely built on land occupied outside formal processes. They have poor quality housing and services, and house more than 20 percent of the urban population. These are usually both informal and illegal. 'Slum designated areas' are those given a statutory status under the 1956 Slum Act in India and might include a range of settlements from JJ clusters to historic neighbourhoods with 'slum-like' conditions. These places are eligible for formal intervention by the state in terms of infrastructure and housing and not all of these are informal or illegal. 'Unauthorized colonies' can also include elite gated communities built on illegally occupied land or in violation of the masterplan – hence they can be planned or unplanned, formal or informal. On the other hand, regularized-unauthorized colonies are those informal/illegal colonies which have been given legal tenure retrospectively. JJ clusters and (rural and urban) villages can be classified as informal settlements since they are usually built outside of (or in violation of) formal planning processes. Yet, rural and urban villages are not 'illegal' in terms of planning and urban development laws. JJ clusters, urban villages, unauthorized colonies and even resettlement colonies are often classified under a more generic language of 'slum', yet the everyday experiences of law, regulation and urban development for those living in JJ clusters differ sharply from those in other types of slums on account of their relationship with law.

Table I.1   Types of settlements in Delhi in 2000. (Planning Department 2001: 129)

No.	Type of settlement	Approx. population in million
1	JJ clusters	2.072
2	Slum designated areas	2.664
3.	Unauthorized colonies	0.74
4	Resettlement colonies	1.776
5	Rural villages	0.74
6	Regularized-unauthorized colonies	1.776
7	Urban villages	0.888
8	Planned colonies	3.308

Despite the divergent connections between slums and law, scholarship on slums is dominated by a conceptual focus on informality. The notion of informality established by scholars on Latin American slums since the 1970s have celebrated the initiative and creativity of those living in these settlements and argued against the 'culture of poverty' logics of urban development (Perlman 1976). Informality as 'a system of spatialized practices' (Roy 2003a: 15) is seen to be produced simultaneously by the modernist logics of urban planning (Roy and AlSayyad 2004, Roy 2005) and by the social networks through which the urban poor procure basic services and goods (Simone 2004). Roy highlights that the informal is in fact produced when the state deliberately suspends formal norms, and it is the state that has the 'power to determine when to enact this suspension, to determine what is informal and what is not, and to determine what forms of informality will thrive and what will not' (Roy 2005: 149). These approaches are useful in understanding the context of squatter settlements in so far as the status quo between the formal and informal city is sustained through the founding and maintaining violence of law and urban development.

Approaching the slum conceptually through informality however, assumes law as tangential to the concerns of the urban poor. Scholarship on informality do not distinguish illegality from informality in that they include both 'legal' and 'illegal' slums within the same frame of analysis. Illegality is often subsumed within the practices of informality both in the examination of everyday lives of squatters and in the practices of the state. Informality (and not illegality) therefore is often seen as the defining condition of everyday life within squatter settlements through which state-citizen relationships are negotiated. In these arguments, 'informal' settlements and 'illegal' settlements become one and the same thing.

While informality and illegality intersect in squatter settlements, they are not quite the same. Informality, understood as the lack of formality (legal or institutional), might refer to the ways that housing, services, infrastructure, and employment are accessed outside of formal mechanisms. Informality can also be morphological, in ways that the building of houses, streets and settlements, and the provisions of infrastructure are laid out without attention to zoning regulations, planning guidelines or building by-laws (Roy and AlSayyad 2004). This does not necessarily mean that informal settlements are unplanned or even illegal. Varley (1998) notes that all informal settlements, there exist degrees of coordinated and organized planning, in terms of appropriating land, building homes or accessing basic services; as well as degrees of legitimacy, whether through political patronage, titles of purchase, or enforceable documents. Further, informal settlements do not necessarily exist completely outside of formal processes. For example in Brazil, informal settlements constructed by the urban poor were not always illegal or unregulated, unlawful, uncontrolled, or even untaxed (Holston 2008). In other words, informal and illegal are not interchangeable terms – they are relational, cultural, and social and are produced for particular political ends.

One of the core arguments around illegality of squatter settlements has been the issue of rights to property. Unlike other types of slums, those who live in squatter settlements do not usually have legal/formal tenure to the land they occupy. That land should be legally owned is not a new concept. In the thirteenth century, public and private property was legally codified in England- landownership was not for the masses, and it was one of the many ways that social classes were spatially differentiated. This notion of property developed later as English common law (from which most Indian land laws are derived), which advocates that a property owner must be protected against trespass or nuisance from those who do not own the land and hence has no rights to it whatsoever. In this notion of land ownership, Guloksuz (2002) notes that 'illegal' settlements are positioned within the relations between a rule of law and property based social relations. State law then upholds a legalistic view of social relations where 'illegal' settlements are seen to be violations of a legitimate property rights system (Fernandes and Varley 1998, Santos 1992).

Despite the conflation of illegality with informality, the distinctions between legal and illegal have recently become crucial for squatters for a number of reasons. First, the role of the post-colonial state, its terms and conditions of urban governance, as well as global development practices has changed radically over the years. Comaroff and Comaroff (2006) point to a general preoccupation in the postcolony now with 'the law' and with the citizen as a legal subject. They note that a 'culture of legality' has pervaded everyday life 'becoming part and parcel of the metaphysics of disorder that haunts all postcolonies' (Comaroff and Comaroff 2006: 14). They describe this as 'lawfare' – the increased judicialization of politics and the use of 'brute power in a wash of legitimacy, ethics, and propriety' (Comaroff and Comaroff 2006: 31). With such a 'fetishism of law' (Comaroff and Comaroff 2006: viii) in urban life, Davis (2006) notes that the urban poor in squatter settlements are now increasingly questioning traditional notions of security and informal networks that were taken for granted since the 1970s. Squatters now find themselves subordinated to and subsumed within the regulatory frameworks of formal and legal mechanisms in the city, and therefore the meanings and consequences of being 'illegal' have become important in their lives. Such a context creates insecurities and uncertainties among the urban poor which Holston and Appadurai (1996) attribute to the changing relationships between cities, civil society and rule of law.

> Such transformations have generated profound uncertainties about many aspects of citizenship which only recently seemed secure: uncertainty about the community of allegiance, its form of organization, manner of election and repudiation, inclusiveness, ethical foundations, and signifying performances; uncertainty about the location of sovereign power; uncertainty about the priorities of the right and the good; uncertainty about the role of cultural identities increasingly viewed as defining natural memberships. (Holston and Appadurai 1996: 188)

Second and related to the previous point, is that squatters realize that their struggles for legitimacy cannot now be realized through informality or political patronage, but through explicit engagements with formal processes. In the case of Mumbai, this manifests into new kinds of 'citizenships from below' (Appadurai 2001) that provide new techniques for accessing housing, water and sanitation. Squatters do this 'by invoking the concept of precedent as enshrined in English common law' (Appadurai 2001: 33). In Brazil on the other hand, as the city redrew its spatial boundaries to exclude the informal settlements on its urban fringes, its residents used a notion of 'insurgent citizenships' (Holston 2008) to assert and legitimize those rights that have traditionally fallen outside the domain of the state.

What happens to squatters' relationship with law and illegality during this moment? Veena Das notes that law becomes 'a sign of distant but overwhelming power brought into the framework of everyday life by the representation and performance of its rules ... and also as a resource for seeking certain rights, although a resource whose use is fraught with uncertainty and danger' (Das 2004: 162). I suggest that this representation and performance of law not just changes the relationship between state and its subaltern citizens, but fundamentally transforms gendered relationships in everyday life. Put another way, while the state seeks to exclude those deemed 'illegal' in urban spaces, those living in squatter settlements often rework and translate these exclusions through a politics of difference within their everyday spaces. Since illegality produces a variety of anxieties around the transience of home and family, local politics becomes precisely about the reworking of power in those spaces where daily struggles and anxieties around living in the 'illegal city' are experienced.

'Slums within slums'

It is widely accepted that slums in the global south began as a result of changing political, economic, and social circumstances in post-colonial cities. A disjunction between urbanization and economic growth in these cities resulted in acute housing shortage, particularly for those rural migrants who were pushed to search for alternative accommodation on public land. This land was usually adjacent to railway tracks or bridges, or near sewage canals contaminated with industrial effluents and were close to industrial and/or middle-class areas, since these locations provided employment. These had different names- *jhuggi jhopris* in Delhi, *chawls* in Mumbai and *bastis* in Kolkata. In Delhi, *jhuggi jhopri* clusters were built mostly on public land and became a common sight alongside canals, riverbanks, railway lines and under bridges (Bijulal 2004). This simultaneous trend in informal settlements and the rapid expansion of post-colonial cities led to a rise in an 'informal urban proletariat' (Davis 2006) in these cities.

In India, 'slums' as a term was first used by the British to describe and separate working-class Indian neighbourhoods from racially white neighbourhoods (Legg 2007). In contemporary India, the word 'slum' has a specific legal force in urban development. Largely regulated by the Slum Areas Act (1956), it includes both dilapidated historic centres as well as progressive informal settlements. To be classified as a 'slum', areas have to be notified by the local authorities as such, which then makes them worthy of physical and infrastructural improvements.

Slums therefore can range from historic neighbourhoods, urban villages, resettlement colonies or squatter settlements known as *Jhuggi Jhopri* (JJ) clusters. If notified as slum, it means that these areas have poor quality buildings, services or infrastructure and are eligible for on-site improvement or resettlement in state sponsored housing projects.

In Delhi in particular, there exists a state practice of providing resettlement to 'eligible' squatters, often located far away from their original accommodation in the city. Most of these were built during the 1970s and 1980s when large scale demolition and resettlement were carried out by the state. Yet overcrowding and lack of maintenance of basic services in these settlements as well as their peripheral location in the city have often led to their turning into slums. The resettlement colonies that were built to counter the effect of slums in the city have often transformed into 'legal' slums.

The settlement that I was studying can be classified as a 'slum within a slum' (Ali 1990). This condition was increasingly observed during the 1990s, when Slum Wing officers began surveying existing state resettlement colonies. One of them, Sabir Ali (1990) observed that most resettlement colonies housed within them, clusters of informal settlements not sanctioned within official plans. These occurred because many of those residents in demolished informal settlements were deemed ineligible to receive state funded resettlement, but at the same time were unable to afford accommodation in the formal housing market. Ali noted that this condition created further pressures on services which were allocated for resettlement colonies in terms of water, sanitation, electricity and waste disposal.

The coming up of squatter settlements or JJ clusters within and around resettlement colonies is a common phenomenon in Delhi and other Indian cities. This location provides security against demolition to the JJ clusters (since this land has low real estate value), yet this very invisibility ensures that they remain outside state proposals for resettlement. We can also see this another way – those who occupy public land around resettlement colonies, must not only negotiate their illegality with respect to the 'legal' city, but they must also mediate this through the social and material differences between 'legal' and 'illegal' slums. This was the condition that participants in my study were confronting everyday – as 'slums within the slums' of resettlement colonies in the peripheries of South Delhi.

Space, law and gender in everyday life

An important moment of understanding, experiencing and negotiating law among subaltern actors begins as Gupta (2006) has identified, through encounters with the state. Citizens encounter the state through their relationships with legal processes at the local level – proceduralism, bureaucracy, rule following, precedent setting and embodied encounters with state institutions and officials within particular spaces produces the idea of 'law' in everyday life (Hansen and Stepputat 2001). Das and Poole (2004) further note that at this local level, legitimacy is attempted often through mimicry of the state, which speaks to a 'community allegiance to the idea of state-instituted law' (Das and Poole 2004: 23) but which is able to claim certain entitlements through state law. There is much to be gained from these accounts of everyday encounters with the state because they highlight the uncertainties and frustrations that are related to wider processes of violence enacted by state rule of law.

Few studies of slums however draw our attention to the fact that 'uncertainty regarding one's right to habitation is also a form of violence' (Chatterji and Mehta 2007: 129). Chatterji and Mehta were asserting this notion of violence in the context of communal riots in Mumbai slums, but we can also consider that for those living in squatter settlements, illegality is a legal, material, and cultural violence that they must confront every day. When their settlement is deemed illegal and hence slated for demolition, their identities as urban citizens are called into question, and their practices of everyday life are threatened through the violent enforcement of law. Negotiating this violence requires a functional and rudimentary knowledge of constitutional rights; it involves knowing what it means to have constitutionally defined identities as a woman, low-caste, Muslim, or a squatter, or any combination of these to use as resources for bargaining with the state for housing and basic services, and it involves the reorganization of social power within the private realm of the home in order to access these resources within the public sphere of the city. This involves finding the right way to do things in different spaces, but there is always slippage in their 'appropriateness', which backfires, or creates confusion, and generates further anxieties.

These subaltern politics of negotiating with the state is that Partha Chatterjee (2004) calls 'moral rhetorics' – the 'hesitant' terrain of political claims in the impossibility of recourse to law. For Chatterjee, moral rhetorics refer to the ways that categories of governmentality are invested with 'the imaginative possibilities of a community' (Chatterjee 2004: 60) so that squatters can use illegality and violence strategically to make moral claims from the state. Such claims form the 'weapons of the weak' (Scott 1985) through which more subtle, indirect and subversive modes of challenging the state can be imagined. Although these approaches are useful in understanding how subaltern citizens encounter state rule of law, it is difficult to examine what happens within local contexts during this moment of encounter. These concepts seem to imagine subaltern citizens as a social group with identical relationships and encounters with the state. The notion of 'moral rhetorics' often lead to a somewhat romantic tendency to view the state and citizen in a morally opposed relationship. In this book, I examine illegality as unevenly experienced and negotiated across different subjectivities in everyday life, and hence consider subjective positionality as an important criterion while encountering and negotiating law in everyday life and spaces. These positionalities determine the exchanges between public and private, legal and illegal, city and slum. They shape how power is distributed across 'community' and how this distribution in turn affects differential encounters with law.

When squatters are deemed as illegal urban citizens and their spaces are subject to erasure by the state, it is the practices of everyday life that are called into question and threatened. I understand everyday life as 'ways of frequenting or dwelling in a place' through mundane acts of cooking, cleaning, eating, sleeping, walking and so on (deCerteau 1984: xxii). The threat to everyday life produces particular subjective encounters with the practices, institutions and agents of the state in ways that are not necessarily resistant modes of action; rather these stimulate exchanges between public identities and a multitude of subjectivities in personal and everyday lives. The 'illegal city' then becomes significant as a space where different hopes, fears, anxieties and aspirations shape different notions of subjective 'justice' as its inhabitants struggle to 'make do' and 'get by' within and across a range of everyday spaces. This can take shape through a range of methods that attempt to reinforce, subvert or challenge the force of law in everyday life. My approach here is to examine how these 'weapons of the weak' (Scott 1985) are not just directed at the state, but also at each other as they negotiate the violence of law in squatter settlements and in the process reproduce some of the very violence that they seek to challenge. They explain how these negotiations also produce squatters as actors complicit in state development and resettlement projects.

Aims of the book

In this book, I examine the relationship between space, law and gender through an intersectional lens. I argue that the gendered distinction between 'public' and 'private' that is so central to law, state and urban development practices becomes the area of contestation and re-examination for squatters in their everyday life. In doing so, I draw upon the work of other feminist scholars (Rajan 2003, Williams 2006) who have highlighted how the state's construction of personal and public law simultaneously 'reinforces existing structures of power and access to resources in the private sphere' (Williams 2006: 12). I suggest that this distinction between public and personal laws affects how 'public' subjectivities of gender, class and caste are encountered during illegality, and consequently negotiated within the 'private' spaces of home and family in squatter settlements.

This book argues that as the violence of law takes away one's choice of inclusion within the urban realm, this lack of choice becomes a significant aspect of producing gendered social agencies within everyday spaces. 'Choice' refers to both its conditions and consequences as well as to what Kabeer calls 'transformatory significance' (Kabeer 1999: 461). The violent impositions of legal, social and spatial boundaries over their settlements make them confront divisions of public/private, legal/illegal, city/slum, centre/periphery in highly subjective ways. These divisions have to be negotiated through specific and 'appropriate' gender performances (Butler 1999) in order to facilitate access to urban public spaces, and these performances can 'operate through consent and complicity as well as through coercion and conflict' (Kabeer 1999: 441).

Further, these performances also have to relate to legal subjecthoods inscribed upon gendered bodies by the state in order to claim rights and entitlements in everyday life. Gendered agencies in this context therefore, involve 'bargaining and negotiation, deception and manipulation, subversion and resistance as well as more intangible, cognitive processes of reflection and analysis. It can be exercised by individuals as well as by collectivities' (Kabeer 1999: 438). This book describes how these agencies not just transform squatters' relationships with law and the state, but also with each other.

Examination of gender relationships during illegality is not to suggest that the transformations of gendered social power in squatter settlements are direct responses to the violence of law; rather that gender and its intersection with other registers of difference are important aspects of the everyday struggles and anxieties around illegality that take shape across different spaces of squatter settlements. The purpose of intersectional lens here is to examine how the categories of 'men' or 'women' are evoked in relation to the other registers of difference during encounters with law, and how these in turn transform gendered relations in everyday life. While gender is a social construction and male/female categories cannot be maintained in dualistic terms, in this book I am interested in what is at stake for gendered power during moments of uncertainty related to the squatter home. I suggest that examination of gender performances across a range of everyday spaces shows how law is spatialized in squatter settlements and how the gendered body is produced during confrontations between law and everyday life. Such a conceptual framework I suggest, allows us to rethink the gendered divisions between city and slums, centre and periphery, public and private, legal and illegal, empowerment and marginalisation – divisions that run at the heart of most scholarship on urban slums and informality.

In using a gendered intersectional lens, this book also departs from the early studies on slums in India, which focused primarily on caste and kinship relations. While caste and kinship relations are still valid and reinforced from time to time in various spaces, the number of national and international development programmes working around women's empowerment in slums makes the gendered body a significant site of analysis across urban, neighbourhood and domestic spaces. Further, the continuous communal politics taking shape across India and globally has made religion a significant register of difference at the neighbourhood level within slums (Datta 2011). Religion is negotiated through customs, festivals and everyday life on the streets but also experienced through religious personal laws at the family and personal level. At a wider urban level, recent literature on slums (Baviskar 2003, McFarlane 2008, Nijman 2008) have underlined the centrality of class in shaping urban segregation and subaltern politics, highlighting how conflicts between middle- and working-class interests produce and shape urban spaces. I argue therefore, that squatters' struggles to be included in the legal city are not simply engaged with one or the other register of affiliation or difference, rather with a variety of social positionalities of gender, caste, class, and religion, each of which are constructed, subverted or resisted during different moments of encounters with law and in different everyday spaces.[2]

Structure of the book

This book is in two parts. The first part includes chapters one to four, which establish the legal, cultural, judicial and urban contexts in Delhi against which the everyday negotiations of law and illegality acquire meaning and significance in squatter settlements. The second part of the book, from Chapters 5 to 8, looks closely at the settlement under study to examine how squatters' encounters with law during the moment of heightened uncertainty about their future, transform gendered power relationships in everyday life.

Chapter 1 begins with examining the nature of what Walter Benjamin (1978) calls 'law-making violence' in the making of the Indian Constitution. The Indian Constitution attempted to deliver justice through law and hence reified a violence of categories of differences in public and personal law. I argue that the Indian Constitution is brought into the rhythms of squatters' everyday lives through a discourse of its original intent as 'just' and its interpretation in law and state policy as illegal. It points to the ways that 'speech acts' around constitutional justice can bridge the gaps between legal subjecthood and everyday subjectivities, between past injustices, present anxieties and future aspirations.

Chapter 2 follows from the previous chapter to describe how the violence of urban development in Delhi produces squatter settlements as 'spaces of exception' (following Agamben's (2005) notion of states of exception). By tracing urban development laws and practices in Delhi since Indian independence in 1947, I argue that the set of special laws and regulations dealing with the exceptional 'problem' of slums are enforced through a rhetoric and force of urban development. These ensure the violence of urban development towards squatter settlements and its enforceability through a 'force of law' (Derrida 1992) in the everyday life of squatters.

---

2   This is supported by increasing data that highlights the intensity of social difference that has been largely unexplored in Indian slums. In 1995 the Indian Social Institute which carried out the first comprehensive count, found that of an estimated 8.47 million registered as squatters in Delhi (quarter of its population) more than 52 percent belonged to Scheduled Castes and Tribes (SC/ST) while more than 20 percent belonged to Other Backward Classes (NIUA 2003). Muslims and 'forward classes' occupied about 12 percent each (Anthony and Maheswaran 2001). South Delhi had 38 percent of all the slum households in the city, by far the highest of all the other parts. But 60 percent of them were registered as SC/ST, while in East Delhi this was close to 39 percent; eight percent in South Delhi were Muslims while in East Delhi, this was 21 percent. Further, more than 86 percent of Delhi slum households classified as 'others' lived in South Delhi – they included Sikhs, Christians, Buddhists, and other sects, castes, and religions. Slum households also stated their ethnic origin from the states of Uttar Pradesh (48 percent), Rajasthan (17 percent), and Bihar (15 percent).

Chapter 3 steps back from the present to a historical contextualization of how the wider politics around slums in the 1970s and 1980s shaped the transformations of homes, families and neighbourhoods in squatter settlements. Through participant narratives recounting the construction of their settlement in the late 1970s, I describe how residents domesticated public land and built their homes in the shadow of resettlement colonies. I examine how encounters with law-enforcement and with residents of resettlement colonies produced a consciousness of the differences between legal and illegal slums, which subsequently shaped their desire to become part of the legal city.

Chapter 4 examines the role of the 'interpretive force of law' (Derrida 1992) vested in the judiciary, in mapping illegality onto squatter settlements. In India, the judiciary has exceptional powers to influence wider societal processes and to exercise a relative degree of control over the state. In recent years, their collusion with the 'public' petitioner has transformed 'informal settlements' into 'illegal' slums. The aim of this chapter is to examine how the violence of judicial decisions maps a homogeneous identity of 'illegal' urban citizens onto the bodies and spaces of squatters and how this then produces among squatters an understanding of resettlement as the only hope for the future.

Chapter 5 begins the second half of this book by looking closely at the 'performative' nature of law through the spaces of collective organization in the settlement – the *panchayat*, the women's collective and the residents' welfare association. I argue that different collective organizations in the settlement reflect the gendered politics that evolved during different moments of uncertainty around the force of law since the 1970s. The aim of this chapter is to show how the contestations for legitimacy among these different collectives reflect the contestations in framing an 'appropriate' response to law and illegality in everyday life.

Chapter 6 follows on the previous chapter to examine how struggles to access water and sanitation shape subjective encounters with the force of law. I argue that the practices of urban development which produce class-based exclusions from the spaces of water and sanitation produce in turn a range of gendered agencies that intersect with class, caste and religious affiliations. The aim of this chapter is to examine how transgression of the boundaries of legal/illegal, city/slum, public/ private and dirt/hygiene during access to water and sanitation transforms gendered relations of power within the streets, lanes and homes of the settlement.

Chapter 7 examines how heightened anxieties around the material annihilation of home inscribe moral authority and power upon the patriarchal family. I explore how squatters articulate the violence of law through a wider anxiety over the 'legitimate' location of gendered bodies across the boundaries of home/outside. This chapter argues that the marginalizing experiences of law in the public sphere lead to a rejection of law in domestic spaces of the settlement. It articulates how the material condition of the single-room squatter dwelling is presented as 'pathological' through internalization of wider discourses of development and modernity. Finally it argues that this pathologization was in effect a 'moral rhetorics' (Chatterjee 2004) to make claims from the state for housing entitlements.

Chapter 8 concludes the book after briefly discussing the sketches that participants made of their future home. By drawing this home as a rectangular piece of land, I suggest that participants visualized the future home as a material entitlement from the state. Through its marked similarity with precedents of state resettlement, the future home emphasized the boundaries between home and outside and the lines that restrained the state from intruding upon their familial and domestic spaces.

The book concludes by reflecting upon the everyday negotiations of illegality in the Delhi squatter settlement and by highlighting the irony and the tragedy of the aspirations for a legitimate future home. It ends on three substantive points – first that legal and cultural constructions of the squatter home are inseparable from the question of how the gendered body is lived and constructed in everyday spaces of squatter settlements. Second that the experiences (and hopes) of becoming part of the 'legal' city produces a terrain of politics that are negotiated through personal and intimate spaces. Third, I note that close attention paid to internal divisions, and to the realm of the intimate, as in this book can help us avoid in the future, simplistic moral divisions that run deep in South Asian scholarship between 'the state' on one side, and the people, or communities, on the other.

Chapter 1
Law, Space and Subjectivity

Researching space, law and gender in a squatter settlement

When I began my research in this squatter settlement in 2002, my initial intention had been to understand the politics of social agency through a study of the women's collective action there. I approached the women's collective through a feminist NGO and was interviewed by one of the leaders of the collective who also worked for the NGO. When satisfied of my intentions, she took me around to introduce me to their members in the settlement. This was during a moment of high activity among the women's collective leaders – they had received funding from NGOs through which they could organize meetings, set up small adult literacy sessions, and a small playschool for the children of residents. At the time, I interviewed about 15 women who had set-up the organization and worked for it. These interviews made me aware that their social and political actions were framed by a strategic engagement with law. It also became clear that the support that these women received from feminist NGOs allowed them to engage with law and legal processes more efficiently than other residents, which helped them achieve a degree of social status and power in the settlement.

In 2002, my study of the women's collective was framed around my interests in gendered spaces of organization. But I also knew that I had not fully explored the consequences of their gender politics in the wider context. If these women's collectives were producing a group of empowered squatter women, how far did they affect the lives of other men and women in the settlement; how did their activism change everyday lives of those who lived in there; and how did those women who joined in their activities perceive their own role in state discourses of empowerment? I wanted to return and get more involved, but it was not till 2005 that I returned to this settlement with a research grant to explore the politics of their everyday lives.

Even before I returned in 2005, I noticed a number of changes taking place in Delhi that affected the course of my research interests. Since 2000, there had been a series of judicial rulings around the 'dirt' and 'filth' that was seen to have infested Delhi. These court rulings were aimed at removing squatters from the city, removing polluting industries and polluting buses from the city – all of which affected the urban poor. My awareness of the consequences of these rulings in everyday life began of course with the demolition of those few houses in 2002, but it was not until 2005, when I returned that I was able to focus on how these were encountered within everyday lives in the settlement.

In the beginning, while I was interested in how participants dealt with the wider power structures of the state and the city, I was also interested in how gender relations of power were transforming across a number of spaces of everyday life. As I began my research, I noticed that participants were anxious about aspects of law and illegality that would affect their future in the city, and therefore aspired to be recognized through legal mechanisms of the state. As illegality and legitimacy began to surface repeatedly in my interviews with participants, it seemed that participants were continually reconciling the boundaries that separated their public life and personal spaces through legal and everyday subjectivities. It seemed then that while they were encountering law and illegality in their everyday spaces, they were also fundamentally transforming gendered social power across those spaces. This observation sometime during my fieldwork began to shape my interviews and analysis from then on.

In the increasing debates on anthropology of the state, ethnography has offered a unique perspective on the practices and politics of life in the 'margins of the state' (Das and Poole 2004). Using ethnography, Gupta (2006) examines how the state affects everyday life in rural areas, in ways that focused primarily on the sites/practices where his participants encountered state agents and bureaucracies. Such ethnographies of the state focus on how everyday practices encounter the institutions, agents and procedures of the state on the one hand, and how the state is constructed through rumour, gossip and humour. Although my research cannot be classified as conventional ethnography, it is nevertheless ethnographically informed through the use of extensive observations and interviews. My research assistant and I kept a regular journal where we noted our interactions outside of interviews. In total, I (with the help of my research assistant) conducted 83 semi-structured interviews ranging from half-hour to two-hour conversations with a variety of participants. Interviews were often group events, where neighbours would collect around to chip in their opinions. At other times, inside the homes, family members would contribute to what began as an individual interview. Interviews with the family were fraught with power hierarchies – older women would hijack the conversations intended with younger women, older male members would overshadow the voices of their female partners, but also often, participants would challenge some of the assumptions that I was making about their everyday lives. Observing and interviewing residents therefore made me aware of the multiple power structures that existed not only across the city, but also the power hierarchies that were being transformed within family, caste, religious and kinship networks during their moments of anxiety and uncertainty.

These power hierarchies were also negotiated continuously with me as a researcher interested in their everyday lives. I was located between the position of an insider and an outsider – I was Indian by birth, I was a *Dilliwali* (Delhi-ite), but I was also middle-class, and I had grown up in those neighbourhoods where many went to work as domestic help, beauticians, drivers, and cooks. I also lived in the UK – I was repeatedly asked how they could be sure that I was not taking pictures to show foreigners the filth that they lived in? I was a woman; often welcomed by members of the women's collective and into private domestic spaces for being interested in 'women's issues' and 'protected' for my forays into spaces of the settlement where young unmarried girls were usually not allowed by their parents. I faced continuous accusations from men about research conducted by feminist NGOs on 'women's issues' – a practice which they felt was not dealing with the 'real' issues in the settlement of male unemployment and lack of access to housing and infrastructure.

I found two ways to deal with these issues. First, my funding allowed me to pay remuneration to participants for the time they spent on the project. Although this was a nominal amount, this token gesture helped assuage some of the doubts about foreigners and NGOs making money from the misfortunes of squatters. It also helped to build more positive relations with my male participants who often suspected that this remuneration was meant only for women (since NGOs often recruited and paid slum women for surveys). Second, I had also unintentionally recruited a male research assistant on this project. His presence and his positive interactions with some of the male leaders served to project us as a research team who were interested in understanding everyday lives of both men and women.

These gender politics during my fieldwork provided interesting opportunities for me to think about the politics of gender during everyday life in the squatter settlement. This was becoming increasingly visible in a context where anxieties about the spatial boundaries around women's bodies intersected with the positionalities of caste, religion, and ethnicity which determined who was able to transgress the socially constructed lines between public and private, and under what conditions. These anxieties were evident in a number of places – houses, streets, markets and public toilets where the aspirations and agendas of different local collectives produced frequent conflicts over the legitimacy and morality of their actions.

'Camp' is a generic name for all squatter settlements (or *jhuggi jhopri* colonies) shown on Delhi maps, which I use from now on to refer to the settlement that I studied. In city plans, camps are always represented as empty spaces – open land that threaten its residents with transience and erasure. However, anyone with more than a passing interest in Delhi's slum geographies might be able to identify this settlement, not only because I have found it essential to the intellectual endeavours of this book to describe its geographical context and hence to a certain extent to reveal its location in Delhi, but also because there are only a few of these settlements now left in Delhi which are still awaiting demolition and resettlement by the state. I have similarly changed all the names and to some extent the personalities of some of the key participants from the women's collective and resident's welfare association in order to make them anonymous, although I am aware that it is likely that some of those working in NGOs will recognize them in this book.

Law, space and subjectivity

Critiques of law have repeatedly highlighted its socially constructed nature and its intimate associations with sovereign power. Much of these critiques are inspired by Walter Benjamin's articulation of two kinds of violence in law – law-making and law-preserving. The first is the founding violence, the one that institutes and positions law. The second is the violence that 'maintains, confirms, and insures the permanence and enforceability of law ... law-making is power-making, and to an extent an immediate manifestation of violence' (Benjamin 1978: 295). Benjamin specifically gives the example of the making of constitutions as the founding violence of law since it guarantees power to the state. Law's maintaining violence can then be recognized as the administrative violence in enforcing this law.

The Indian Constitution put together in 1950 marked the founding of the newly independent Indian Republic. Written during the moment of transformation from a colonial state to a 'sovereign, secular, socialist, democratic republic' (Indian Constitution 1950: Preamble) the Indian Constitution remains the final treatise on law and policy in India. The 'founding violence' of the Indian Constitution is marked by a transfer of power from the colonial to the postcolonial state giving its subjects therein a legal citizenship to the sovereign state and establishing a rule of law – fixed rules that are universally applicable, but whose 'connotative qualities are more expansive, covering everything from a sense of equality under the law to the political ideals of justice and individual dignity' (Hussain 2003: 8). The Indian Constitution in its very making attempted to resolve the issue of justice through law. While equality was maintained through legal citizenship to all its subjects, it was also differentiated through rights across particular social groups. The constitution went about very explicitly creating laws that would in effect remove 'social ills' and institute as it saw forms of justice for those historically marginalized within Indian society. In doing so, it produced a violence of categories – low-castes and tribal identities became what Chatterjee calls 'population groups' (Chatterjee 2004: 61), distinguished from 'citizens' on account of the classificatory schemes produced by governmental institutions in order to deliver social justice. In public life, the constitution instituted a process of positive discrimination across these enumerated populations, while in private life it recognized religious laws over gender equality. Thus the founding of the Indian Constitution constructed a relationship between law, space and subjectivity by spatializing and differentiating legal subjecthoods across public and private life.

The Indian Constitution instituted that 'Law' would include 'any ordinance, order, bye-law, rule, regulation, notification, custom or usage having in the territory of India the force of law' (Indian Constitution 1950: 6). Derrida has described the 'force of law' as 'the force implied in the very concept of justice as law' (Derrida 1992: 927). This force can be 'direct or indirect, physical or symbolic, exterior or interior, brutal or subtly discursive and hermeneutic, coercive or regulative and so forth' (Derrida 1992: 927). The Indian Constitution can be seen to use this force of law in bringing about social change – formulating special laws and regulations that positively discriminate towards enumerated population groups. But as Derrida notes, the institution of a rule of law in this manner cannot be equated to justice, since justice cannot be equated to law. Feminist scholars also rightfully question the potential of law as a transformative or emancipatory instrument for marginalized groups (Menon 2004). For example, Menon argues that law emerged in postcolonial societies during the double moment of modernity and colonialism, and therefore cannot be granted the same emancipatory force as it might have had in Europe in its transformation from feudalism. These debates around the 'justice' embedded in equal citizenship through positive discrimination in India are continually contested and deliberated, and have provided much ground for marginalized social groups to organize around their rights against discrimination in public life. While this is of great interest, I am more concerned here in understanding how the notion of legal subjecthood embodied in the Indian Constitution permeates through to different spaces of everyday life and subjectivities.

In this chapter, I argue that while the Indian Constitution attempted to deal with social justice through subjective categories, it is brought into the rhythms of everyday life by squatters through a continuous interpretation of its 'original intent' as 'just'. This is different from Derrida's (1992) force of law where he does not actually differentiate between what law is to what law does. This is also different from how Das highlights the different ways that the state acquires a presence, which she calls 'magical, in the life of communities through local practices' (Das 2004: 224). Das notes (following Derrida) how the state has a continuous presence in low-income neighbourhoods through its writing technologies – as a 'signature', which grounds the spectacular in everyday life. Das was discussing police First Information Reports (FIRs) filed after communal violence in Delhi slums, which through their rewriting of violence made the state 'illegible' in everyday life. I argue on the other hand that it is the threat of law-preserving violence experienced through the demolition of their homes, which ensures a continuous discursive presence of the Indian Constitution as the final arbitrator of justice and legitimacy for its subaltern citizens. This does not necessarily speak to emancipation or transformation; rather it points to the ways that 'speech acts' around constitutional justice can bridge the gaps between legal subjecthood and everyday subjectivities, between past injustices, present anxieties and future aspirations.

Legal subjecthood and the Indian Constitution

Article 15(1) The State shall not discriminate against any citizen on grounds only of religion, race, caste, sex, place of birth or any of them. (Indian Constitution 1950: 6)

Article 15(3) Nothing in this article shall prevent the State from making any special provision for women and children. (Indian Constitution 1950: 6)

Article 15(4) Nothing in this article or in clause (2) of article 29 shall prevent the State from making any special provision for the advancement of any socially and educationally backward classes of citizens or for the Scheduled Castes and the Scheduled Tribes. (Indian Constitution 1950: 6)

The rich scholarship around Indian law has noted that 'law' during the colonial period was an amalgam of earlier autochthonous systems of Hindu legal tradition and the Islamic *Sharia* laws, which had governed different parts of society (Galanter 1988). Galanter notes that the British introduced a system of precedent based on available texts, which served to crystallize the flexible application of Hindu *shashtras* into a body of rule known as 'Hindu law'. Along with this, the British Raj, in an effort to produce equal representation of 'minorities', began for the first time to categorize and measure the population within different castes and religions in India. Such efforts had two outcomes – on the one hand, it produced a crystallization of caste and religious identities that till then had been quite amorphous in everyday life, and on the other hand, low caste and tribal groups (named for the first time as 'Scheduled castes and tribes') became structurally enumerated identities which could be used by the state to 'measure' representation and development (Srinivas 1957).

A number of scholars (Khilnani 2005, Saberwal 2005) have argued that democracy in India was not the product of popular action and claims for rights; rather democracy entered India through the engagement and relationship of the political elite with western and colonial law. As Nandy notes, the notions of rights and democracy arrived in India 'riding piggyback on an oppressive colonial society to establish lasting bonds with established stratarchies in society' (Nandy 2002: 35). The founding authors of the Indian Constitution, Jawaharlal Nehru (India's first Prime Minister) and Dr B.R. Ambedkar (first low caste Indian to pursue an education in India and a law degree in the West) put together a mixture of legal and subaltern rights within a notion of equality of citizenship (Khilnani 2005). They organized the constitution around two different legal norms – one the Fundamental rights, which were legal and enforceable, and second the Directive Principles of State Policy, which were non-binding socio-economic and cultural guidelines to the state to legislate on policy. The Fundamental Rights, which Galanter (1984) suggests, was modelled on the United State Bill of Rights, included a range of universal and differentiated rights in the social, cultural and political spheres. Article 14, 15(1) and 29(2) of the constitution, stressed equality of citizenship which stated that the state shall not discriminate against any individual on the basis of caste, religion, ethnicity, and gender. The right to shelter was left implicit under the Directive Principles, which also included right to education, right to work, and so on. While Fundamental Rights could be enforced by law, right to shelter was neither an enforceable nor a fundamental right of all citizens. The 'founding violence' in the Indian Constitution was the further recognition of right to property as a Fundamental Right, which meant that those without legal rights to their land or homes could be justifiably removed by the state without compensation.

Although distinctively modern (in following Western models) in guaranteeing universal equal rights as fundamental rights, the constitution produced a socially differentiated citizenship in public life where individuals could enjoy rights by virtue of their membership to structurally identified communities of identities. In so doing, the constitution attempted to strike a relationship between 'a set of ideal and formal rules and social practices, between 'law' on the one hand and 'culture' on the other' (Khilnani 2005: 66). This was translated into state policies on caste reservations. 'Scheduled Castes', who traditionally consisted of lower castes of sweepers, scavengers and toilet cleaners (also known as untouchables), as well as Scheduled Tribes, which included a large number of indigenous tribes, were provided with a range of entitlements including a 22.5 percent reservation of seats in public sector education and employment, as well as reservation in many state-funded development programmes. Such a formulation of equal rights on the one hand and reservations for the marginalized on the other were based on two significant assumptions. First, as Kaviraj (2000) notes, those identified as marginal and oppressed in Indian society were meant to achieve development and progress through the state. Second, that representation in the public realm of those historically excluded from public life was expected to ultimately lead to material and economic transformations in marginalized communities. Khilnani notes that it also made another crucial assumption – that reservations in public life would be supported by intensive state welfare programs on education, housing and infrastructure provisions. This distinction between civil/political and social/ economic rights embedded in the Fundamental Rights and the Directive Principles of State Policy meant that while the civil/political rights were enforceable by the judiciary, the social and economic rights were only to be regulated and interpreted in the context of their violation of the fundamental rights (Baxi 2005).

As Khilnani argues, the constitution embodied a blindness about the 'potential implications of introducing political equality in a society of great social and economic inequality, without questioning how the nature of political representation and the status of rights might change over time and in their relationships to each other' (Khilnani 2005: 67). In this approach, rights were treated as 'plastic in relation to the state's interpretation of the character of political community at any given time, and therefore of how it was appropriate to treat its members' (Khilnani 2005: 76). This was a paternalistic notion of citizenship where the state determined appropriate rights for its citizens and downplayed the notion of rights as a form of agency and political action. Crucially in these exercises, as Saberwal (2005) points out, the existence of a western notion of civil society – a space where individuals participate as equals was taken as given.

The Indian version of modernity therefore, used law as a way of changing society, and used the Indian Constitution as the ultimate treatise on law (Galanter 1988). What was particular about the constitution though was the idea of judicial supremacy, in that the judiciary could strike down any law or policy proposed by the state that was deemed as 'unconstitutional'. Further, the government could acquire property for public purposes, and state land reform law could not be subject to judicial review. Although the power of the judiciary has never been completely accepted by the politicians (indeed during the Indian emergency in 1975–77, the state actively tried to seize this power from the Judiciary), it has produced an intriguing dynamics in everyday perceptions of law, rights and entitlements.

Since the constitution clearly delineated law-making and law-preserving across institutions, the judiciary (in particular the Supreme Court) now has the final say in the interpretation of law and legal documents. For example, Article 21 of the constitution states that no person will be deprived of their property apart from by law. This could be interpreted as those who do not have legal rights to property could be legitimately removed from their property by the state. But the right to shelter of squatters, not a fundamental right in itself, could also be interpreted as an aspect of the fundamental right to life. As we shall see in Chapter 4, the judiciary has used both interpretations from time to time.

These issues raise important questions about the changing relationships between law, space and subjectivity. First, that since the Indian Constitution saw the welfare state as the main driver of housing development; it focused on removing socio-cultural marginalizations in public life through reservations. In 1991 however, the 74th and 75th amendments to the Indian Constitution established a three-tier system of local governance, which decentralized powers to local authorities and to Urban Local Bodies (ULBs). In light of this, local authorities began to function as institutions of local self-government by engaging in public-private partnerships in the delivery of housing to the poor. These changes, made on the basis of recommendations by the UN[1] have seen the retraction of the states responsibility for housing, and the increased role of NGOs and the private sector in delivering housing and infrastructure. Second, precisely because of the lack of legal recourse by squatters to resist the demolition of their homes, they must now find a different kind of legal language to claim their entitlements from the state. The legal subjecthood embodied in the constitution as fundamental rights, as low-castes, or as women has now become the only political resource towards making claims to shelter.

---

1   The UN articulated the Agenda 21 objectives, which required participation at the local level in planning and implementing environmental, social, and economic policies – the focus was particularly on empowering women, children and local communities. Recognizing the need for infrastructure, especially for the urban poor, Agenda 21 recommendations were to provide this through 'adequate pricing policies, reduction of subsidies, and recovering the full costs of environmental services such as water supply, sanitation, and waste management' (UN-Habitat 2003). It also stipulated that the role of non-governmental organizations and local level governance should be strengthened in the signatory countries to achieve these objectives. This was further reinforced in the Istanbul declaration on human settlements as part of the Habitat Agenda, which argued for a 'new era of cooperation' between the state, civil society and private sector to create sustainable human settlements (Future Cities and Habitat II 1996).

Gendered spaces of law

The codification and reform of Indian laws carried out by the British and later through the Indian Constitution has further produced a disjuncture between public and individual identities. While the reform of public life in terms of political equality and social reform, followed a process of 'compensatory discrimination' (Galanter 1984: 41), the reform of personal law on the other hand was seen by the authors of the constitution as a space where they should maintain non-interference. There has then emerged a clear division of the 'legal subject' across public and private spaces – while laws were reformed in the social, political and religious institutions and in public life, laws relating to the home and family were left largely intact from the colonial period (Menon 2004, Williams 2006). The founding violence of law in the Indian Constitution was therefore also a gendered violence in so far as it reinforced and validated a patriarchal logic of home and outside.

While the constitution constructed public life through caste and tribal identity, private life was largely constructed through religious identity. The constitution attempted to modernize and purge Indian society of its gendered 'social evils' (such as dowry, bride burning and so on), but this was achieved through the reform of religious practices. Further it was only Hindu Law that was seen by the constitution as requiring reform. Articles 17 and 25(2) of the Indian Constitution required the state to make laws reforming Hindu personal and religious life. Yet personal and religious laws of religious minorities could only be reformed if demands were made from that community to do so. Personal laws including laws on marriage, divorce, maintenance, inheritance, succession, adoption and guardianship, were largely defined by citizens' locations within religious communities. As Rajan notes, 'even at the cost of supporting differential laws and discrimination against women' (Rajan 2003: 16) gender became an aspect of religious identity, codified through religious personal laws.

Public and private life cannot of course be conceived as distinct social and spatial arenas; rather they are continually produced through the intersections between home and outside, self and other, law and society. Yet, the constitutional coding of particular forms of identity across different spaces of the home and outside, works to regulate particular forms of legal subjecthood across these spaces. Thus while the state regulates gendered behaviour within the home, it refuses to intervene within certain spaces of the home. For example, while the state has passed a series of acts to reform Hindu personal laws in their treatment of women (dowry, bride burning and so on), the state has been relatively less proactive in other arenas of the 'private' sphere, such as parenting or in equalizing gendered relations of power within the family, or indeed in equalizing differences between male- and female-headed households. In interpreting personal law on the other hand, judiciary has subsequently ruled that neither Article 21 (right to life) nor Article 14 (right to equality) as fundamental rights have any place within the private sphere (Williams 2006). As an example, the Dowry Prohibition Act, passed in 1961, criminalizes the giving and taking of dowry; amendments in the early 1980s recognized abetting to suicide as a special crime, made cruelty to a wife a non-bailable offence, and made police investigation mandatory on cases on which a woman died within seven years after marriage. Yet, it also reflects particular notions of 'family values' and 'tradition' (Ahmed-Ghosh 2004) and normalizes gender identity of women as mothers and wives, 'as economically dependent, as passive, dutiful and self-sacrificing ... It is an example of the often-homogenizing nature of legal discourse, which obscures the multiplicity of differences between and among women, and the very different ways in which women live in and experience their families' (Kapur and Cossman 1996: 101).

For the Indian Constitution and state then, the 'emancipation of women' presents a paradox. On the one hand, Indian law supplants gender identity with religious identity in personal law, yet on the other hand, it attempts to protect women from the violence faced within patriarchal families. This paradox is carried through the formulation and enactment of a variety of development programmes around women's empowerment offering women a new kind of 'agentic identity' (Rajan 2003: 27) despite their recognition as religious subjects in personal law. While the state constructs squatter homes as backward, illiterate, parochial, and misogynous, it simultaneously takes a paternalistic role towards its women as the victims of this home and hence the 'burden of the state' (Rajan 2003: 25). As scholars have argued, the state reinforces its legitimacy and power in defining public and private identities since public and personal laws are always negotiated through the state. And when the law comes to represent identity (whether gendered or religious or caste, or a combination of these), then it means that identity itself has to be negotiated through the state (Williams 2006). And in so doing, social affiliations of caste, religion, gender, and their associated legitimacies and identities have to be mediated through law.

Rights and entitlements in everyday life

> Law as a concept depends on the state's mythical qualities, the practices of solemnly encoding certain rights in constitutions, of entrenching and interpreting these rights in judicial practices and invoking them in political rhetoric also hinges on the efficiency of the imagination of the state as a guarantor of these rights. If that imagination is ineffective, the discourse of rights is inconsequential.
> (Hansen and Stepputat 2001: 18)

There is a recurrent debate in South Asian scholarship that the state has survived in popular imagination, particularly among the working classes as the repository of social justice and rights. Kaviraj (2005) notes that the state is seen as a distinct entity by subaltern citizens by cutting it loose from political parties, bureaucracy or governance and making it a moral repository of rights in everyday life. This allows subaltern citizens to make claims to state benefits through a 'moral rhetoric'

(Chatterjee 2004), to demand 'justice, equality, dignity, assistance' (Kaviraj 2005: 295) in its name, even if the state cannot deliver any of these. Law enters this equation through the notion of legal citizenship to this state, through its relationship with the state and with the constitution as Hansen and Stepputat (2001) rightly point out. Yet, the discourse of rights is significant even if the state cannot be imagined as the guarantor of rights. Among participants in the camp, this was precisely so. Seen as corrupt, inefficient, elitist at best and murderous at worst, none of the participants evoked the Indian state as a guarantor of rights, even in its most abstract form. Rather they continually evoked the Indian Constitution as the treatise of law and justice, which had been misinterpreted and wrongly practised by the state and its agents.

This notion of justice formulated by participants was not imagined through the state; rather through the structurally enumerated identities in public life that was guaranteed by the constitution. The constitution was therefore interpreted through its original 'intent' as just, and the state in its interpretation of the constitution as unjust. Lower caste participants rejected state policies and practices as unconstitutional, since they seemingly went against the notion of positive discrimination adopted in the constitution. This interpretation of justice was based on linking the founding moment of the constitution with low-caste empowerment. Its co-author Dr B.R. Ambedkar, a low-caste intellectual and nationalist had been instrumental in writing positive discrimination into the constitution. In making such links, low-caste participants presented the Indian Constitution as an essentially 'just' treatise that preceded and transcended the state. In so doing, the constitution was cut loose from the state and made the location of justice, empowerment and morality.

> I've been born in a poor environment and as the honourable Dr. B.R. Ambedkar sahib had investigated, he had said that wealth and land should be distributed. So until wealth and land are distributed, this country will not benefit. But there is no place for the poor in this land. Tell me one thing, come with me, to Sainik Farm, it is close by. People have built farmhouses extending over 25 acres each. At the same time there is talk of demolishing a poor person's hut, why? [Ramlal]

Ramlal, one of the participants in the settlement that I was studying, reinforced the point that Derrida (1992) has made, that law is not justice and justice cannot be equated to the correct enforcement of law. Ramlal refers here instead to a violence of law that originates in its relationship between the rights to property and geography of disorder mapped onto squatter settlements. Those elite classes who live in Sainik farms in Delhi's urban fringes are safe from demolition even though they have built their houses in violation of urban zoning and landuse laws. While it is not just squatter settlements which are 'illegally' constructed, the force of law under the cover of legitimacy and development is applied brutally only against squatter settlements. Since squatters fall most easily within the dialectics of law and disorder, their spaces are subject to coercion and erasure.

Residents in the settlement I was studying, continually evoked the Indian Constitution as a representation of historical and social 'justice' by those marginalized by the threat of law-preserving violence. This was because in the absence of fundamental rights to shelter, it was harder for squatters to articulate any discourse of rights to housing from the state. Already marginalized within normative legal spaces, simple recourse to law (through courts) was not possible (Santos 1992). Rather their struggles were politicized in a way that replaced illegalities through a discourse of legal subjectivities embodied in the Indian Constitution. In 2005 when I was in the settlement, low-caste participants were increasingly referring to housing and basic services as entitlements afforded through particular constitutional subjecthoods – as low-castes, and minority communities.

But in order to stake their claims, participants recognized that they would also have to enact their identities according to those prescribed in the constitution. Constitutional identities then became a performative force in the lives of those who had to live by its regulations, procedures and categories.

> It is because of the benefits afforded to us by the government that we are contesting an election; otherwise these others [upper castes] wouldn't have let us. This is why the government did this, reserve seats for them [lower castes]. Until that is done, no one will let them contest. There are many muscle men; they won't even let this man stand. [They will say] sit down quietly on the floor, we are the moneyed, we will contest. That is when it becomes a compulsion. That is why we have to agree that we are inferior. [Radha]

Participants like Radha articulated their socially 'inferior' positions less in terms of everyday cultural practices than in terms of competition for territory, resources, and political inclusion within wider society. The construction of an inferior position was first and foremost in relation to the entitlements sanctioned by the Indian Constitution for lower-castes. Claims to these entitlements had to be made from a position of lower social status, since these were not automatically acquired. Here Radha specifically asserted her right as low-caste to participate in political life. This was not an entitlement that Radha intended to take up personally, but claiming this entitlement as a low-caste afforded her a sense of inclusion within wider society in a way that her identity as urban poor had not.

Radha therefore presents a 'speech act' when she calls herself 'inferior'. This speech act attempts to bridge the gaps between legal subjecthood and everyday subjectivities. Asserting low-caste status is not an assertion of lower social position in everyday life (as Radha explains); rather it is an assertion of the right to be provided certain entitlements in order to become equal – an argument which is as much historical as it is political. Participants then saw their exclusion from the city as part of their socio-historic marginalization from Indian society, a practice whose continuance in modern India was 'unconstitutional'. Such an argument however was a paradox – while participants might make claims as 'lower castes', in everyday life, their identities did not conform to such narrowly defined categories. So while an articulation of lower caste status might have provided certain entitlements in public life, participants were constrained when other aspects of their identities such as gender or class came to the fore in their private or everyday lives. Similarly, while articulations of gendered subjectivity might have worked to make claims to economic and social developmental projects of the state at another time, participants were similarly constrained when other identities such as caste, class or religion intersected with gender in their everyday lives. These intersectional dynamics and politics of entitlement in particular spaces and places of their everyday lives served to transform participants' relations to law, state and power. I will discuss this in detail in the rest of this book.

Chapter 2
Violence of Urban Development

The founding violence of India's Constitution can be considered in many ways to also be the founding violence of urban development in postcolonial India. As I mentioned in the previous chapter, in framing the constitution, its authors (Jawaharlal Nehru and BR Ambedkar) took the view that development enable the path to justice. The relationship between development and justice was reinforced through a series of government obligations – 'the progressive implementation of policies, programmes and measures that disproportionately benefit and empower the impoverished masses of India' (Hasan, Sridharan and Sudharshan 2005: 38). In other words, the authors of the constitution focused on removing social inequalities through law but left the responsibility of formulating policies around economic inequalities on the state. This meant that housing for the urban poor was to be dealt with through national and urban development plans.

Immediately after independence in 1947, the National Planning Commission was set up in India to formulate five year plans. The intention was to manage the planning and growth of Indian cities (Planning Commission 2001), which had gone into decline during the colonial period and was forecast to increase their economic activities after independence. These five-year plans were to have clear developmental goals which would be monitored, evaluated and amended every five years in line with the changing demands from economic development. The First Five-Year Plan (1950–55) therefore proposed a major rehabilitation program mainly for refugees of partition through large-scale construction of row houses in the capital. During the Second Five-Year Plan (1956–61), the government began to pursue the policy of slum clearance and rehabilitation, borrowing from the experience of British slum clearance programs of the early twentieth century (Wadhwa 1988). From the Third Five Year Plan (1962–66), the intention was to control the perceived haphazard and unplanned growth of cities like Delhi. The fourth and fifth five year plans in the 1970s recognized mass impoverishment in cities and set up of a number of programmes to reduce poverty in urban areas. These numerous programmes on development and poverty alleviation directed at the 'exceptional' spaces of slums and squatter settlements reinforced New Delhi's sovereign power over slum dwellers.

These programmes have also shaped the force of urban development in many Indian cities, which often became sites of squatters' violent confrontations with law. In Delhi, this has been particularly significant through attempts to enforce an orderly masterplan since the 1960s. The often violent enforcement of this masterplan through demolition of squatter homes and (if 'eligible') resettlement of squatters, shapes everyday experiences of the power of 'law', and it influences everyday practices through which home and family life are negotiated in squatter settlements. Law is constructed through 'the way that right to property is put in abeyance when they squat on government land' (Kaviraj 2005: 295); in ways that the demolition of their homes can be delayed through bribes to corrupt agents of the state or hastened by judicial rulings; and in ways that the state retracts from any direct responsibility for providing shelter to the urban poor.

Urban planning has attempted since the colonial period to legitimize forms of governmentalities (Legg 2007). But as Chatterjee notes, 'it was in planning above all that the postcolonial state would claim its legitimacy as a single will and consciousness – the will of the nation, pursuing a task that was not universal and rational: the wellbeing of people as a whole' (Chatterjee 1993: 205). The use of planning as a form of sovereign power can then be seen as a continuum from colonial to post-colonial spaces. The violence of urban development in this chapter then refers first, to the force of urban development in Delhi that could not have been legitimized in a postcolonial context without a degree of sanction from the Indian Constitution; second, to the enactment of a number of policies and programmes that attempt to bring about improvement to urban slums in line with global development goals, but are in themselves a function of the powers vested in the state and its institutions to formulate laws and policies to this effect; and finally, to the maintaining violence of these laws and policies that continue to produce the myth of resettlement among squatters.

Squatter settlements as 'spaces of exception'

The state of exception as articulated by Agamben is a necessary component of a rule of law. For Agamben the state of exception embodies an 'anomic space in which what is at stake is a force of law without law' (Agamben 2005: 39). The force of law then refers 'not to the law, but the decrees that the executive power is authorized to issue in some situations, particularly in the state of exception' (Agamben 2005: 38). What is significant in the state of exception is a spatialization of the conditions of exception, which produces differential geographies of power and authority across social groups. For Agamben, the state of exception is an empty space. Yet exception works precisely through its inscription upon specific places which are deemed as 'justifiably' outside of law. This is a space where the universality of a rule of law is abandoned in order to produce a special set of acts, regulations, and programmes specifically to monitor and govern these spaces.

There is much literature on the colonial state as a state of exception (Galanter 1988, Hussain 2003, Legg 2007) which has particular modes of relationship to law and to sovereign power. Hussain's work on emergency law in the colonial state has pointed to how emergency rule produces a problematic relationship between law and sovereign power, in which law can be 'legitimately' suspended in order to maintain sovereignty. Hussain's perspective about the conflict of the absolute sovereignty of the state and the rule of law as universal, rational and formal, suggests that the use of exceptional conditions justify the suspension of all civil and fundamental rights and maintains the state in absolute power. In postcolonial states, the state of exception is initiated at the moment of emergency powers of the sovereign state, when law is suspended, a moment which is outside the 'norm'. Much of this analysis has been devoted recently to human rights violations of terror suspects which relates to the notion of 'bare life'- the stripping off of all rights from the human body. These states are indeed exceptional and the collusion of law and sovereign power in its making is more obvious and visible.

I argue however, that exceptionality also works through the 'ordinariness' and normalization of state control over squatter homes and settlements. My approach in presenting this argument explores squatter settlements as spaces where law is differently conceived from the rest of the city *as if* that were the norm. This approach is closer to that taken by Das and Poole (2004) who examine the state at its margins, and suggest that exception lies both inside and outside the law. The notion of squatter settlements as spaces of exception works on the basis that special laws and regulations are formulated and enacted in order to deal with the exceptional 'problem' of slums without threatening 'the overall structure of legality and property' (Chatterjee 2004: 137). In India, these special laws are the Slum Areas Act, judicial rulings, various housing schemes for the urban poor, state schemes for slum upgradation, and innumerable global/national development programmes for empowering women in slums. These laws are enacted through a rhetoric and force of urban development. In so doing, squatter settlements are treated differently to the rest of the city, through a set of institutions that document, enumerate and repeatedly survey the spaces of slums. Such practices claim to secure particular eligibilities to state entitlements, but in turn lead to a sense of marginalization among squatters. They are seen to penetrate the spaces of home and destabilize the boundaries between public and private, home and outside, centre and periphery. These special set of laws, regulations and institutions ensure the sustenance of squatter settlements as spaces of exception and produce the relationship between law and everyday life.

Urban planning and development has always been an important aspect of the legitimacy of sovereign power in the capital city. Indeed New Delhi's claims to sovereignty began through its visualization and aestheticization in colonial urban planning (Legg 2007). The colonial state had begun this process through forms of governmentality, planned order and sanitized modernity. Legg (2007) suggests that colonial New Delhi was produced as a space of sovereign power through an undemocratic process of its relocation from Calcutta to New Delhi, through the ways that planning of this new city evoked colonial grandeur and supremacy, and through a reinforcement of social and spatial distance from 'Old Delhi'. Like most colonial cities, New Delhi functioned as a state of exception, realized through the extensive programmes of slum clearance from within its boundaries carried out by the Delhi Improvement Trust (Legg 2007).

In the postcolonial state, the 'illegal city' is constructed by sovereign power as an 'unruly' and 'disorderly' space. The illegal city can be seen as a necessary counterpart of the legal city, which can be brought under control only through a force of law that treats this as a space of 'exception'. Illegality in the case of squatter settlements therefore is not where law ceases to exist; rather where law and space have a distinct relationship with the rest of the city. This relationship is one of uncertainty and undecidability, which underlines the relation between legal and illegal city.

Slum Areas Act 1956

Delhi was the most important city of sovereign power in postcolonial India. But at the time of independence in 1947, it had not experienced much formal development beyond the British imperial city of New Delhi. The coming of the squatters into this orderly city after independence presented a moral attack on the city's sanitized order – it was haphazard, disorderly and chaotic against a vision of a modern city symbolic of the Indian Republic. The need to clear up the city of what was increasingly seen as a 'public nuisance' led to the institution of one of the most important acts in India that regulate slums till today. In 1956, the Indian Parliament passed the Slum Areas (Improvement and Clearance) Act, which provided a legal meaning to the word 'slum' in India as a place where buildings were unfit for human habitation as a result of 'dilapidation, overcrowding, faulty arrangements and design of buildings, narrowness or faulty arrangement of streets, lack of ventilation, light or sanitation facilities, or any combination of factors detrimental to safety, health or morals' (Slum Areas Act 1956). The use of 'slum' was specific to Indian colonial history (since the British has coined this term for specific indigenous neighbourhoods in India) with its connections to British urban planning and therefore had enormous symbolic force. Although Slum Areas Act at the time was to cater for the declining historic walled city which during the British rule had been racially segregated and denied basic infrastructure and services (Legg 2007), 'slum' as a legal term within this Act was used to include both declining inner-city areas and slums across Delhi that had substandard housing and lacked basic services.

This legal force around the word 'slum' is particular to India. In a global context, 'slum' has a developmental force – reinforced and framed by the United Nations as one of the areas in which the global south has to formulate and enact a number of policies to eradicate poverty and bring empowerment to its women. The 'slum' in India however emerged as a legal terminology over and above its associated developmental status to deal with those 'anomic' spaces within the city. The Slum Areas Act as a law of exception was used to include a range of building typologies and tenure, seen as outside the norm. Under this legal terminology, not all slums were informal, nor were they all illegal. The 'slum' in India could range from historic neighbourhoods, urban villages, resettlement colonies, or the squatter settlements known as *Jhuggi Jhopri* (JJ) clusters in Delhi. The term 'slum' could be used as law to bring about demolition, upgradation and/or resettlement in any of these spaces.

This Act had tremendous consequence not just in the ways that the state has notified and dealt with slums since then, but also how residents of squatter settlements have imagined their identities, eligibilities and routes to the legal city. In order to be eligible for improvement or upgradation, areas had to be first notified as a 'slum' by a competent authority (municipal officers from the Slum Wing), which made particular settlements eligible to receive certain material and social entitlements from the state, determined by the number of slum development programmes launched since the 1960s. The legally designated status as 'slums' would permit the local authorities to take up in-situ upgradation, infrastructure improvements and collect 'betterment charges' from the beneficiaries. Slum clearance of these areas was to be carried out only if the land was needed for 'public interest'. Becoming a legally notified 'slum' however, is a paradox – on the one hand, residents of squatter settlements have strived to convince slum officials of notification since this would mean the provision and improvement of basic services, but on the other hand, designated slum areas have led to a lowering of property prices, to urban decay, and to social and material segregation from the rest of the city.

Masterplanning 'illegality'

The creation of New Delhi was part of a contested developmentality which involved a huge restructuring of Delhi's urban landscape. This rationale of development began during colonial period when the city was spatially and racially demarcated across types of population – native, civil servants and white British, and across types of landuse -parks, institutional, residential, industrial and commercial zones. Most of these were enacted through a series of byelaws formulated by the New Delhi Development Committee, a regulatory body which had jurisdiction over the new city of sovereign power and the Delhi Improvement Trust with jurisdiction over old Delhi (Legg 2007). After independence however, a number of enquiries into the ineffectiveness of different regulatory bodies led to the demands for a masterplan and a single regulatory authority across the Delhi metropolitan area. There were two rationales behind this – the first was to manage the planning and growth of Indian cities which had gone into decline during the colonial period and was forecast to increase their economic activities after independence (Planning Commission 2001); and the second was driven by a desire for planned order that was seen to have been lost as a result of the 'ad hoc' settlements that had erupted across the city after independence.

In 1960, the Delhi Development Authority (DDA) was created by a statutory act of Parliament and became the single planning authority responsible for the development and disposal of land in the capital. Under the DDA, experts from

Ford Foundation in USA collaborated with members of the Indian National Planning Commission to produce the first ever Masterplan for Delhi (1962–81). Its intention was to acquire urban land for capital development projects, reduce urban sprawl by building a green belt around the city, and to remove 'surplus' population to a series of 'satellite towns' around Delhi. Land use was to conform to a set of statutory restrictions around zoning- commercial, industrial, residential and retail areas physically separated from each other. Infrastructure and services were to be provided in these zones based on their sanctioned land uses in the masterplan. The notion of DDA becoming the sole owner of all public land in the city was related to a strong desire among urban planners for regulation of public property and civic space by a state institution in the context of intense anxieties over the 'squatter problem' in the city. The idea was that DDA as a statutory institution of the state would be able to control, maintain, and develop public land for the shared use of the public.

To this end, the Indian Parliament passed the Urban Land Ceiling Act in 1976, which provided a ceiling or an upper limit to the amount of land that could be owned by an individual. Using this Act, the Delhi Development Authority (DDA) acquired 36,000 acres of urban land (Bhargava 1983) – its aim was to use this for future development of housing and various infrastructure projects in the city. Significantly, through this acquisition, the DDA came to have over 62 percent share in the number of squatters in the city, which could now be demolished and resettled under the statutory power of DDA. It is then that the label of 'unauthorized colonies' became significant because this referred to the curiously unofficial status of squatter settlements within the classificatory systems of the Delhi Masterplan. In Delhi, since the 1960s then, the process of acquiring and owning public land has been highly regulated and formalized through the practices of the Delhi Development Authority and the Urban Land Ceiling Act.

In Delhi, much of the 'illegality' vested in squatter settlements is related to the violations of the Delhi Masterplan. The masterplan selectively dealt with areas of the city as 'spaces of exception', as violations of zoning and landuse – allocating slums and squatter settlements for resettlement and demolition while elite farmhouses built on the fringes of wildlife sanctuaries, five-star hotels and warehouses built in violation of the zoning guidelines were overlooked. In Delhi in particular, it is argued that one of the reasons behind the rapid growth of squatter settlements since the 1970s was due to the failure of the Delhi Masterplan to provide adequate and affordable housing to the poor, and the DDA to build even the housing numbers prescribed in the masterplan (Nigam 2002). As Nigam (2002) notes, in the 20 years from 1951 to 1971, the number of squatter settlements in the city increased from 199 to 1,373, housing more than 98,483 households. The removal of squatter settlements to the urban peripheries then became imperative, because they were occupying 'public land' (owned by DDA). The masterplan therefore designated separate zones near the fringes of the city where the squatters were to be relocated. Such interlocking notions of property, public land, and masterplanning produced a planning environment in Delhi where the removal of squatters to the resettlement colonies on its peripheries was justified in terms of their 'legitimate' place within the masterplan. During 1961–77, the Delhi Development Authority (DDA) developed 47 resettlement colonies of about 200,000 plots accommodating about 240,000 households on the fringes of the city (Department of Urban Development 2006).

Emergency planning (1975–77)

In 1975, Indira Gandhi declared State Emergency which meant the curtailment of all democratic rights, including the freedom of speech. To do this, she suspended the judiciary which in the Indian Constitution was empowered to strike down any law formulated by the state as 'unconstitutional'. This was a state exerting an absolute form of ideological power – both in terms of reconfiguring Delhi's urban geography as well as in shaping its future population. The Emergency State then launched a 'city-beautification program' which entailed forced and often violent eviction of slums from across Delhi, as well as a 'population control' program which entailed forced sterilizations of the urban poor. These two initiatives were executed through a suspension of laws, rights, citizenships, national policies and democracy. Not only that, the Emergency was spatialized in so far as it was inscribed on the spaces and bodies of squatters themselves and thus removed the distinctions between public and private bodies in law.

The Indian emergency declared in 1975–77 has been likened to a state of exception (Tarlo 2003). As Tarlo shows through her analysis of the Indian Emergency (1975–77), the spatialization of this state of exception was most effectively inscribed onto Delhi slums. The population control programme was regularly adopted within the structure of Delhi's Slum Wing, who took decisions on demolition and resettlement of slums based on sterilization of slum dwellers (Tarlo 2003). Location and visibility of the slum were important in these decisions – slums on prime urban land and city centre locations were provided with alternative land when demolished, while those on marginal and less visible land (such as next to contaminated land) were not provided with resettlement until an adult member of the household participated in the sterilization programme. City centre slums such as those in old Delhi, and near middle-class residential areas were cleared under the 'city-beautification' scheme sanctioned by Indira Gandhi and enforced under the aegis of her son Sanjay Gandhi and the vice-chairman of the Delhi Development Authority.

The slums constituted a 'site of disorder' within an Emergency state that strived to produce order. This was of course based on Western notions of modernity, urban planning and the public realm. Slums provided the justification for suspending law and civil rights during this moment – they became the sites of exception from where order, modernity and beauty could be reintroduced into a postcolonial city. To do this, the vice-chairman of the Delhi Development Authority, Jagmohan set about his dream of saving the capital 'from turning into a veritable slum, a

death trap for future generations, a symbol of national degradation and shame'
(Jagmohan 2005: 87). Tarlo notes that according to official statistics alone,
'around 700,000 households were evicted from the city centre and relocated in
resettlement colonies in the urban fringes, and 161,000 persons were sterilized
during 1975–77'. (Tarlo 2001: 69)

Tarlo (2003) suggests however, that law was subverted at the local level
through a combination of violence, trickery and market forces. Slum dwellers
negotiated and worked their way around a difficult situation not because they
colluded with state ideologies; rather because they had very little choice in terms
of their resettlement and sterilization. Thus Tarlo notes that they used 'pure
pragmatism' in trying to make the best of a situation that provided them with little
options – strategies of avoidance and transfer became important in such situations
of extreme fear and coercion. Families decided who amongst them could become
part of the state schemes in order that the benefits of resettlement could be enjoyed
by the family. This meant that older members or those who already had children
would volunteer for sterilization while those young or unmarried would be
shielded from its reach. This was also gendered in so far as the sterilization drive
was largely directed towards and taken up by men in the families. Tarlo's account
of the Emergency thus challenges the myth of the 'victim' of sovereign power as is
common in literature around rule of law and the state of exception. Rather it shows
the gruesome reality of how unwilling actors within sovereign rule get drawn into
becoming participants of a force of law. I will explore this aspect in detail in the
second part of this book.

Moving to the peripheries

By 1982, the number of squatter households in Delhi had increased by record
numbers to 113,000 (Banerji 2005) largely as a result of the relocated squatters
moving back into the city from its peripheries. In 1982, a newly revised Masterplan
(1982–2001) promised resettlement to around 49,000 squatter households, with
provisions of income earning opportunities within or in proximity of resettlement
colonies. During 1981–2001 the DDA was expected to construct 160,000 dwelling
units, of which 70 percent were intended for the economically weaker sections and
low-income groups. Yet, this period saw the construction of only 55,000 houses,
of which only 58 percent were allotted to the urban poor (Banerji 2005). The
resettlement colonies constructed on the city fringes did not take into account
squatters' needs to remain close to employment opportunities and infrastructure
facilities. Much of these colonies remained unoccupied as its residents moved
back into the city to other squatter settlements. Further, as the city expanded, it
drew these peripheral colonies of the 1970s towards itself in the 1990s, so much
so, that some of these colonies began to be located close to the new upmarket
commercial and retail centres.

The relationship between centre and periphery in Delhi has always been temporal. The area outside the administrative setting of Delhi and New Delhi (denoted as National Capital Territory or NCT), have tended to exist as villages with a largely agricultural population. These areas on the periphery of the city belonged to the neighbouring regional states of Haryana, Rajasthan, Uttar Pradesh and Uttarakhand, which once urbanized became known as 'urban villages' within the Delhi masterplan. Within the administrative context these were exceptional places, which could be developed at a large scale for generating 'counter-magnets' to the city. These became places where new centres for urban migration were to be realized.

The urbanization of Delhi's peripheries followed a very different model from other North American or Latin American cities. The north-east, north-west and south-east zones of the urban periphery were developed as large-scale squatter resettlement projects for slums demolished in the city centre. The camp that I studied was located near one of them. The eastern and south-western zones of the periphery on the other hand were developed into 'satellite-towns' for the middle-classes – these were Gurgaon, Faridabad, Noida and later Greater Noida (see Figure 2.1 later in this chapter). Thus unlike American cities, Delhi's urban peripheries were not exclusively wealthy suburbs, and unlike Brazilian cities the peripheries were not exclusively the realm of the urban poor to whom subdivisions had been sold without legal validity (Holston 2008). Rather the spatial segregation along Delhi urban peripheries was based upon geographic separation of middle-class and resettlement colonies into different satellite towns. This counter-migration to the peripheries of Delhi was a huge state-led initiative which began even before the Emergency, but which has continued to this day.

In the 1990s, slum upgradation and tenure legalization were the most expensive solutions for the urban institutions involved. Under pressures of land values, demolition and resettlement remained a widespread strategy. Legal tenure through resettlement became the panacea of the 'problem' of slums – it was evoked time and again by politicians, media, NGOs, development agencies and grassroots organizations. Move to the peripheries in this context epitomized the official route to legitimacy since it was in the peripheries that squatters were provided with some form of legal tenure by the state. Of course this was as much a myth as utopia, since not all squatters could be resettled, and space standards actually reduced over the years to make some resettlement colonies worse than squatter settlements.

These resettlement initiatives were assessed by independent planning committees, which from time to time shaped the range of measures towards demolition and resettlement. One of the most significant reports undertaken by the Buch Committee in 1996 stated that none of the resettlement schemes undertaken by the DDA have worked since the squatter population in Delhi had risen by 85 percent from 1990–94. They recommended that vacant land be protected against encroachment and that the Delhi Government immediately identify land to be cleared of encroachment, described as follows.

Lands of strategic importance, right of way for a road or railway, land earmarked for essential services such as a sub-station or a hospital, land need on a priority basis for public use, land reserved for a specific purpose whose use cannot be transferred to another site; land with intrinsic high economic value which can only be realized if the land is out to the earmarked use; JJ clusters which are a *direct nuisance* [my emphasis] and cause of social tension in the area; clusters exposed to the vagaries of nature such as Yamuna Bandh. (Planning Commission 2002: 68)

Buch recommendations and those of several successive reports have shown the way for further demolition and resettlement of squatters to the peripheries of the city. The 'nuisance' discourse initiated by the Buch recommendations is what Ghertner (2008) notes as the performance of a semiotic task that transforms the discourse of 'slums are dirty' to 'slums are a nuisance'. This transformation Ghertner suggests, 'carries out much deeper ideological work' to reorient 'the terrain of citizenship, social justice and access to the city' (Ghertner 2008: 11). The Buch recommendations' adoption of the nuisance discourse shaped policy and urban development practices in the 2000s and was reinforced through the subsequent court rulings since 2000.

The myth of resettlement

State resettlement is not without financial or social cost to squatters. Resettlement of squatters to the peripheries is often driven by geographies of urban land values, and provides legal tenure conditional upon removal from prime urban land. The very early resettlement schemes in Delhi gave freehold rights to a plot of land on cash-down payment. From the late 1970s, resettlement was provided on leasehold plots on a subsidized mortgage (Ali 1990) and squatters were also liable to pay a nominal leaseholder fee each year. But since the mid-90s, allotments of plots have been made as five or ten year 'license of inhabitation' (Kundu 2004), in which residents have no rights to sell or rent these units. In more recent resettlement schemes after 2000, the licensee receives a photo identity card on which the plot number and license number are clearly marked, and has to be shown to officials from the Slum Wing during inspections. If this card cannot be produced during inspections the Slum Wing officers can seal these plots on the justification that this was not being inhabited by the licensee.

Over the years, space standards provided in resettlement colonies have also steadily declined. The Delhi masterplan in 1960s provided for 80 square metre plots within resettlement schemes. During the 1970s this was reduced to 40 square metres. In 1982, plot sizes were further reduced to 25 square metres. After 2000, two types of plot sizes were proposed – 18 square metre plots for those with identity cards before 31 January 1990, and 12.5 square metre plots for those with voter registration cards after this date but before 31 January 1998 (Dupont

2008). The actually allocated plot sizes in the resettlement colonies however are usually 12.5 square metre (Menon-Sen and Bhan 2008) – barely large enough for a medium sized room and often smaller than some of the squatter homes in more established settlements. These are also based on a notion of self-help labelled as 'incrementality' where the residents are expected to add to the structure and make improvements to their houses at a later date. Tenure was provided through joint titles for men and women in the family, or only to women in women-headed households.

These declines in standards produce a range of marginalizations. After all, 12.5 square metres is a room not larger than three metre by four metre in each direction, and difficult for a family to live in. This is consistent with various reports on slums which note that environmental conditions in resettlement colonies are often worse than the slums from which they had been relocated (Ali 2003). Half of Delhi's resettlement colony residents do not have individual water connections, there are few individual toilets and community toilet facilities are far from adequate, garbage is rarely collected from these colonies by the municipality, the roads are in severe disrepair, street lights do not work, and education and health facilities are grossly inadequate. Despite some form of formal legal tenure, these places are characterized by lack of infrastructure, crime and no material improvement in their standard of living (Bhan 2009, Ghosh 2008, Menon-Sen and Bhan 2008).

There has also been a lack of clear allocation of duties and responsibilities of low-cost housing projects between DDA and Municipal Corporation of Delhi (MCD). These two authorities shared the responsibility of slum clearance (through the Slum Wing) in an ambiguous manner; the former undertook the development and capital investment projects while the task of maintenance rested with the latter. The Slum Wing has also moved between these two departments various times, which has made it very difficult for slum dwellers to hold any institution accountable for their condition.

In addition, the Census and MCD figures are very different in terms of the total slum population in Delhi. The Planning Commission (2002) noted that the MCD count of slum population in 2002 was three million, whereas the Census reported a number of 1.85 million. This discrepancy also exists in land ownership. As mentioned earlier, a large proportion of squatter settlements are now under DDA land, but as the Planning Commission notes, much of this land is shown in land records as under dual ownership with other institutions. But with both DDA and other institutions denying ownership of these jointly owned lands, improving services or providing resettlement to squatters on these lands have remained a challenge.

More recently, the first survey of resettled squatters in Delhi since 2000, notes that while the residents of the squatter settlements were promised legal tenure in plotted development outside the city, in reality only less than half of them were considered eligible for these plots (Menon-Sen and Bhan 2008). But these did not come free; those eligible had to pay subsidized rates for purchasing these plots (in addition to bribes to municipality officials) which were then given on five year leases. Above all, these resettlement colonies were not connected to urban basic services – water, electricity and sanitation were not provided by the state but subcontracted to private companies. Menon-Sen and Bhan note that far from freeloading on state services, these resettled residents were paying more than the rest of the city to access infrastructure. Legalization through resettlement then was a myth since it had pushed those in 'legal settlements into illegality in order to meet their basic needs' (Menon-Sen and Bhan 2008: 55).

Housing policies for the 'urban poor'

State schemes of providing housing for the 'urban poor' have tended to require a minimum level of 'worthiness' from squatters in order to be included. This includes the use of particular idioms and representations of legal subjecthoods that make squatters eligible for state housing. This produces a performative force in the lives of squatters in order to be eligible for state housing measures – it means that slum dwellers must find ways to argue for their eligibility under these schemes through particular subjecthoods of caste, tribal affiliation and poverty.

One of the main idioms of self-representation has obviously been that of economic disadvantage. The Delhi Development Authority delivers finished housing schemes for different social classes zoned across different parts of the city – Economically Weaker Sections (EWS), Low-income group (LIG), Middle-Income Group (MIG) and Higher-Income Group (HIG). Housing for resettlement is provided under the EWS scheme, which has relied on providing serviced plotted developments based on incremental housing models. But as I have discussed elsewhere (Datta 2008), squatters and slum dwellers find it very hard to invest financially in these models, and have traditionally sold these to speculators. They have also benefited the least from this scheme since most of the housing by DDA was developed for MIG and HIG groups (Banerji 2005).

Economic disadvantage is usually easier for squatters to present as their most marginalizing condition. Their location in squatter settlements usually makes them eligible (under certain conditions imposed by the state) but dependent on state programmes of development. Much of these housing policies for the poor are related to the National Housing Policy of India drafted in 1988 which described itself as a 'war against human indignity' (Planning Commission 1988: 1). It laid down legal and regulatory reforms to speed up the process of housing construction for the urban poor since lack of housing 'compels the needy to turn to unauthorized construction and the growth of ugly slums which today totally disfigure the national landscape' (Planning Commission 1988: 9). The argument was that resettlement housing would provide much needed space to squatter families who were living in overcrowded conditions. Since then the policy has undergone several revisions and amendments. The current version drafted in 2005 aims to 'promote sustainable development of habitat in the country, with a view to ensure equitable supply of land, shelter and services at affordable prices'. (Planning Commission 2005: 3)

In the late 1990s, the Ministry of Urban Development put forward a draft National Slum Policy for consultation, which addressed all under-serviced settlements – unauthorized occupation of land, congested inner-city built up areas, fringe area unauthorized developments, and villages within urban areas and in the periphery, irrespective of tenure or ownership or land use. In many ways, this policy was a significant change in the political approach towards squatters since it made it mandatory for slum evictions to be accompanied by the simultaneous provision of alternative housing sites. It also highlighted the different needs of men and women in the slums stipulating that livelihoods and women's particular needs were to be carefully addressed through the provision of childcare, primary healthcare, and literacy campaigns. The National Slum Policy did not expressly seek to legitimize squatter settlements per se – rather it proposed a 'city without slums'.[1] This rhetoric was significant – on the one hand, it aimed to reinforce particular imaginations of a sanitized and rationalized modern city, while on the other hand, it seemed to suggest a connection between state policy and social justice. The National Slum Policy however, was never ratified in the Parliament. Indeed Kundu (2004) notes that in the future, provision of land even in peripheral settlements on a massive scale seems unlikely because of rising costs. He predicts that if anything, the eviction process is likely to be strengthened in the future, quite independent of which political party wins the election.

In 2001, the Indian state announced the *Valmiki Ambedkar Awas Yojana* (VAMBAY) scheme 'to ameliorate the conditions of the Urban Slum dwellers living below poverty line' (Government of India 2001). These made high proportions of reservations for particular subjecthoods – not less than 50 percent for 'Scheduled Castes and Tribes', 30 percent for 'Backward Classes' and 15 percent for 'Other Backward Classes' as defined by the State government, and five percent for physically & mentally disabled and handicapped persons. Not only did it emphasize the connection between poverty and lower caste status, the cultural politics of this scheme is also worth noting. In its naming, the scheme

---

1   This notion draws upon the action plan 'Cities without Slums' drafted by the Cities Alliance in 1999. It was subsequently endorsed by 150 heads of state and governments (including India) attending the UN Millennium Summit in September 2000. Among many other policies, the action plan stressed the need to provide a legal system where property rights and security of tenure are seen as sustainable approaches to slum upgrading (Cities Alliance 1999). The UN Millennium Development Goals (MDGs) which emerged from the Millennium Summit were particularly relevant in this context. Goal seven of the MDGs aimed to make 'significant improvement in the lives of at least 100 million slum dwellers by the year 2020' in line with the 'Cities without Slums' initiative. Goal seven had targets to 'halve, by 2015, the proportion of people without sustainable access to safe drinking water' and 'proportion of people with access to secure tenure'. However, there are many complex forms of housing tenure in informal settlements 'ranging from the existence of national legal rights to subjective assessments of security, through to actual evictions' (UN-Habitat 2003: 8), which has led to prolonged debates over what the target value of security of tenure should be.

invoked saint *Valmiki* – a low caste dacoit in Indian mythology who moved up to the caste of a priest through meditation, and subsequently wrote the Indian epic story of Ramayana; and it invoked Dr B.R. Ambedkar a low caste Indian intellectual educated in the west, leading political figure in Indian independence, and architect of the Indian Constitution. The word *Valmiki* also refers to those low-caste (historically referred to as untouchables) groups who see themselves as direct descendants of saint Valmiki and belonging to the same caste as Dr Ambedkar. In its naming, this scheme then attempted to join the mythical to the modern, indigenous knowledge to western rationality, symbolize hope, and ultimately underline the idea of social mobility of low-caste citizens.

The entry of such cultural politics in housing policies resonates with what Nandy (2002) notes as the changing terrain of cultural difference in India. By connecting constitutionally defined identities with housing entitlements, these policies attempt to crystallize cultural differences in everyday life. They have been important in producing a solidification of the 'self' that is highly fluid and intersectional within everyday life, into a 'self' that is defined by constitutional law. It has facilitated the making of moral claims to 'entitlements' from the state as I discussed in Chapter 1, and it has made it possible to demand from within the normalizing 'slum' rhetoric, a future in the 'legal' city.

In 2009, the government further launched a special housing scheme called *Rajiv Awas Yojana* (RAY) aiming to create a 'slum free India' (Government of India 2010) in five years. The aims are to provide investment through the *Jawaharlal Nehru National Urban Renewal Mission* (JNNURM) to regional states to build housing for people living in slums. The first part of this scheme is to encourage regional states to create a GIS survey of all slums and squatter settlements and biometric surveys of all slum dwellers in the cities where this would be implemented. Investment released under this scheme will attempt to create 'slum free city plans' which would provide affordable housing to eligible slum dwellers in terms of housing, infrastructure and interest subsidized loans. In the second stage, states are required to assess the 'rate of growth of the city with a 20 year perspective, and ... specify the actions proposed to be taken to obtain land ... and promote the construction of affordable EWS houses' (Government of India 2010: 11). Significant in this is the potential of delivery through public-private partnerships and the flexibility to each federal state in determining their own legislations towards 'slum free city planning'.

In the RAY policy however, cultural politics have given way to more judico-legal interpretations of rights and eligibility to resettlement. Thus it is no longer public subjectivities of caste or tribal affiliation, rather squatters' temporal relationship with the city which has become the criteria for eligibility. The first product of RAY housing scheme launched in Delhi in 2010 however, consisted of a mere 7900 houses . The Slum Wing had received more than 250,000 applications for this housing, but had kept eligibility to be determined by possession of ration cards from 1998, which significantly reduced the number of beneficiaries.

State housing schemes for the urban poor therefore have taken a remarkable trajectory since the 1970s in recognizing and reinforcing particular registers of difference of its 'beneficiaries'. By shifting these over the years from economic disadvantage to caste, gender and tribal affiliations to temporal links with the city, these policies have determined how particular forms of 'public' identities become part of the politics of demolition and resettlement, inclusion and exclusion from the city.

After 2000: Delhi's worldly aspirations

In 2004, Delhi won the bid for the 2010 Commonwealth Games. Soon thereafter, the Chief Minister of Delhi, Sheila Dixit announced her intentions of using the Games to invest in the city's infrastructure, to improve its urban environment, and turn Delhi into a global city. Yet, as Delhi suffered from the worst power cuts and water problems in 2006, slogans began to circulate of a 'walled city, not world city' being produced in the capital, referring to the dualisms between the historic old city of Shahjahanabad and New Delhi, between the past and future, and between underdevelopment and modernity. This was important since the Commonwealth Games were seen as a springboard for its 2020 Olympic Games bid.

Delhi's world-city dream is facilitated by a series of changes since 1991 that has led to the devolution of power to Indian cities and an increasing intra-national competition to achieve world city status. First, at the national level, various states made changes to their constitutional frameworks to incorporate the structure of participatory governance encouraged by the UN.[2] Till 1991, India had always functioned as a federal system, while local level institutions only had statutory status under state law. In 1991, the 74th and 75th amendments made to the Indian Constitution established a three-tier system of local governance giving increased powers to local authorities and to Urban Local Bodies (ULB). Although Delhi was particularly unique in this reorganization as a capital city that had always maintained a certain degree of autonomy, these amendments nevertheless empowered and entrusted local authorities such as the Municipal Corporation of

---

2   The UN articulated the Agenda 21 objectives, which required participation at the local level in planning and implementing environmental, social, and economic policies – the focus was particularly on empowering women, children and local communities. Recognizing the need for infrastructure, especially for the urban poor, Agenda 21 recommendations were to provide this through 'adequate pricing policies, reduction of subsidies, and recovering the full costs of environmental services such as water supply, sanitation, and waste management' (UN-Habitat 2003). It also stipulated that the role of non-governmental organizations and local level governance should be strengthened in the signatory countries to achieve these objectives. This was further reinforced in the Istanbul declaration on human settlements as part of the Habitat Agenda, which argued for a 'new era of cooperation' between the state, civil society and private sector to create sustainable human settlements (Future Cities and Habitat II 1996).

Delhi and the Delhi Development Authority to function as institutions of local self-government – to elect its own Mayor, to manage and fund their own programs and to engage directly with local community groups.

The devolution of power means more responsibility and financial burdens to local authorities which places an increased reliance on public-private partnerships as key to the efficient supply of housing for the urban poor.[3] This has led to a newly formed land market which shapes decisions on the resettlement of slums. The urban government usually makes land available to private developers at a subsidized rate for which the developers have to take the initiative to develop and deliver housing for the urban poor. This means that such land can then be speculated upon by private investors to prioritize their projects – while prime urban land can be used for more profitable projects like offices, retail or commercial purposes, it is only the marginal and underserviced land which makes it financially viable for housing the urban poor. As Sanyal and Mukhija (2001) note, the process of negotiation and management of low-income housing delivery through partnerships have also often hindered rather than facilitated the smooth delivery of legal housing for those in squatter settlements.

Further to this, the devolution of power has also encouraged local authorities to initiate new forms of participatory governance using ordinary urban citizens. In Delhi, the *Bhagidari* or 'share-holding' scheme initiated by Shiela Dixit, Delhi's Chief Minister provides civil society groups, NGOs and Residents' Welfare Associations (RWAs) with deliberative powers through participatory processes. This includes initiatives like giving the responsibility of the upkeep of parks and public places to Residents Welfare Associations (RWAs) in order to prevent encroachment on public land. However, this is limited to 'authorized colonies', and not squatter settlements in which 60 percent of Delhi's urban poor reside. One of the striking effects of this in Delhi is the ways that the urban middle-classes have become actively involved in the making of cities and urban spaces through their involvement in RWAs, and have often taken recourse to legal institutions in order to reclaim urban spaces from slums and slum dwellers (Fernandes 2006).

Such processes produce conditions where the removal of squatters from the city is linked to market-led land development. In a selective enforcement of 'slum clearance', it is those slums which are on prime urban land that are the first to face demolition. Thus in 2001, slums along the Yamuna riverbanks near Gautampuri made way for the Commonwealth athletes' village (Verma 2002), while other

---

3   The transformation in the Indian housing sector began in 1988 with the United Nations General Assembly of the Global Strategy for Shelter to the Year 2000 (GSS) which recognized the severity of the 'housing problem' and called for the adoption of new roles and responsibilities of various actors in the shelter-delivery process including the crucial role of women and women's organizations in solving the crisis of adequate housing. Although it did not propose that governments should withdraw from housing, it placed significant responsibilities on the public-sector agencies for creating an 'enabling environment' and ensuring the availability of shelter for all (United Nations Chronicle 1988).

slums demolished from prime urban land in AIIMS, Nehru Place, and Hauz Khas made way for new metro stations and capital investment projects (see Figure 2.1). Those removed from these sites were moved to the outskirts of the city – to areas like Narela, Bhalaswa, Puthkalan and Papankalan to the north and west of the city and Kalyanpuri, Madanpur Khadar, and Molabund to the East.

These demolitions and resettlements were carried out in a rush before the new masterplan came into force in 2001. In the new masterplan, the redevelopment of slums has been envisioned through vertical development of tower blocks where they would be resettled by private developers. In this conceptualization of resettlement is embedded another set of assumptions around home, which is markedly different from those made few decades ago. The 'solution' of high-rise blocks presumes a static notion of family and households as against the dynamic nature of incremental housing embedded in the earlier resettlement plots. While it was possible for earlier resettled families to expand their floor space by constructing vertically, the high-rise apartments will make that option impossible.

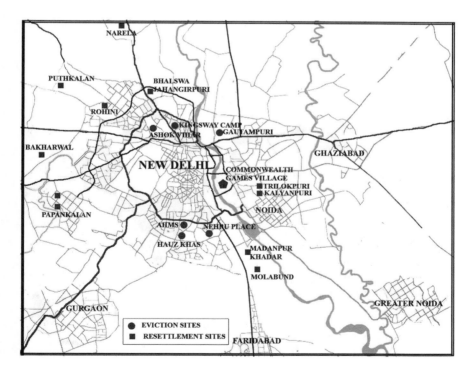

Figure 2.1   Resettlement and eviction sites in 2001. (Based on Department of Urban Development 2006: 6–8)

The discussions in this chapter have highlighted that those living in squatter settlements are suspended between law and exceptionality, between resettlement and demolition and between legal and subjective identities. The violence of urban development which inscribes illegality on their lives and spaces is also the violence of naming, identifying and enumerating particular population groups based on legally identified categories, which provides them with particular idioms of representation through which to stake their claims to the legal city. This violence cannot be categorized through the making or maintaining violence of law; rather it is related to the violence of everyday life where squatters have to live under the continuous threat of demolition while performing public identities of caste, class and gender in order to prove their 'worthiness' to forms of legality constructed by the state and judiciary. This violence is related to an exclusion from the city by law, which shapes the politics of everyday life and becomes a conscious mode of distinction, not just from the city itself, but also from others like them living in 'legal' slums. I turn to this in the next chapter.

Chapter 3
Construction of Squatter Settlements

In the 1970s, Delhi went through some tumultuous urban transformations. Around 2000 hectares of land on its urban fringes was developed for a massive slum clearance project during the Emergency period (1975–77). Lakshmipuri resettlement colony located on 31.5 hectares of land was one such project planned to re-house slum dwellers from the city centre to the commercial and industrial areas on the southern fringes of Delhi's metropolitan boundaries. The rationale was to create an 'orderly city' by removing the symbols of decay and deviance from the city and giving them tenure security in neatly planned 25 square metre plots of land in which to legally build their homes and live. The Lakshmipuri resettlement project required the clearing of parts of the southern edge of an urban forest, one of the largest green belts in South Delhi tracing its history to the Delhi Sultanate period (1320–1413 AD). This location was attractive since the northern edge of the forest was making way for various middle-class colonies which could draw upon the residents of these resettlement colonies for service sector work. This is how in 1976, Lakshmipuri resettlement colony became part of the 'legal' city.

It was during this time that word spread that land was available in the area and small clusters of makeshift hutments crept up along the fringes of the resettlement colonies bordering onto the urban forest. These were not built on allocated land – rather they were on land appropriated by those who had not been eligible for resettlement plots. The adjacent vacant land became a suitable place to encourage others to settle there. The earliest residents who came to acquire land along the peripheries were mainly relatives or kin of those allotted plots in the resettlement colonies. Once they built a temporary home for themselves, they invited those they knew to join them. Current estimates of the number of residents in this squatter settlement put the figures at around 4,000–5,000 residents, living in an agglomeration of about 1000–1500 homes.

In Delhi, a large proportion (38 percent) of the slum population is concentrated in more affluent South Delhi, in places like Lakshmipuri, while the city centre, as a result of the slum clearance programmes of the 1970s houses only eight percent (Anthony and Maheswaran 2001). The labelling of these places as 'slums' however is in many ways a flexible terminology as mentioned in the previous chapter – in common use, it refers to the variety of formal and informal settlements in poor state of accommodation and basic infrastructure. The 'Lakshmipuri slums' are similarly a collection of these settlements – the planned resettlement colonies which were built by the state during the emergency years in what was then the urban peripheries, and the informal settlements that crept up alongside these resettlement colonies during this time. It is the latter that I focus on – those labelled as 'slums within slums' (Ali 1990) or 'camps' within Delhi's cartographical representations. These 'camps' reflect the 'illegal' city – they have no formal status within urban legislation and masterplan and therefore susceptible to demolition.

The making of Lakshmipuri camp

There is a widely held belief that a large part of squatting in Delhi was made possible by the land mafia who were given protection by the politicians. This land mafia is understood to have exploited the rural migrants who arrived in the city and who were then confined to the informal and illegal land market. Participants in the camp however had lived in other parts of Delhi before they squatted there. Their narratives of numerous movements across the city challenge more orthodox accounts of slums as 'cities of peasants' (Abu-Lughod 1971, Roberts 1979). In the camp, participants had roots in rural areas around Delhi and in neighbouring states, but had lived in the city long enough to become aware of particular opportunities that would allow them to appropriate land, build their homes, and live there for a reasonable period of time.

> I lived in Jangalpur earlier, near Lady Sriram College [South Delhi]. Lived there on rent, then some friends of his came, of my man [husband]. They said there is this place, *jhuggis* are being put up there, you come too. Then they came here to check it out, to see the place. They liked the place. At the time, they got tarpaulins, mats, and built a small *jhuggi*. [Asha]

Asha, who came into the camp during the late 1970s, narrated stories of 'finding' this camp through their social networks. Most residents like Asha were tenants in other parts of Delhi, paying rents which they could barely afford. Others had grown up in slums, which were demolished and resettled by the government during the Emergency. Avtar was one of them – his family had built a house in the Govindpuri camp in South Delhi which was demolished in 1977, but his family was not resettled since they did not have 'solid proofs' of eligibility. Avtar's family then came to Lakshmipuri, having heard from neighbours that land was available for squatting, took the permission of the local leader and began to build their house.

The last survey conducted on slums and squatter settlements in Delhi in 1995, notes that most slum dwellers come from the neighbouring states of Uttar Pradesh (48.7 percent), Rajasthan (17.5 percent) and Bihar (15 percent) (Anthony and Maheswaran 2001). Yet, while participants had roots in rural areas, and would indeed provide names of their villages when asked where they were from, they were what could be termed as 'long-term migrants'. My findings thus fall in line with more recent observations in Delhi (Dupont 2008) and Cairo (Bayat and Denis 2000) that squatter settlements have redistributed populations rather than housing new rural migrants.

Participants seemed to be aware even at the very start of this process, that in order to secure their future on this land it was important to do this in large numbers. One of the earliest residents, Moinullah who came in the camp during the late 1970s began to spread the word about available land for settlement.

> Approximately in 1977–78, everyone was making their *jhuggi* so we also made ours ... Had we wanted at that time, we could have taken much more [land] because the area at back and on this side was vacant, but then I thought that we are poor and that other people should also get a place. So, I requested others. I was here, there would be more, and then one more and then all of us would be together. It feels nicer when there are more people. Poverty becomes easier. If ten poor people get together then they can deal with hunger and thirst comfortably. [Moinullah]

Moinullah, moved here from North Delhi from where he used to face a long commute to work in South Delhi. He knew that the land on which he was building was not legally his, but on inviting others like him to live alongside, they would be able to deal better with legal complications in the future. By building many homes, and living similar lifestyles, the earliest 'settlers' then were not only staking their claims to a piece of the city, they were pioneering the production of squatter settlements in the city.

The early residents therefore made use of a variety of opportunities – the presence of vacant public land, their own social networks, and the negligence of law enforcement agencies, which would secure their stay in the city. In their radical appropriation of public land, their public identities were perceived by the urban planners, bureaucrats and urban elites as that of 'rural' migrants. But despite their strong rural links, these squatters who settled in the camp were part of the wider reordering of the city, displaced from city centre slums and priced out of rental properties, moving into liminal spaces bordering on resettlement colonies, and attempting through clumsy and haphazard efforts to secure a place in the city for their future generations. At this moment, 'illegality' was not their prime concern; in the absence of affordable housing, they perceived this as ways of 'making do' in the city.

Domesticating public land: the making of squatter homes

One of the first actions in the process of settling constitutes the clearing of land in order to make the ground suitable for building. The land which the squatters were settling upon was part of an urban forest in South Delhi which had a combination of dense undergrowth and rocky soil. Further, as they were adjacent to the resettlement colonies, which at that time did not have adequate sewage facilities; their land was often used for defecation by residents from these neighbouring resettlement colonies. Removal of human faeces was one of the few tasks in preparing the land for building homes, and the disposal of this rubbish became one of the many ways that camp residents began their interactions with the resettlement colonies.

Building their houses in this open land was a process of domestication of public land. Domestication meant appropriating and reordering the 'malevolent' outside into a home – a space of the inside, the realm of gendered reproduction of the family. Building a home however required bodily labour, not just in clearing the land but also digging into the rocky soil, and levelling the ground. Most of this labour was provided by the family, the men dug the ground, while the women removed the debris, sewed together plastic bags and sacks to cover the roof and walls. The contribution of men, women and even young children was crucial to the remarkable speed with which they build the houses, before they could be intercepted and removed by the police or municipality. The first houses were made of bamboo, timber pieces, sacks, plastic sheets or whatever building materials residents salvaged from across the city and brought with them to the camp. The boundaries of these houses were demarcated by erecting four bamboo poles in four directions, enclosing it with sacks and covering it with plastic sheets or straw.

> There were such ditches, deep ones. It was hilly terrain but people filled it up and built. We had stones on our land there was a heavy stone in the middle, another this side which is why this [house] is at such a height … So we built a kind of veranda first of stone …yes, then began keeping some stuff on it, then gradually, then we had done the floor, the second time, then we beat it down, we cut it a little, then put some soil mix, and made it even. So that the stones don't show, there are a lot of stones underneath. [Shabbu]

In appropriating land which was not under private ownership, the residents argued that they were domesticating a 'no man's land', turning over its soil and land through their embodied labours and creating a home for themselves. I hesitate to call this a 'non-western' notion of public space, but it is worth considering what Kaviraj notes as the marked discrepancies between two competing notions of public/private divisions (Kaviraj 1997) which produce contestations of urban land in cities like Delhi. For many participants, the land that they occupied was similar to Kaviraj's notion of 'public' that awaited its fulfilling through their embodied labours; it awaited the performance of their everyday domesticities, and it could only achieve its full potential through the building of their homes, through the taming of a 'wild forest'. In this context, illegality was seen merely as a matter of property codification, not a social and material ideology that could be enforced through a rule of law.

'Emergency' promises

During the Indian Emergency (1975–77), when large numbers of city centre slums were demolished, the camp residents were placed in a precarious situation. As a slum within a developing resettlement colony, they would have been removed from the land they occupied. Many of the informal leaders of the camp joined the mass protests during this time through a hunger strike in front of the Indian Parliament. Those familiar with Indian political history would know that Indira Gandhi was removed from power in 1977 and placed under house arrest for her role in the Emergency. But soon afterwards, she came back to power with absolute majority and began a very different political strategy where the urban poor were patronized for their votes. One of my participants, Shalu claimed that it was at this time that her grandfather secured a promise from Mrs Gandhi.

> During the '76 time [Emergency], they [grandfather and other residents] were on what do you call it – hunger strike. There was a hunger strike at the India Gate. He was there and then Indira Gandhi had said that you will not be displaced from this camp … If you are removed from here, you will be resettled in some other place. You stay here. If you have any problems, please come and meet me. [Shalu]

Shalu's account of her grandfather's political action as leader of the camp was confirmed by other older participants as one of the 'successes' of the 'pioneers' who set up the camp, a testimony of his worthiness as leader of the camp. There are divergent accounts of the exact order of the events that took place during this time. Some residents claim that assurance from Indira Gandhi was received in 1977 after the hunger strike. Others claim that following Indira Gandhi's re-election as Prime Minister in 1980, she personally visited these Camps across Delhi and other Indian cities and gave assurances of security. No one knew exactly what the terms were, and of course these assurances had no legal validity. But most of the physical improvements in the camp such as the construction of open drains, paving of the roads and so on were carried out by the Municipality after these events. These verbal assurances and the physical improvements in the camp gave residents a sense of legitimization and security in the 1980s and 1990s.

A note on tenure legalization in India

Indira Gandhi's promises to the residents were made in the context of the 1980s, when 'slum upgrading' practices became popular in India. In 1985, during the seventh Five-Year Plan, the Indian state on direction from UNESCO launched the Urban Basic Services Scheme (UBSS), which aimed at improving the infrastructure facilities in slums through the inter-agency coordination and a 'community' approach. It provided water supply, environmental improvement, health services and education for eight major slums in Delhi. This was not the first time however, that attempts were made at improving physical conditions in slums. In 1972, the Ministry of Urban Development had launched a scheme for Environmental Improvement and Upgrading of Slums (EIUS) which aimed to provide basic physical amenities in urban slums. This included one water tap for every 50 residents, drainage for waste water and storm water, one bathing space for every 20–50 persons, one water closet for every 20–25 persons and one electric pole every 30 metres. Around the same time, it also launched an in-situ upgradation programme, where three JJ clusters in Delhi were re-planned by redistributing the dwelling units as 10–12.5 square metre plots across the encroached land.

In 1991, the Government revised these programmes as 'Urban Basic Services for the Poor' (UBSP) and integrated them with earlier urban poverty alleviation programmes such as the Environmental Improvement of Urban Slums (EIUS), and Low Cost Sanitation (Banerji 2005). The objective of the UBSP scheme was to provide both social and physical amenities to the urban poor – water supply and sanitation, employment generation, and education and childcare for women. It saw the role of NGOs as crucial in the process of delivery through their role in collectivization and mobilization of community support and participation in these programmes in order to provide efficient delivery and take-up. From 1985–99, 503 pay-per-use toilet complexes were constructed, while 917 water hydrants and 601 hand pumps were provided from 1985–1990 (Banerji 2005). These were shared amenities provided at 'neighbourhood' levels. These basic improvements however, provided a sense of security to the residents since these programmes were not sanctioned by the state without the assurance from DDA that these settlements would not be demolished in the subsequent 10–15 years.

The argument for slum upgradation can be traced back to the 1960s in Turner's visions of 'self-help' in Latin American settlements, which suggested that those living in slums should not be criminalized; rather seen as entrepreneurs who were able to provide alternative solutions to the housing crisis in the global south (Turner 1967). In the 1980s, this argument was further developed by deSoto (1989, 2000) who proposed that giving legal tenure to those living in informal settlements was the only way of providing them with access to a range of economic benefits and ultimately improving their conditions. Tenure and upgrading involved the provision of the most basic services – water and sanitation, drainage, roads, footpaths, accompanied by community facilities and security of tenure. These projects did not involve house construction since these were largely based on assumptions of 'self-help' with loans for house improvement. Legalization was seen to facilitate access to formal finance mechanisms, to formal housing market economies, to offer the security to make investments in squatter homes, and in general to offer opportunities of accessing a wider range of services and benefits not usually available to illegal settlements.

These approaches were also produced from a global context of post-war international development which sought to reduce and define entire post-colonial nations as underdeveloped and in need of aid from the West (Sachs 1999). De

Soto's (1989) arguments were taken up by the United Nations and World Bank as a solution to informal settlements particularly in Asia and Latin America where slum upgradation was undertaken at a large scale during the 1980s (Gilbert 2002). The Indian state signed up to a host of global agreements with the UN in the 1980s, to formulate urban development policies in its metropolitan cities across the developing world.

Around this time approaches to the 'problem of slums' was also undergoing significant transformations in two related trajectories, both of which fused into a solution as 'legal tenure'. The first trajectory mobilized slum upgrading as a route to poverty alleviation in the third world. This was the deSoto (1989) argument around the relationship between legal tenure and socio-economic benefits. The second was to specifically engender slum upgrading as 'women's issue' and to empower women through this process. Successive reports on gender and development produced by the UN in the 1980s and 1990s repeatedly made the case for providing land titles to women, particularly in women headed households and to single women to simultaneously address the 'feminization of poverty'. Legalization of 'illegal' settlements through tenure and slum upgradation therefore became a catch-all in the 1980s for a range of national and urban development policies.

Tenure legalization has rightfully come under sustained criticism from development scholars. There are a number of reasons for this. First, scholars (Fernandes and Varley 1998, Gilbert 2002, Varley 1998, 2002) highlight concerns with the way that the legal/illegal dichotomy is used to introduce the urban poor to capitalist economies, without making any real difference to their lives. Differences between legal and illegal are seen to have been exaggerated by global development agencies, suggesting that 'the proponents of formalization share a belief in the efficacy of legalization as an engine of social and economic change that depends on the binary opposition of 'legal' and 'illegal' (Varley 2002: 450). They note that this dichotomy needs to be rejected in favour of a legal-illegal continuum. Gilbert goes so far as to suggest that legalization does not make any material changes in the lives of the urban poor since housing improvements and the informal housing market exists irrespective of secure legal status (Gilbert 2002). Legalization does not necessarily decrease overcrowding, improve sanitation or reorganize any of the social power relations that still exist in these settlements. Indeed, it is said that tenure absolves the state from providing anything more than the bare minimum (Davis 2006) and may turn squatters into speculators reinforcing some of the locally entrenched inequalities (Neuwirth 2006).

Tenure legalization was often used to political ends by the ruling parties to promote patronage, to prevent grassroots political action, and to remain in power. In making promises to those like Shalu's grandfather, Indira Gandhi also secured a number of votes for her Congress party and remained in power till 1984 when she was assassinated by her bodyguard. Significantly, just as in the case of urban Mexico (Varley 1998), the gesture of regularization brought about a political integration of the urban poor within a state framework of law. My purpose here is neither to support the deSoto argument of empowerment through tenure legalization, nor to suggest that tenure legalization is inconsequential. I find that both approaches are essentially addressing the issue of the role of the state and law in delivering welfare to the urban poor. As I have already mentioned at the start of this book, this issue cannot however be separated from how tenure legalization and illegality are both perceived and in turn transform gender power relations in everyday life. I turn to this issue next.

Legal and illegal slums

The residents of the camp soon realized that while they might be demographically similar to those residents of neighbouring resettlement colonies, in reality, they were perceived by those in these colonies as 'illegal', or those that had no right to be there. Part of the reasons behind this were that squatters were seen to directly compete with the residents of Lakshmipuri resettlement colonies in terms of resources – water, sewage, land and so on; but also that those in resettlement colonies wanted to move away from the stigma associated with informality and illegality. Here, with state sanction, those in resettlement colonies had finally entered the legal spaces of the city through a neatly ordered planned development with legal tenure. But they soon found out that this did not reduce their proximity or association with the illegal city. The symbolic and material associations with squatting produced particular contestations of space over the use of open land where the camp was situated.

> They [those in resettlement colonies] used to dump their faeces in this land, and we have moved it with buckets and thrown it in the jungle, people used to defecate sitting on the stones there, and there were insects and worms in the rainy season. Then we threw all that in the jungle and dug up the ground to cover up this place, there was a big hole which we have filled with our own hands. [Salma]

This was a double and contestatory 'publics' emerging in Lakshmipuri in the 1970s and 1980s – the notion of open land used for defecation by those in resettlement colonies[1] and the same land domesticated by squatters. There was a tension over what constituted 'public' land – one that was not privately owned and hence

---

1   Resettlement colonies usually provide a 'serviced plot' to its beneficiaries. Water, electricity and sewage connections are provided along the roads where the plots are laid out on. This means that when residents first move in they do not have any basic services. It is only when they build their house on this plot that they begin to add private connections to water, waste and sanitation. In the early years of Lakshmipuri resettlement colonies therefore, its residents faced similar struggles for basic services as did residents in the camp. Over the years however, residents of these resettlement colonies have built toilets

could be 'used' by all; and one that was the 'outside' and hence available for domestication (Chakrabarty 2002). The urban forest served both these notions of public land for the squatters and the resettlement colonies – for the former, it was dangerous and to be subsequently tamed and domesticated, whereas for the latter, it was the outside – a place where faeces and rubbish could be placed.

While the contestations of public and private between the squatters and the urban elites have received enough attention (Chakrabarty 2002, Kaviraj 1997), less attention has been paid to the relations between 'illegal' and 'legal' slums. Residents in these two settlements were demographically remarkably similar, and they also experienced similar struggles around access to material resources (such as water, sanitation, electricity). Yet those in resettlement colonies were seen as radically different by residents in the camp. These conceptualizations were produced not least through the harassment faced by those in the camp from agents of the state (such as municipality or police), but also because these two areas were markedly different in terms of morphology and built forms.

The resettlement colonies were planned on a linear grid, with 25 square metre plots laid out along straight roads; whereas the camp was more 'haphazard' and amorphous, with narrow winding roads often leading into cul-de-sacs and alleys, emerging into small clusters of houses and not following any clear settlement pattern. More significantly, the 'illegal' status of the camp was clear from the open drains that ran along each lane, which carried the wastewater out of the camp. Lakshmipuri resettlement colonies were connected to the municipal sewer and water lines. Over the years its residents had built private toilets in their houses and thus like the rest of the city had managed to keep its 'infrastructure' out of visibility.

Residents in the camp however perceived themselves as rightful claimants to urban infrastructure. While the rest of the city considered residents of these settlements as 'parasites' who were to be blamed for the power outages and water shortages in the city, residents often saw this as their entitlement.

> During V.P. Singh's [Prime minister of India in 1989] time electricity had been made free for us. So, during his time electricity was made free for poor people living in *jhuggis*. It had come in the [news] paper as well. So, people used to connect wires to get electricity. This was in the open. Thousands and lakhs of people are using electricity. There is nothing about stealing here. The Prime Minister had taken pity on the poor and had made such a statement, so we were using the electricity. [Moinullah]

Of course, V.P. Singh did not make electricity 'free' as Moinullah claimed. Other participants noted that this was indeed an illegal practice which the government would not obstruct since they were in effect huge vote banks for V.P. Singh, the

---

in their houses, have private water and waste connections and no longer use the forest for defecation.

Prime Minister at the time. Most squatters in the city including those in the camp made use of such practices to access 'benefits' such as electricity or water from politicians and political parties.

Participants therefore articulated their entitlements from a position of marginalization. As I mentioned in Chapter 1, such a position allowed them to make moral claims to their entitlements using specific constitutional privileges. Articulations of difference on the basis of class or caste or religion were common even to stake their entitlements to 'public goods'. Even though participants understood that their exclusion from basic services such as electricity, water and so on was on account of their illegal status; yet their social and economic marginalizations were seen to justify a seizing of public goods, as 'legitimate' entitlement to what was denied to them by law.

Residents in the resettlement colonies and the camp largely shared common histories and memories through extended families and kinship structures, but it was the differentiation on the basis of their relation to urban planning laws that determined how differences between these two places were perceived and negotiated by their respective residents. While they shared the marginalities of class

Figure 3.1   **Lanes inside the resettlement colonies (left) and camp (right).**
              Photo: Author 2005

with respect to the rest of the city, social, material and morphological differences between the camp and Lakshmipuri resettlement colonies, ultimately shaped the hopes, aspirations, and anxieties among those deemed to be on the 'wrong side' of the law. This produced a symbolic hierarchy among the residents – those in the resettlement colonies regarded themselves as legitimate citizens whereas those in the camp aspired to one day achieve legitimacy like their neighbours, and be freed of the social and material struggles that they had to undertake everyday.

Housing 'legitimate' subjects

Till the late 1980s, participants had understood their relationship with the rule of law primarily through their marginalized positions as urban poor. Although caste-based privileges had been written into the Indian Constitution, in the appropriation of public land, in differentiating themselves from the legal slums and in understanding their marginalization from other urban citizens, they had largely described themselves through class-based disadvantages in the public realm.

All this changed in 1989 when V P Singh, the leader of the Janata Dal political party became Prime Minister of India and began a process of legalizing squatters in Delhi. Known as the 'transition man' his term was the shortest (less than a year) in Indian political history but his rise to power was on the basis of his manifesto on caste-reservations. As soon as he came to power, his party voted in favour of introducing 27 percent reservations for 'Other Backward Classes' (OBC) over and above the already existing 22.5 percent reservation for Scheduled Castes and Tribes (SC/ST). The OBCs identified as both Hindu and non-Hindu castes, included *gujjars* (sportsmen), *dhobis* (washermen), *gwalas* (milkmen), and *kasais* (butchers). These social groups saw themselves at a higher social order than the *dalits* (untouchables), yet were in many ways also marginalized by structural conditions of poverty. Unlike the SC/ST list however, the OBC was to be a dynamic list where social groups would be taken on or off it depending on review every ten years. These differentiated privileges became extremely significant in 'legalizing' squatter households in Delhi, where a large proportion were lower castes.

In 1989, Janata Dal, the ruling political party began a scheme of issuing identity cards to squatters in the city. These identity cards offered voting rights, food ration cards, and hence for the first time – legitimate status as urban citizens. Along with this, the ruling party also started a token allotment system, where each squatter home became entitled to resettlement from the state in case of demolition. These documents issued to those living in slums allowed them to achieve degrees of legitimization not imagined before and became the only possible route to imagining a 'legal' future in a resettlement colony.

These documents became the markers of what Chatterjee (2004) calls both 'citizen' and 'population'. Although these two terms were produced by different processes, they intersected in particular ways in the claims to resettlement. In these documents, the squatter 'population' was an enumerative category produced from the practices of governmentality of the VP Singh regime. These documents allowed squatters to be classified under this population group for the purposes of state developmental goals. 'Citizen' on the other hand, was what the residents of the camp were laying claims to through the symbolic meanings attached to these documents – it facilitated their regularization and hopes for resettlement in the future. Enumeration as squatter population then allowed residents to stake moral claims of the state in terms of belonging to the legal city.

These set of documents also turned squatter homes overnight into precious economic capital – a material possession that in the combination of the right set of documents could provide a legitimate urban home in the future. Although squatter homes which were bought and sold did not have legal validity, stamp paper receipts from 'owners' or prior occupants with signatures of local leaders, or legal personnel such as notaries confirmed the 'transfer of the structure of a house' following payment by the present to the previous occupant. Many squatters supplemented this 'informal legitimization' by participating in the activities of political parties, establishing deals with the local MPs, councillors and functionaries of political parties, acting as mobilizers of party vote banks and gaining a range of informal assurances from these parties in return.

Political patronage is not new or unique to Delhi – it is common in cities like Rio, Karachi, Mumbai, Kolkata and other parts of the world where there are large slum populations. Under this process, the state or the agents of the state, namely political parties and their leaders use the marginalization of the urban poor as resources in electoral politics. Vote-banking is a common and established informal strategy used by most political parties where particular social groups would be promised certain benefits on successful election. V.P. Singh's political patronage of 'backward classes' worked through the mapping of India's cultural politics (namely that of caste and religion) across 'illegal' squatter settlements of the city. These political patronages attempted among many things to give what Nandy notes as 'India's traditional plurality a different kind of psychological basis. Instead of being a burden in contemporary times, culture has become a means of monitoring politics' (Nandy 2002: 31). And it was during the V.P. Singh regime that cultural difference as a legally framed subjecthood became a way of monitoring the politics of entitlements to the legal city.

'Abusing the system' – Transforming homes, households and lanes

A more 'private' transformation to that taking place across Delhi slums however, went largely unnoticed during the mass legitimization of squatters. As differences of caste, religion, and ethnicity were made visible in Delhi's slums, homes and households in squatter settlements were also becoming more differentiated. During this moment, many extended families presented themselves as separate nuclear households. Where parents and married sons had lived in a small room earlier, they partitioned parts of their homes which were used for a kitchen or for washing into separate rooms. This way each household maximized the number of housing entitlements they received from the government. This meant that in the future if their homes were to be demolished, each nuclear family unit within the extended family would be eligible for a separate resettlement plot.

> The camp has expanded like anything. There weren't many people here to begin with, but then when our V.P. Singh came as a Prime Minister, he started carting people here by the truckloads…and then he started the token allotment system and people abused it. On one token they often built two shacks. People even kept a stove in the latrine that was constructed and claimed that they lived there. [Rajkishore]

While Rajkishore did not have enough physical space to partition his home and called this 'abusing the system', other residents did not necessarily see these manipulations as unlawful. Living in one room for a large family was incredibly difficult, and when 'tokens' were allocated, it made sense to get one for each nuclear family unit within the extended household. It was also possible then that once they had these tokens, they could sell their homes in the informal market. They could now also use this address to register themselves as voters, get food ration cards, credit cards, passports and so on. Thus while their legal status as urban citizens was still ambiguous, the tokens associated with their homes could provide them with a legal plot of land in a future resettlement colony.

Apart from these social and material changes in their homes and households, the regularization drive of the late 1980s meant that overnight squatter homes increased in economic value. Many families sold their homes immediately and moved to more 'legalized' colonies with established infrastructure. Residents made their houses more permanent by constructing proper foundations, building their houses with bricks and concrete and covering the roofs with stone slabs or tin sheets. Some residents took loans from building shops or banks, others bought second-hand bricks, and still others salvaged building materials from nearby middle-class neighbourhoods. Yet, while their homes became increasingly linked to social and economic capital, the legal ambiguities in their status continued to make both buyers and sellers uneasy about their transactions.

Many participants voiced this unease about the future value of their property. Not all who I interviewed came in the 1970s, some had moved in during the late 1980s in the peripheries of the camp. Others had bought their homes in the informal market during the 1990s. Utpal was one such participant who had lived on rent in the camp since the 1980s, but in the 1990s managed to put together enough money to buy his landlady's house. But he realized later that he did not receive all the documents associated with the purchase.

> An old Madrasi [South Indian] woman lived here, I bought this from her. She didn't give me the card given by V.P. Singh. The red card, she hasn't given it to me; to this day it is with her. The ration cards have been made in our name,

but that one thing she hasn't given. She keeps threatening to arrive with the V.P.
Singh card when the *jhuggis* are demolished. [Utpal]

Such practices were common in the camp, as part of the control exerted over newly
purchased squatter homes by pre-1989 residents. Those who left the camp did not
really want to live here – the homes were overcrowded, the streets were congested,
and there were no services. Those who bought these houses were doing so for a
future in the city – in the hope that if demolished they would also be resettled. But
with the 'informality' of the purchase, sellers were able to manipulate the terms
of the sale, keeping the buyers in confusion about the validity of the documents.
Thus these homes began to occupy two simultaneous spatio-temporal aspirations
– one in the present where people needed an immediate place to live; and one as
an investment into a legitimate future in the city.

Even while leaving the camp, earlier residents continued to shape the
spatialization of difference along its lanes. I asked one of my participants how it
was that most of her neighbours along her lane were Bihari (from the East Indian
state of Bihar who share linguistic and cultural practices). She answered as if it
was obvious – they had all come together to settle here. 'But, have none of them
ever sold their houses and left?' I persisted.

When that man [neighbour] began to sell his *jhuggi*, when he decided to sell, he
asked us 'we are selling the *jhuggi*; if you have any relatives, who want to buy it,
then we'll sell it to you, otherwise some Muslim will come and live here'. I said
'no, we have no relatives who will buy it; and we don't have that much money;
we won't take it'. He sold it to a Muslim. So the rest of this lane is Bihari from
top to bottom; just the one Muslim home. [Ratna]

Ratna noted that this spatialization was in order to make sure that those who came
later would be 'accepted' in the lane. Ratna and her husband themselves had
purchased a few homes from those who were leaving, and invited their extended
family or kin from their village to come and live there on rent. As these new
families made their livelihoods in the city, they had bought the home from Ratna.
That way Ratna and her neighbours had kept control over who lived along their
lane. In more recent years, Ratna could not afford to buy any more houses and
therefore her neighbour had reluctantly sold his house to a Muslim family, who had
turned out to be a 'very undesirable neighbour', because he refused to take turns
in cleaning the open drain running through the lane. Stories such as Ratna's were
common among participants who described how they played a part in choosing
their new neighbours as earlier residents left the camp, and thus strived to maintain
more or less the socio-spatial geographies of the original settlement pattern.

What is remarkable is the disjuncture between these accounts of neighbourly
agencies in maintaining spatialized difference, with the reality of wider politics
of regularization shaping Delhi's squatter settlements in the early 1990s. While
residents assured me of their 'choice' in determining their future neighbours,

in reality, after the regularizations in 1989, there began a huge influx of new residents into the camp, which they had little control over. These new residents came primarily from the OBCs (Other Backward Classes), patronized by V.P. Singh's Janta Dal party. As they moved into the camp, they transformed the earlier dynamics of interactions between the residents on the basis of caste, religion and ethnicity. While the OBCs came from marginalized social groups they still saw themselves on a higher socio-historical hierarchy to the low-caste Dalits in the camp. Thus while the residents normalized an exclusionary politics of spatialized difference in the informal buying and selling of homes, in reality, they had little hand in the larger politics of the state which sanctioned the arrival of a new social group of squatters and the transformations of homes, households and lanes in the camp.

Here then was a moment of regularization in the camp in the 1980s, but this was never complete or absolute. Each of the bureaucratic processes involved in the surveying, counting, mapping, notifying residents, maintaining accurate registers, allocating tokens and coordinating across the DDA and MCD was both physically challenging and time-consuming for the officials involved. And between the time that this process began and was completed, more houses had been subdivided and more residents had moved in.

Encounters with law enforcement

Knowledge of the workings of law is required ever more so in 'illegal' slums. In order to receive identity cards and those grey documents of tenure legalization which became so coveted in the 1980s, residents had to prove their temporal attachment to the city through their home. If this home as a physical structure was perceived to be a recent addition, it would invariably be demolished by the municipality. But this also gave certain individuals within law-enforcement agencies to misuse their powers and extort money from residents during such inspections. Most of this harassment was when the police would ask residents for a payment during building work, and they would be arrested and taken to the police station if they could not pay the police. The home then formed a significant site of encounters with law and law enforcement. Given that this encounter largely shaped participants' attitude towards the police as corrupt and devious, meant that this brought forth the discourse of a 'home under threat' (both physically and socially) into wider circulation within the camp. This home had to be protected and the first step involved the understanding of their legal rights.

One participant, Kishan noted that he was forced to understand his rights to put an end to his continuous harassment by the police. Kishan noted that harassment happened to those who 'do not know the law' and that living in the city since the 1970s and being under continuous threat of erasure of his home had helped him slowly acquire a functionalist knowledge of his legal rights. In more recent years, at every instance that the police made unannounced inspections, illegitimate demands and unprovoked arrests, he would challenge the legality of their actions. He would ask to see warrants, refuse to pay bribes, and complain to senior police officers about the 'misdeeds' of their junior staff.

> They don't mess with those who know the law, those who don't know, simple people, they go to them to demand ... simple people, end up giving [money]. When someone invests 20,000 [rupees] in a house, he will have to give 300–400 [rupees]. If he doesn't give, the police will pick him up and sit him down in the police station – will lock him up. It is blind; it is the law of the rich. [Kishan]

Kishan made an important observation about the rule of law as 'blind and the law of the rich'. By this he meant that the middle-classes were able to ignore and manipulate particular aspects of law when it suited them, whereas this opportunity was not available to the squatters. It is this perception of the unfairness of law and the procedures through which law enforcement operates in the city, which produced anxieties among participants about their future in the city. If the rule of law could not be relied upon to deliver them with a home in the city even if they were eligible for resettlement, then they needed to know the law, to understand how they can 'get by' its many unfair and informal processes in everyday life.

Gupta (2006) notes that for most Indian citizens, the state is encountered through government bureaucracies. Within this level, the discourses of corruption circulated by those negotiating this in everyday life draws attention to the 'powerful cultural practices through which the state is symbolically represented to ... citizens of the nation' (Gupta 2006: 221). Gupta draws a clear distinction between entitlement and empowerment, and although he was referring to the discourses of development, rights and political action, participants like Kishan found that a functionalist knowledge of law and legal processes was a form of empowerment. This knowledge provided them with the possibilities to claim their rights and entitlements from the state and even challenge agents of the state for corrupt practices.

By the mid 1990s the urban poor in Delhi's squatter settlements had learnt a new vocabulary of rights, marginality and law to construct a discursive terrain of entitlements towards the legal city. This required an understanding of duties and responsibilities of different state institutions towards urban citizens. While the functions of urban and state institutions were shrouded in complex legal language, bureaucratic procedures and corruption, this very opaque process of law-making and law-enforcement encouraged squatters to construct a parallel system of legitimacy that was purely functionalist. This helped them avoid getting into trouble with law enforcement as well as finding ways to legitimize their claims to housing and infrastructure. They did not claim to know the finer workings of legal codes, yet at the same time, exercised a working knowledge of law, which helped them deal with corruption within law-enforcement agencies, demand infrastructure from utility companies, and accumulate a range of documents which would in some way or the other prove their rights to resettlement.

The transformation of the camp and its homes was possible because of the residents' ability to find within the exclusionary spaces of the city, opportunities of mobilizing a variety of calculations around the availability of empty land, building and consolidating their homes, accessing livelihoods and then legitimizing these in a variety of ways. In making this observation, I depart from the classic Latin American studies on informality, which implicitly takes illegality as tangential in the lives of squatters. Rather, I suggest that it was a desire to find opportunities from within the spaces of law that produced the transformation of squatter homes both socially and materially. Squatters negotiated their illegality through a 'whole series of procedures and permits, some of which may be followed while others ignored' (Bromley 2004: 278). In the ever-changing vocabulary of legality till the 1990s, the squatters negotiated largely productive relationships with the rule of law in their everyday life.

Chapter 4
Becoming 'Illegal' Urban Citizens

Establishment or creating of slums, it seems, appears to be good business and is well organized. The number of slums has multiplied in the last few years by geometrical proportion. Large areas of public land, in this way, are usurped for private use free of cost. It is difficult to believe that this can happen in the capital of the country without passive or active connivance of the land owning agencies and/or the municipal authorities. The promise of free land, at the taxpayers cost, in place of a jhuggi, is a proposal which attracts more land grabbers. Rewarding an encroacher on public land with free alternate site is like giving a reward to a pickpocket. The department of slum clearance does not seem to have cleared any slum despite its being in existence for decades. In fact more and more slums are coming into existence. Instead of 'Slum Clearance' there is 'Slum Creation' in Delhi. (*Almitra Patel vs Union of India* 2000)

In 2000, a landmark judgment was passed by the Indian Supreme Court. Widely known as the *Almitra Patel case*, this ruling overturned the implicit understanding of shelter as a basic human right and constituted a qualitative shift in the approach to slum dwellers. During the summing up of a Public Interest Litigation brought by a 'concerned citizen', the judge labelled slum dwellers as 'pickpockets', 'encroachers' and 'trespassers' – referring largely to the squatter settlements which are built on public land and are seen as illegal.[1] Ignoring earlier case law on implicit rights to shelter, the judge interpreted and translated squatting on public land as an act of 'trespass'.

The *Almitra Patel* ruling used a formal and 'objective' interpretation of law, and constructed slum dwellers as 'citizens without a city' (Appadurai 2001: 27). Since the *Almitra Patel* ruling, reference to slums as 'illegal encroachments' gained increasing discursive popularity. While the Indian courts till 1980s had followed an implicit understanding that access to affordable shelter and infrastructure services was a basic human right, this ruling set the trend for interpreting squatting as a criminal offence in most regional states of India.

In 2001, the Delhi High court called in contempt the municipal authorities for failing to comply by the Supreme Court order made in 2000 about clearing up 'illegal' encroachments along the city's river Yamuna. The municipality hastily began to remove all squatters along the riverbank and in other parts of the city while denying resettlement to most of its residents. At the same time, the Delhi

---

1   The judge was using the word 'slum' in this case as a generic term although not all slums are illegal encroachments.

Development Authority which owns most public land in Delhi decided to enforce its powers through removal of all 'illegal' structures which had come up in violation of the Delhi masterplan. This became a mass demolition of all slums in the city.

Understandably, there was huge uproar from academics, activists, and politicians– each with different justifications for opposing and challenging this ruling. What emerged in the months following the indiscriminate demolition of many squatter settlements in Delhi, Mumbai, and other Indian cities, was a debate on the 'legality' of this ruling – whether it was in keeping with the Indian Constitution, human rights laws, or indeed UN development guidelines (Muralidhar 2004, Ramanathan 2005). Lawyers and legal sociologists claimed that this was landmark ruling in the sense that it had overturned every possible welfarist value that the Indian state had stood for since it was conceived in 1947.

As discussed in the previous chapter, the Indian state's practices on ground towards addressing the 'problem' of slums had usually been ensconced in development discourses around the empowerment, resettlement and upgradation of slums. Implicit in these approaches had been the view that squatters were 'victims' of rural underdevelopment who came to find work in the city and hence should be treated with compassion. The 2000 ruling was a new trend in the sense that law could now be used in a punitive, selective and indiscriminate manner against 'trespassers'. As Bhan notes, this was a turning moment since it was 'not that illegality suddenly became apparent but, rather, that the terms by which it – and those who lived within it – were represented and recognized, changed' (Bhan 2009: 136).

The aim of this chapter is to examine how the violence of judicial decisions maps a homogeneous identity of 'illegal' urban citizens onto the bodies and spaces of squatters and how this then produces among squatters an understanding of resettlement as the only hope for legitimacy and urban citizenship in the future. I am ultimately interested in how an interpretive force of law produced in squatters a heightened consciousness of their 'illegal' status. This was not only a violence of the founding and maintaining aspect of law which Benjamin (1978) refers to; but also a form of violence in law that has to do with a judicial interpretation of rights and citizenships of those already located within 'exceptional' spaces of the city. In taking this approach, I am not only following Derrida (1992) in disengaging any notion of justice from law, but more importantly focusing on the ways in which judicial interpretations of law became instrumental to the reordering of public identities and aspirations of squatters in the city.

Judiciary and the 'public petitioner'

> The juridical institution promotes an ontological glorification. It does this by transmuting regularity into rule, factual normalcy into legal normalcy ... In this way the juridical institution contributes universally to the imposition of a representation of normalcy according to which *different* practices tend to appear

deviant, anomalous, indeed abnormal and pathological. (Bourdieu 1987: 846–7) [Original emphasis]

So far in this book I have been referring to a force of law articulated by Derrida through the 'paradox of iterability' (Derrida 1992: 1007). In doing so, I have focused on the various ways that the founding and maintaining violence of law are translated in the context of squatter settlements through a performative and interpretive force of law (Derrida 1992). But what is the role of the judiciary in instituting this violence? For this, I turn to Bourdieu who provides a critique of the 'juridical field' as a form of symbolic power and 'a tool in the service of dominant groups' (Bourdieu 1987: 814).

For Bourdieu, the juridical field functions 'in close relation with the exercise of power in other social realms and through other mechanisms' (Bourdieu 1987: 807) – one of these being the state. This does not mean that the judiciary is an arm of state power. Rather that both the law and judiciary has a complex and often antagonistic relation with the exercise of other forms of power – which Bourdieu calls 'Force of Law'. For Bourdieu, force is power, and the power of law stems from the law's ability to codify and formalize social norms, which in turn is taken as a sign of law's objectivity and hence neutrality. Bourdieu claims that it is this formalization and codification that grants power to the judiciary to deliver judgments based on law.

The juridical 'field' in India has always been an important space where the question of illegality of squatter settlements has been debated. Armed with a discourse of laws, regulations, rights and responsibilities the judiciary in India has time and again made particular judgments towards resolving the vexed question of illegality surrounding urban slums. Accepting their ruling of 'illegality' in the case of slums means accepting the rules of landuse planning, regulations, zoning and a whole set of statutory acts and laws through which this legal decision was arrived upon. As Derrida (1992) argues, it also means accepting the power of the judiciary to influence and determine in part how the law will deal with a particular issue during specific cases of conflict.

Bourdieu however clarifies that the limits of the power of judicial decisions or the power exerted by the judiciary is related to the 'position of the juridical field within the broader field of power' (Bourdieu 1987: 823) including the state, society, and a number of institutions which codify and enforce laws and regulations. In India for example, the judiciary is independent of the state, which means that the judiciary can strike down any regulation or law passed by the state which is deemed unconstitutional by the judiciary. This independence grants the judiciary exceptional powers to influence wider societal processes and to exercise a relative degree of control over the state.

As Galanter notes, courts are 'passive institutions' (Galanter 2000: 57), in the sense that they have to be moved by citizens in order to deliver decisions backed by a rule of law. Galanter suggests that 'for a legal order to flourish, it requires not just the leadership of judges and mediation of lawyers but also active participation of its citizenry' (Galanter 2000: 57). Yet the public has very low expectations from the courts to deliver 'justice' in India. They try to avoid the lower courts as much as possible since juridical processes are characterized by long delays, mounting expenses and meagre damage awards. Thus those who benefit most from judicial processes are those who are already satisfied by the status quo between middle/ working classes and between legal/illegal cities.

In India in the 1980s, an increased awareness among the judiciary about the 'failings' of the courts manifested in a form of judicial activism known as Public Interest Litigation (PIL). During this period, the judges responded proactively through a series of unprecedented initiatives including responses to grievances brought to their attention by third parties (Galanter and Krishnan 2004). PILs were intended to use the powers of the judiciary to protect powerless groups and to secure entitlements that were going unredeemed. Also called 'social action litigation' this process 'enabled any citizen to bypass ordinary legal proceedings and appeal directly to the Supreme Court to protect his/her fundamental rights' (Rosencranz and Jackson 2003: 230). This has had remarkable effects on the number of cases brought forward since it enabled third parties such as NGOs and civil society groups to make petitions on behalf of disadvantaged groups. Galanter and Krishnan (2004) note that PILs in India have promoted several important social changes including promoting citizen action groups, accountability of government and local authorities, and increasing public awareness on a number of issues. The most important social change however has been the increased legitimacy of the judiciary through assertions of constitutional rights to aggrieved parties.

The earlier PIL cases in the 1980s dealt with a number of landmark cases and key rulings including those on the rights of prisoners, bonded labourers, pavement dwellers, and children. Since the 1990s however, PILs have produced an emergent figure of the 'public petitioner' (Sharan 2005: 70) seeking rights to environmental goods in public spaces. Since PILs have always worked on the basis on a judicial interpretation of one of the fundamental rights such as rights to life or rights to freedom and so on, the public petitioner who seeks redress through the Supreme Court against environmental damage argues that pollution in some form or the other infringes on rights to life. In metropolitan areas, these PILs are increasingly related to the 'dirt' of cities – air and water pollution, sewage, sanitation and soiling of green space and seek to make the state accountable towards ensuring clean-up. The courts have usually interpreted this through a fundamental right to life often granting aggrieved parties rights to clean-up operations by reprimanding local authorities responsible for urban public spaces. The *Almitra Patel* case was one such PIL.

Since Indian liberalization in 1991, the urban middle-classes have become actively involved in the making of cities and urban spaces through their initiative in preventing environmental ills in cities and urban regions. This has often resulted in recourse to the Supreme Court in order to reclaim urban spaces from slums and slum dwellers (Fernandes 2006). One of the striking effects of this in Delhi is the increasing focus on dirt and pollution, where the urban middle-classes through their presence in civil society organizations have time and again drawn the attention of the courts to the inefficiency of the state in maintaining and policing urban public spaces from 'filth' and a range of other 'civic disorders'. There emerges therefore this figure of the 'public petitioner' in recent years – one who is environmentally conscious, well educated in order to draft a PIL suit, and quite obviously middle-class. This public petitioner attempts to speak on behalf of the urban public sphere on issues which affect all urban citizens.

The frequency of these PILs to claim environmental goods has increased in recent years on account of a simultaneous transformation in forms of participatory urban governance. In Delhi for example, the *Bhagidari* or 'share-holding' scheme initiated by Shiela Dixit, Delhi's Chief Minister provides civil society groups, NGOs and Residents' Welfare Associations (RWAs) with deliberative powers. This includes initiatives like giving the responsibility of the upkeep of parks and public places to RWAs in order to prevent encroachment on public land. However, this is limited to 'authorized colonies', and not squatter settlements. As we shall see in this and subsequent chapters, RWAs have frequently filed PILs in the Supreme Court to remove squatters as 'environmental ills' from public green spaces such as parks and urban forests. The judiciary over the years therefore has produced a middle-class urban petitioner who attempts to exclude squatters' access to urban public spaces through an assertion of the former's fundamental rights to life.

Whose Right to Life?

> Article 21 No person shall be deprived of his life or personal liberty except according to procedure established by law. (Indian Constitution 1950: 10)

Whose right to life is sustained when squatter settlements are demolished in order to keep public spaces 'clean' and free of pollution? Is it the right to life of the squatters who would be homeless once their settlement is demolished, or is it the right to life of the middle-classes who experience these spaces at a distance yet fear disease, dirt and pollution emanating from these? Since the 1980s, the judiciary has deliberated on the future of urban slums using Article 21 of the constitution – the fundamental rights to life, enforceable by law.

A seminal judgment passed by the Indian Supreme Court in 1985 was in effect the first judicial ruling in favour of rights to shelter in the city for urban poor across India. A Public Interest Litigation (PIL) between the *Bombay Municipal Corporation v/s Olga Tellis* arose when the former wanted to forcibly evict Bombay's 4.8 million pavement dwellers on account of their 'inhuman existence' on the streets. The Supreme Court held that evicting them would mean a loss of livelihood which amounted to a denial of their 'right to life' under Article 21 of the Indian Constitution. The judge ruled that

> If they were forcibly evicted they would lose their livelihood along with being de-housed which would result in the denial of the right to life, the right to life and the right to work being interdependent. … The eviction of the pavement or the slum-dweller not only means his removal from the house but the destruction of the house itself. And the destruction of a dwelling house is the end of all that one holds dear in life. (*Bombay Municipal Corporation vs Olga Tellis* 1985)

Ramanathan (2005) argues that the interlinking of right to shelter and livelihood being part of a 'right to life' by the judiciary was an important interpretation of rights to the city in the absence of legal or statutory rights to housing. The Supreme Court recognized the important contribution of slum and pavement dwellers to Bombay's urban economy and noted that it was the non-implementation of the city's master plans and of the Urban Land Ceiling Act that had resulted in their increase. Significantly, they were not to be seen as 'trespassers' but as victims of 'economic hardships'.

Consider another important ruling in 1995 which further used the right to life argument to defend the rights of scheduled castes and tribes to a secure a home in the city. In this case, land acquisition by the State for a special scheme to provide housing for the Scheduled Castes was upheld by the judge.

> The right to shelter when used as an essential requisite to the right to life should be deemed to have been guaranteed as a fundamental right. As is enjoined in the Directive Principles, the State should be deemed to be under an obligation to secure for its citizens … To bring the Dalits and Tribes into the mainstream of national life, providing these facilities and opportunities to them is the duty of the State as fundamental to their basic human and constitutional rights. (*Chameli Singh vs. State of UP* 1996)

Thus in the history of Indian case law, although the rights of the poor to shelter had not been framed as a fundamental right, they were interpreted as implicit within a fundamental constitutional 'rights to life'. Further, these rulings emphasized and reinforced the differentiated citizenship rights accorded to marginalized social groups under the Indian Constitution stressing that the state had a duty of care towards preserving the rights to life particularly of these groups. While urban planning models pushed the poor further to the margins through landuse and zoning, urban development institutions struggled to cope financially and logistically with the sheer enormity of the numbers to be resettled and the land to be made available, subsequent judicial rulings continuously reminded various urban governments of their responsibilities of accommodating slum dwellers 'into the mainstream of national life'. But these were also related to accommodating those lowest in the social hierarchy, the Dalits (untouchables) and Scheduled tribes who were entitled to special provisions under the constitution. The judiciary therefore reinforced two kinds of subjectivities through this interpretation of law – first, the legal subjectivities of lower castes as disadvantaged and marginalized, and second a form of spatial subjectivity that emerged from the connections between marginalized constitutional subjectivities and illegal slums.

In order '(t)o be just, the decision of a judge, for example, must not only follow a rule of law but must also assume it, approve it, confirm its value, by a reinstituting act of interpretation, as if ultimately nothing previously existed of the law, as if the judge himself invented the law in every case' (Derrida 1992: 961). In the rulings during the 1980s and 1990s, the decision of the judge attempted to follow a notion of justice based on particular set of interpretations of constitutional rights, landuse and zoning regulations. These decisions can be understood as creative reinterpretations of constitutional guarantees and state responsibilities towards those marginalized, which sustained connections between the rights to shelter and the fundamental rights to life.

The decisions during this period also reinforce another important link made by the judiciary – between the legally enforceable fundamental rights to life and the non-enforceable Directive Principles of State Policy. This was based on simultaneous cases in India in which judges ruled out constitutional amendments made by the state that were deemed to violate what Mehta calls the 'basic structure' (Mehta 2005: 179). It refers to the Supreme Court view that the Directive Principles were basic to the Fundamental Rights, even though the former were non-enforceable. Mehta argues that in doing so, they put a 'legitimate form of pressure on the state to accomplish policy goals to ameliorate the conditions of vulnerable groups within society' (Mehta 2005: 180). This basic structure approach however changed in the late 1990s as middle-class groups began to mobilize and demand the protection of environmental goods from the state using the Public Interest Litigations as a tool to achieve their goals. Urban environments then began to be seen by the judiciary as equally important to the fundamental rights to life.

There is nothing new about middle-class concerns with the decline of city's public spaces. Even during colonial rule, the Indian middle-classes have been repeatedly concerned with the presence of the urban poor in Indian towns and cities (Gooptu 2001, Kaviraj 1997). These concerns echoed Victorian anxieties over slums in eighteenth and nineteenth century England, which were addressed through rational and orderly town planning strategies. As Gooptu notes in the interwar years, the Indian middle-classes were 'keen to see the towns modernized and expanded into clean new zones for their own use, the squalor ridden slums eradicated, and the poor kept at bay and under control' (Gooptu 2001: 83–4). In post-colonial India, these middle-class anxieties over public space increased with what was seen as the ineffectiveness of local authorities in enforcing landuse and zoning plans, keeping public spaces free of trespass (associated with the growth of slums) and effectively keeping 'dirt' (pollution, waste and sewage) away from cities.

In 1996 Mrs Almitra Patel, an environmental activist moved the Supreme Court on a writ petition concerned with the apathy of urban municipalities to effectively remove urban waste from metropolitan cities like Bangalore, Bombay, Chennai, Calcutta, and Delhi. The PIL was not concerned with slums; indeed it had not mentioned slums at all in its script. On delivering the judgment in 2000, the Supreme Court Judge however drew a link between the proliferation of slums in these cities and the increase in 'domestic waste strewn on open land in and around urban slums' (*Almitra Patel vs Union of India* 2000). As Ramanathan (2005) notes, this ruling became one of the defining moments when the 'problem' of garbage disposal effectively transformed into a 'solution' of slum clearance in India's metropolitan cities. It defined the terms under which the urban poor became illegal through a conflation of state and middle-class anxieties over the spatial transgressions of 'dirt' from slums onto urban public spaces. In one moment, slum dwellers had not just been criminalized; they had also been associated with the filth of cities.

> Domestic garbage and sewage is a large contributor of solid waste. The drainage system in a city is intended to cope and deal with household effluent. This is so in a planned city. But when a large number of inhabitants live in unauthorized colonies, with no proper means of dealing with the domestic effluents, or in slums with no care for hygiene the problem becomes more complex. ... This in turn gives rise to domestic waste being strewn on open land in and around the slums. ... It is the garbage and solid waste generated by these slums which require to be dealt with most expeditiously and on the basis of priority. (*Almitra Patel vs Union of India* 2000)

In 2001, the Ministry of Urban Development in an affidavit to the Delhi High Court used the *Almitra Patel case* to stress the need to provide a policy for relocation of slums. The Delhi High Court in turn held the Delhi Development Authority and Municipal Corporation of Delhi in contempt for not preventing 'further encroachments' and urged them to use their statutory powers to strictly enforce urban development policies and to remove 'illegal' squatter settlements which 'pollute' urban environments. In March 2003, a Delhi High Court order directed 'all authorities concerned' to remove unauthorized structures, including slum clusters. Regularization based on the red identity card scheme from the VP Singh period, led to the announcement of January 1990 as the cut-off date for eligibility to resettlement (Bijulal 2004). Following mass protests in 2000, the cut-off date was extended from January 1990 to December 1998 (on the basis of most squatters holding food ration cards until this date). However this included a differentiation in entitlements – a 18 square metre plot of land to pre-1990 squatter families, and a 12.5 square metre plot of land to families possessing ration cards post-January 1990 up to December 1998 (Dupont 2008). But, since the beginning of February 2004, the Municipal Corporation of Delhi (MCD) and the Delhi Development Authority (DDA) have reportedly demolished 40,000 homes of slum dwellers and forcibly evicted 200,000 people without adequate and equitable resettlement (Anthony and Maheswaran 2001).

The *Almitra Patel* and subsequent rulings in different cities across India have seen the radical reinterpretation of the fundamental rights to life by the judiciary. While before, the rights to life was associated with the rights to shelter and livelihoods of the urban poor, now the rights to life is interpreted through its associations with the rights to environmental goods. The judiciary often expressly holds the state and local authorities in contempt for violation of legislations, masterplans, and landuse regulations, and issue warnings to rectify these when it deems that environmental goods are not protected. Indeed, the judiciary has warned that if their rulings are disregarded by urban local governments then the courts would enforce them through police force (Kumar 2006).

These new judicial interpretations of law related to the urban environment is not just a transformation of the judiciary's approach towards the urban poor, but as Ghertner notes – a 'more subtle production of a new aesthetic ordering of "the public" and its "proper uses"' (Ghertner 2008: 2). Examining the legal and technical mechanisms through which slum demolitions are authorized and validated, Ghertner argues that recent judicial rulings around the slums in the city have reinterpreted earlier nuisance law by reconstituting the 'meaning of "public interest", defining distinctly (bourgeois) private interests as public matters and projecting a vision of urban order i.e. a "world-class aesthetic" founded on property ownership' (Ghertner 2008: 2). This reinterpretation of 'nuisance' is purely aesthetic, tied to judiciary and middle-class (or the public petitioner's) understanding of acceptable conduct and visual order. This violence of legal interpretation makes squatters' rights to the city conditional upon their current (legal) status.

'Strange laws continue'

This radical shift in judicial interpretations of law places squatters firmly within the murky illegal spaces of a city, spaces from where they cannot articulate any formal discourse of rights. By reinforcing the need of a rule of law to remove 'illegal' urban citizens from metropolitan cities however, the Almitra Patel ruling was not as articulate on the nomenclature and typologies of slums. Squatter settlements that are not notified slumsare not under the state list for upgradation. At the same time, as a JJ colony, squatter settlements are typologically unplanned (informal) settlements with no legal rights to the land occupied. For the state therefore the ruling made it easier to remove 'illegal' slums (or squatter settlements like the camp) on the basis of violations of property rights.

For the residents of the camp then, slum nomenclature was critical to their experiences of law, space and subjectivity. While 'illegality' was prescribed on their bodies and spaces, residents began to articulate a series of arguments in order to challenge this nomenclature. Very early on in the research, participants emphasized that their camp was illegal only on the basis of property rights, which to them was mere technicality. They would show me numerous documents – ration cards, voters' identity cards, bank passbooks and food ration cards with their names and addresses in the camp, to question the law that classified them as 'illegal'.

They would argue that they were as illegal as the elite farm houses and affluent middle-class gated communities which were built by acquiring agricultural land in the urban peripheries through dubious deals. In making such comparisons, participants were drawing upon their working knowledge of how Delhi's urban landscape was being transformed through obfuscatory legal processes which attempted to selectively marginalize them. They knew that while a normative rule of law was used during demolition, the law itself was subject to interpretation by the judiciary. The key issue under such circumstances was to make claims to a legitimization based on common law – the procurement of a range of documents which would prove their own identity and their long-term residence on the land.

> The thing is that this is unauthorized by the government. But when the electricity bill is coming here and passports are also being made with this residential address, I do not think it is unauthorized. People have gone to Dubai and Saudi Arabia. Several have gone from here. I have a driving license and credit card on the same address. It's a *jhuggi* in name and nothing else. [Pradeep]

In Pradeep's view, slum nomenclature was irrelevant in a context where the most decisive document of legal citizenship – the Indian passport is issued on the basis of their 'illegal' address in the camp. The assertion that the settlement was not unauthorized therefore was a challenge to their positioning under a nomenclature that made them 'illegal' despite very little 'real' experience of illegality in terms of seeking transnational employment, accessing credit and basic services, and providing proof of identity.

Despite these assertions, the changing ideologies of the state and its associated laws and legislations were symptomatic of the distrust participants felt for legal discourses and consequently the insecurity of their location within the squatter settlement. Emerging here was a wider meaning attributed to the role of law in bringing about justice and legitimacy to the urban poor.

> I have received no help from the government to this date. The government eats, drinks, and is happy. The prime minister changes every five years, every three years. The laws change too. This is the biggest problem in Hindustan [India]. Everything is wrong here, strange laws continue, and keep changing, and [court] cases keep running. [Utpal]

Das and Poole point to the 'different spaces, forms and practices through which the state is continually both experienced and undone through the illegibility of its own practices, documents, and words' (Das and Poole 2004: 8). In their investigation, the security of identity and rights can become destabilized through the illegibility of bureaucracy, proceduralism and documentation. Utpal's narrative is resonant with this illegibility of the state where law, legitimacy, rights and citizenship can be violently unsettled. He became anxious that it would be families like his, without adequate income who would suffer the most if the camp was to be demolished.

He worried that even if they were provided with resettlement, he would not have the money to pay for the licensee fee or the mortgage. Despite being eligible for resettlement, he would probably have to live on rent if the camp was demolished. He pointed to a couple of houses along his lane insisting that those families would not worry because they were rich – because they owned many such houses in this camp and they had thousands of rupees saved away in their banks.

One important development that has added to these anxieties since the demolitions began across Delhi is that it has become very difficult to sell homes in the camp. The uncertainty surrounding all squatter settlements across the country and particularly in Delhi devastated the informal housing market in the 2000s – those who had homes were simply 'sitting it out' even though their employment and family circumstances might have required otherwise. Owners of homes in the camp were neither able to sell and move on, nor interested in spending more money to make improvements in their houses. For many residents it was this uncertainty which came in the way of getting on with their everyday lives – taking up a new job in another part of the city, getting their children married, adding another floor to accommodate an increasing family and so on. Sitting it out and waiting for resettlement was like keeping their lives on hold.

The anxieties that participants associated with impending demolition were also related to how they were positioned for the future. Demolitions of other squatter settlements in Delhi had used 1990 as the cut-off date. Those who had the documents from the 1989 regularization knew they were entitled to receive resettlement from the state. Those who had documents to prove their residence since 1998 also knew that they would receive a resettlement plot albeit smaller than those settled since 1989. But in other similar cases across Delhi, documents such as voter identity cards and food ration cards had not always been honoured by the authorities (Menon-Sen and Bhan 2008). Those who bought their houses at a later date also felt unsure about their eligibility. Some did not receive all the documents from the previous owners as I noted in the previous chapter, and even if they did, they were unsure whether their purchase in the informal housing market would be recognized by the state. Those pre-1989 owners, who despite selling their property had not let go of their regularization documents, knew that the moment demolition of the camp was finalized, they would return to claim resettlement from the state.

Anxieties therefore differed according to the number and nature of grey documents that one possessed, between those who were the original settlers against those who bought their homes in the informal market, between those who were eligible for a number of resettlement plots (because they had subdivided the original squatter home during the regularization drive as discussed in the last chapter) against those who owned a single 'illegal' home in the camp. These differences were in relative terms, between those who felt more or less secure about the future. Participants were convinced though that since the 'illegal' city in its present form would cease to exist, resettlement as the journey into the 'legal' city was their only hope for the future.

'That is the only hope'

> ... a wide range of popular stories around successful slum relocation programs
> in the 1970s and 1980s, when land and resources were more widely available,
> mythologize resettlement plots as equal in standing to private plots. Furthermore,
> the DDA and Municipal Corporation run slum surveys prior to removing a
> slum to establish resettlement eligibility, which, in addition to enumerating
> and registering slum households, construct a compelling image of resettlement
> colonies as fully serviced, permanent, and integrated residential spaces,
> something akin to a private plot. (Ghertner 2011: 12)

Current research by NGOs report that most slum residents want 'to move, on
condition that they were guaranteed secure tenure and an appropriate location'
(Patel, d'Cruz and Burra 2002: 161). As I mentioned in the Introduction to this
book, Chatterjee suggests that the assertion of the desire for resettlement among
the urban poor is a 'neoliberal dogma' (Chatterjee 2004: 69), which allows the state
to acquire prime urban land from squatters and maintain the status quo between
the legal and illegal city. I have suggested however, that we pay greater attention
to the reasons why resettlement comes to be the only possible future and hope
for squatters and hence presented by the state and NGOs as a form of 'justice'. I
suggest that resettlement became attractive in a context where it allowed squatters
to escape from the 'spaces of exception' and enter the legal city with the automatic
rights and entitlements enjoyed by other ordinary citizens. Further to this, is the
mythologizing of resettlement as Ghertner (2011) notes above which gave this
the symbolic status of private land. This was a powerful moment since it allowed
squatters to think of themselves as 'equal' citizens in law. However, instead of
accepting NGO claims of squatters' unqualified desire, or seeing this as a form
of free-market appropriation of marginal spaces, I consider this as a 'fetishism of
law' (Comaroff and Comaroff 2006: viii) from below with the terms of inclusion
into the city understood and articulated through a legalistic framework. Could we
then see this as a way for squatters to simply imagine an escape from 'illegality',
from the interpretive violence of law, and from the anxieties of temporality and
annihilation associated with the squatter home?

Asserting a desire for resettlement is a moment of paradox in the lives of
participants. While in the past they could broker deals with local politicians
and secure informal promises of future legitimizations, in the aftermath of the
judicial rulings, there has existed a quandary. Voting rights have not provided the
same bargaining power with politicians since the politicians have now become
increasingly aware of the ways that middle-class political identities are also
significant in their re-election. This issue was evident to some participants who
pointed out that while in the 1980s and 1990s, political leaders such as Indira
Gandhi, Rajiv Gandhi, or V.P. Singh would make personal visits to their houses, in
more recent years, these visits were limited to local MPs 'who do not even bother

to step out of their cars'. Under these circumstances, residents found that their only option was to demand resettlement from the state.

> We celebrated 14th August [Independence Day], and had called [local MP]. So he had come, so we raised the topic of – 'please give us a place somewhere'. So he said 'When Indira Gandhi was displacing you, and giving you homes, why did you refuse? You should not have refused'. So we said, 'See those who refused are no more, but think of how to set this camp right, we can hardly live here for the rest of our lives'. So he said, 'don't worry, these *jhuggis* will be converted into DDA [flats]'. [Shalu]

As one of the few literate women, intermittently assisting NGOs in development research, Shalu was aware of much of the wider processes taking shape across the city and India around demolition, relocation and resettlement. Her narrative around the desire for resettlement thus made a break from the political and historical connections of her family around securing the camp. The reader may recall that in Chapter 3, her grandfather along with the early pioneers of the camp had secured promises from Indira Gandhi after the Indian Emergency. In explicitly stating to the local MP that these pioneers were 'no more' Shalu and other residents in the camp were distancing themselves from earlier forms of legitimacy that relied on informal promises and political patronage. Shalu however was not undermining the contribution of her grandfather; rather responding to the spatio-temporality of a law which would not sustain their current material and legal conditions. In desiring resettlement from the politicians then, Shalu and other residents were demanding recognition as legal citizens of Delhi.

Thus, while particular hegemonies of the State, judiciary, and urban governance produced a variety of uncertainties about their future in the city, participants attempted to work with the shifting dynamics of a rule of law to articulate their demands according to realizable possibilities. They realized that in Delhi, their small aspirations for permanence would have to accommodate its lofty world-city aspirations.

> In 2010 there will be the Olympics [Commonwealth], and before that, they want to demolish all these lanes. They say no, demolish it, there shouldn't be such a thing in Delhi, the *jhuggis* shouldn't be there. I have read the chief minister's statement once or twice. Sheila Dixit had said the other day that this [city] should be made even better than Paris, by the time of the Olympic [Commonwealth] Games. 71 nations are taking part in this – the Commonwealth. So I don't think these crooked lanes will be spared [laughs], these will be demolished. [Rajkumar]

Such meanings were constructed in the belief that squatters did not have any place in the future of Delhi. Images of Delhi's drive for order and sanitization flashed in the small television screens in almost every home. Participants were glued to their televisions during the news since often this news was about slums being demolished across India – images of broken homes, material possessions strewn around the debris of these homes, and municipal bulldozers dominated discussions of their ultimate fate. These images produced a contrast in their minds – of a Delhi, the symbol of modernity and the 'Paris of the East', against squatter settlements representing chaos, disorder and parochialism. In this contrast, squatter settlements were perceived as the most contested sites of modernity, which convinced participants that the world-city vision would only be possible over the rubble of their 'illegal' homes.

What seemed to increase the uncertainties was that while slum demolitions were being carried out across Delhi, Sheila Dixit, Delhi's Chief Minister promised to regularize all unauthorized colonies in the city while at the same time, local MPs were assuring them of relocation to high-rise apartments. These conflicting processes left participants worried about their future – leaving the camp was not possible until their future was confirmed; living in the camp meant that they would ultimately have to accept whatever 'solution' was deemed appropriate by the Delhi government. Most realized that in the absence of legal tenure their everyday struggles with illegality – police harassment, absence of basic services like water or sanitation and much other direct and indirect exclusion from urban spaces will remain. Yet, they were also hesitant in demanding demolition since they were uncertain whether and who will be entitled to resettlement and whether this will be conducive to their everyday lives in the city.

> I would like to build a small house somewhere, keep my children there, but where is the possibility? I will have to continue living in this camp until [pause] the government keeps talking of eviction, I don't know when it will happen. Where we will get a plot or whether we will get one at all. There is no permanence here. Even if we get one, it may be outside Delhi. Work is here, if they give us a plot outside Delhi, I cannot work here. This is not permanent, that [points across the road to resettlement colony] is permanent. *That is the only hope* [my emphasis]. [Prempal]

On the one hand, participants knew that the camp would cease to exist in its current 'illegal' state, yet on the other hand, they were also uncertain about their housing entitlements from the state. In this context, the legal and spatial condition of their neighbouring resettlement colony became 'the only hope' for the future. Living in such close proximity to the Lakshmipuri resettlement colonies provided such aspirations of legality – to receive a plot of land where they could build without being harassed by the police, to be provided with regular water and sewage connections, and to feel secure about their future in the city. Whilst accepting that resettlement might mean that they would be removed from the city altogether, Prempal saw resettlement as the only hope of sustaining their lives in Delhi.

As I have already mentioned, the reasons behind such arguments for a legitimate future under the rule of law were related to what many scholars have noted as the current conditions of neo-liberalism where land is increasingly privatized, surveilled, and less readily available for squatting (Davis 2006, Holston and Appadurai 1996). Similarly, during the moment of Delhi's transformation into a world city, participants understood that only legal tenure provided in the form of resettlement could be taken as a secure future. Prempal's narrative reflected this paradox of a squatter home, which had been put together over two decades, but was still considered transient and impermanent. This paradox was also the tragedy of a squatter home.

But even as the residents in the camp continued to aspire towards the legal city, they were constrained by the geographies of capital in a city that selectively enforced the rule of law in certain areas deemed to be desirable for investment and development. I have discussed this uneven geography of demolition in Chapter 2 where particular squatter settlements in the city were removed since 2001 in order to make way for the Commonwealth Games infrastructure. Participants were aware of these logics of demolitions and resettlement and they knew that the only reason that their wait had been prolonged was because the camp was located in close proximity to resettlement colonies – on land that was not valuable for capital investment projects and had not increased in real estate values. Their location had ensured their security since the 1970s, but this location was also an impediment towards a legal home in the future. In brief, they saw their 'problem' as one of geography.

> I feel that we are in a bad area, that's why the government is not listening to us. The government has no need for this useless area, the day they need it, this will automatically become okay. They have no need for this camp [land]. Had this been in the standard area, the well-to-do people would have asked the government to have the slum removed. That's why the *jhuggis* in Nizamuddin and Nehru Place [office/retail neighbourhoods] got removed faster; they were all in the standard area, in the good area. [Sukhdev]

Participants perceived their prolonged wait as an indication of the relative marginality of the land they had appropriated in Delhi and by extension of their own marginalization within state 'benefits'. Sukhdev's perspective should not however be seen as passive acceptance of the state rule of law – rather as a way to negotiate the system on its own terms. In this narration of removal, the middle-classes are seen as allies rather than adversaries in their access to legitimate housing in the city. Further, those who were forcibly removed from 'standard areas' in Delhi, were now subjects of envy because they were given legal titles and resettled on government land.

In these different narratives, the camp was constructed as inadequate and unliveable through the rhetorical use of phrases such as 'bad' area', 'could hardly live here', 'useless area' and so on. It is not that they inherently believed in these descriptions of the camp, but these descriptions were evoked in order to present a space of dirt and disorder, where a demand for state intervention could be produced. The state as the violent enforcer of their illegality was thus also put forward as the one responsible for mediating their legitimacy. This was another form of the evocation of 'moral rhetorics' (Chatterjee 2004: 60) through which participants like Shalu and Prempal made claims to their rightful 'benefits' from the state. These rhetorics were produced in a context where resettlement was the 'only hope'. And it was only in this context that resettlement was narrated as the provider of better housing and basic services. In other words, resettlement became the myth and utopia of the legal city.

As I have already discussed in Chapter 2, quality of life in resettlement colonies have steadily declined since the 1970s. Most participants knew that squatters removed from Nizamuddin and Nehru place were relocated to the outskirts of Delhi from where they faced much harder struggles to access urban infrastructure and livelihoods in the city. This knowledge clearly was also the source of their uncertainties about the future. But in charting their route to the legal city, they tended not to acknowledge the material conditions that accompanied resettlement, which had been reported to be worse than other slums in the city (Menon-Sen and Bhan 2008). Rather they focused on the symbolic meanings associated with resettlement, which would lead them into a future where their legitimate status would be able to give them the legitimacy they so desired.

These narratives highlight how the force of law, is exercised through the complicity of those most dominated by it. They point to a wider cultural and symbolic shift that was produced in the aftermath of the court rulings. As more and more 'illegal' slums were demolished, the differences between resettlement colonies and squatter settlements were widened through discourses of permanence, security and legitimacy. Participants spoke at a moment where the differences between 'legal' and 'illegal' slums were felt profoundly, in a city that punitively imposed a rule of law over its 'illegal' citizens. But these symbolic differences were not related simply to an abstract notion of law (although they were related) – they were also part of the social, cultural, and material violence suffered by participants in their everyday spaces on account of their illegality within the rule of law. Above all, these differences mobilized constructions of themselves as inhabitants of 'pathological' spaces in order to demand that the state fulfil its duties as a protector of marginalized social groups (I will discuss this notion of pathology further in Chapter 7).

In these first four chapters, I have focused on the notions of illegality constructed by the state and negotiated by participants. I noted that the perceptions of transience, impermanence and unfairness that the state rule of law produces among participants actually laid the foundations of a deep-seated belief that there was no place for *jhuggis* in contemporary Delhi. They knew that the camp will be demolished in the near future, but while they were waiting, they increased their familiarity with their legal rights and political entitlements and attempted to maximize their legitimate status within the framework of a state rule of law. But the irony of their condition was that even as they desired a legitimate part of the city as their home, the material conditions of resettlement colonies reported by researchers were very similar to those in the camp. In many ways then, these chapters form the context of illegality and its resultant anxieties among participants, against which I will position the discussion in the remainder of this book.

The second half of the book from now treats my central argument around the politics of space, law and gender in the illegal city. I examine how the variety of anxieties around legitimacy and urban citizenship which I have raised, are negotiated in a number of spaces in the camp. I explore how anxieties over appropriate and legitimate forms of social and political action produce hegemonic controls over the location, materiality and performances of gendered bodies in everyday spaces; how anxieties over limited access to urban basic services in everyday places produce the reinforcement of social hierarchies and the desire to control those places associated with these services; and how anxieties over the material erasure of home produce violent and hegemonic forms of control to make this home socially resilient to erasure. These processes show how everyday places in the camp become the primary sites of contestation of law where squatters negotiate their relationships with the city and with each other.

Chapter 5
'Legitimate' Social Organization

The camp is not difficult to reach but it is difficult to find if you do not know where it is. It is close to one of the main arterial roads in South Delhi, dividing the middle-class colonies from the resettlement colonies built in the late 1970s. But the only way to reach the camp is to take the road that branches off from the main arterial road, and passes through these resettlement colonies. One is aware that the road has reached an ending of sorts because the surface suddenly becomes dirtier, muddier and unkempt. This is the start of the camp. This is where I usually asked the driver to drop me off.

The main road leading into the camp divided it from its neighbouring resettlement colonies. This road had over the years turned into an economic and retail thoroughfare. Its spaces were however delineated according to certain implicit and explicit cultural rules governing the use of space, including the 'appropriate' location of men's and women's bodies in specific places of this road, and the inscription of gendered codes on these bodies. For example, while the shopkeepers were mainly men, women were the main patrons of these shops, their presence increasing during the mornings and evenings. The focus of the main road however, was the square where larger shops and a temple attracted groups of men (young and old) under the only tree. It was unusual to see women 'hanging around' or engaged in conversation with men here, although one had to go past this square to enter or leave the camp. Women participants would often narrate stories of cat-calls from these young men, and would pull their saris over their heads as they passed by the main road to avoid these calls. Thus, although women were always visible on the main road, the meanings of the main road were primarily constructed through discourses of aggressive and deviant youth masculinities practiced there.

As I walked into the camp for the first time after a few years, I was trying to remember my way through the myriad lanes of the camp to Zahira's house deep inside. As one of the leaders of the women's collective, Zahira had introduced me to participants in my earlier visit. This second time too, Zahira seemed very happy to meet me and we talked for a long time about the most recent developments in the camp. After a bit of hesitation, Zahira informed me that she was no longer involved in the collective, that she had resigned from her leadership there and now she worked mainly with a feminist NGO in the resettlement colonies in the outskirts of the city, where those evicted from the Commonwealth sites had been relocated. I was disappointed with news of her resignation because I had hoped to follow the activities of the women's collective more closely during my visit. Zahira said that she did not feel part of the women's collective anymore and that she was still ready to help anyone in the camp who came to her, but as an employee of the NGO, not as a leader of the collective. She said to me, 'I have been part of this collective for so many years, so I feel very bad about this. But I could not continue any longer. You will hear many stories about me when you talk to others during your research; it is up to you whether you believe them or not. But I will not lower myself by criticizing or blaming others. You will have to make up your mind about it'.

Zahira was right, over the next few months I heard different versions of the breakup of the women's collective leaders. Most of these stories took sides between the two leaders Zahira and Neeti, and many were contradictory. What emerged from my conversation with Neeti later was that Neeti had wanted to break away from the feminist NGO and start an NGO on their own, which Zahira had initially agreed to. But when Neeti handed in her resignation, Zahira refused to do so and remained employed, while Neeti lost her job. The other story which was also repeated by a few participants was that Zahira's daughter-in-law had approached Neeti claiming that she was being harassed by Zahira and her family. But before Neeti could intervene, Zahira heard of this and accused Neeti of interfering in her 'private' matters and inciting her daughter-in-law against her. Since Zahira had chosen not to speak about these to me, these stories were one-sided and cannot be confirmed.

In this second part of the book, I am interested in how local politics in the camp engages with law and illegality within a range of everyday spaces. I suggest that this engagement is at once performative in that participants attempt to enact the various subjecthoods that make them and their actions legitimate in the eyes of the 'Law'; and also at the same time transformative, in that such enactment requires fundamental changes in the gendered relations of power across private and public spaces. In this chapter, I am particularly interested in the genealogies of local social organizations as they evolved in the camp since their settlement in the 1970s. I argue that the social action of different organizations such as the women's collective or *Mahila Mandal*, the male *panchayat* and the more recent Residents' Welfare Association reflect the gendered politics that have evolved during different moments of uncertainty and encounters with law around the squatter home since the 1970s. During these moments, law was not taken simply as an imposed order; it was also used productively to engage with law enforcement, statutory authorities and with normative patriarchal ideologies in the homes, streets and lanes of the camp. Further it was not that informality ever became redundant in their everyday struggles; rather that informality was reworked into the discourses and performances of law in order to legitimize particular spaces in the camp as 'appropriate' sites of power and authority of social collectives. These spaces were then used to sustain gendered hegemony and control over the terms and nature of participation of others. Contestations of these different collectives in different spaces of the settlement reflect the contestations in their gendered constructions of 'appropriate' response to law and illegality in everyday life.

Much of the mediations with the state or agents of the state that these gendered collectives engage in, might appear at first to be captured by Chatterjee's notion of 'political society' (Chatterjee 1998: 136). For Chatterjee political society lies between civil society and the state and consists of 'institutions and activities where several mediations are carried out' (Chatterjee 1998: 136). The mediations between the state and gendered collectives in the camp suggest that even though the latter are excluded on account of their illegality to participate in legitimate civil society associations, they are able to 'channelize and order popular demands of the developmental state' (Chatterjee 1998: 140) in ways that Chatterjee calls the 'exercise of democracy'. Thus while the developmental state makes a number of policies in order to make certain sections of its population worthy of welfare (such as in the promotion of women's collectives through NGOs), political society might work in the camp by perceiving these to be democratic rights and entitlements.

Following Chatterjee, Hansen notes that political society in India, can be 'unruly and unpredictable, a theater of dispersed, sometime anarchic, sometimes highly organized collective performances and protests, ritualized violence in public spaces and equally ritualized destruction of public property' (Hansen 2001: 230). I agree with Das' critique of this bleak portrayal of dissent as lacking a clearer understanding of the 'fine networks or cleavages within which violence comes to be located' (Das 2004: 181). But I also find that both Chatterjee's and Hansen's notion of political society relies on an understanding of 'political' as that performed in public places – through protests, resistances and acts of public representation *against* the state. In remaining silent around the subjective relations of power between subaltern actors, they both reinforce the clichéd and moral division between state and subaltern citizens in political society.

In this chapter, my interests are twofold. First, is to understand how law and illegality becomes part of a politics of gendered organization in the camp. Second, is to understand how illegality in everyday spaces is tied fundamentally to the question of how the gendered body is constructed during political organization. These concerns begin with the contention that gendered relations across personal spaces are intimately linked to those in public spaces during social organization and political action. I propose here that political society is not just enacted within public spaces through spectacular performances; but also within neighbourhood and private spaces, and through a gendered politics directed towards dealing with illegality in the camp. Here law is not just an abstract terrain of regulations and procedures; rather it creates a space from where one's power in the local context could be manipulated and alternative models of legitimizing one's location in the city could be imagined. In other words, law becomes a terrain through which the state can be seen both as a 'threat and guarantee' (Poole 2004: 52) – a productive space, from where different types of gendered relationships with the state, and with each other can be negotiated. The contestations over space that I describe in this chapter then attempt to answer the question of what is at stake for gender during 'legitimate' social action. More crucially, it asks, how is law 'read' into the gaps between informality and illegality, and how does that shape the politics of gendered social action?

Informal leadership of the *pradhans*

Very early on in the settlement of the camp, a few residents became informal gatekeepers to the land that was occupied. Those who came later and wanted to settle on this land had to pay them a commission in order to build their houses. These transactions were inevitably informal but more or less honoured by both sides. These gatekeepers later became the unofficial leaders or *pradhans* of the camp who became more important as the camp was rapidly populated in the late 1970s. Simultaneously, police harassments began of the increased building activity and the *pradhans* became unofficial spokesmen for those in the camp, settling disputes, negotiating with the police and so on.

While there are numerous accounts of the 'land mafia' making huge sums of profits from subdividing urban fringe land in Latin America and South Asia, the role of the *pradhans* in producing the camp suggests a more localized politics of place making that was enacted by residents of squatter settlements during the late 1970s and particularly during the Emergency. This was altogether biased and exclusionary in the sense that patronage of the *pradhan* was an essential element of gaining entry to the camp and access to land within it, yet it provided legitimacy to the *pradhans* in the urgency of the Emergency period. As they heard rumours of proposals being drawn to demolish the camp the *pradhans* mobilized a group of residents from the camp and joined the mass protests taking shape in Delhi. As I have already mentioned in Chapter 3, the hunger strike in front of the Parliament that earliest *pradhans* participated in resulted in verbal assurances from Indira Gandhi, India's Prime Minister which validated the social status and power of these *pradhans* in the camp.

Soon afterwards a collective of these *pradhans*, who by now commanded enough social and symbolic power within the camp, formed a *panchayat* – a traditional form of governance whereby the different *pradhans* became part of an informal collective that would represent the demands of the residents of the camp and negotiate on their behalf with the wider urban public sphere. *Panchayat*, as a model of self-governance is common in villages, and is formed of five village elders (usually men) who arbitrate disputes. As in rural *panchayat*s, in the camp too, the *panchayat* was self-appointed – with the oldest leaders making a collective.

The *panchayat* was important since their marginal status in the city in the 1970s meant that residents were not able to rely on law enforcement agencies to solve their disputes; indeed, most residents avoided as much contact with the police or municipality as possible. The *panchayat* however, drew inspiration from systems of social justice in rural areas, which gave preference to leaders on account of social privileges of gender, caste, and generation. The *pradhan* as one who was more educated and of an upper caste became their spokesperson, allocating land to newly arrived squatters, arbitrating between neighbours and family members, negotiating with the police and municipality, negotiating with utility companies for water and electricity and so on. In the contingency of land appropriation, the *pradhans* and the *panchayat* became the symbolic 'guardians' of squatters on the camp and informal gatekeepers to public land.

The importance and significance of informal leaders has been noted in many studies of slum informality (Jha, Rao and Woolcock 2007, Linden 1997). These studies claim that informality has been a continuous feature of leadership and social organization in urban slums through which urban basic services have been accessed. In African slums Simone (2004) notes that creativity and imagination in the informal economies and social networks are crucial to the procurement of basic goods and services. For Simone, informality uses 'a proficiency in formal institutions to elaborate new spaces of operation' (Simone 2004: 24), although it maintains its dependence on relations with customary authority – a *marabout*, which combines religious leader, sage and merchant, and can be both spiritual leader and political authority. But these local leaders are also seen as schemers and fixers who are able to manipulate their social networks and contacts. Simone's framing of the access to power of these figures of local authority relies on the gaps between institutional and informal forms of transactions in everyday life. For Simone, the power of these informal structures of authority emerged from their economic collaborations, and allowed new types of mobilization across diverse identities, even without any formal opportunity to do so.

The informal collective or *panchayat* in the camp however came together very differently from the economic nature of collaborations noted by Simone (2004) in Africa. The *pradhans* in the camp formed a 'political society' of sorts, through which they accessed basic services and goods from the state. Their location within this political society was related to their privileged access to urban land, to law-enforcement, and to political networks. The *pradhans* had appropriated land along the main road occupying the larger houses – these indicated material signs of their higher social status in the camp. During visits from MPs, police or local political leaders, these *pradhans* then took centre stage in any activity which involved 'speaking for' or on behalf of squatters. This involved giving bribes, eating or consuming alcohol with them. These privileges were related to the caste, gendered, ethnic and religious positionalities of the *pradhans* – they were all male, middle- and upper caste Hindus from particular villages in Uttar Pradesh, Bihar, and Rajasthan. Each *pradhan* was also a member of a political party, which determined how the needs of their particular community of affiliation (ethnic, religious or kinship) were to be protected. In return each *pradhan* would keep a list of camp residents belonging to their caste or kinship based community who were encouraged to vote for those political parties which patronized them. In maintaining their power and control over the informal spaces of authority in the camp, the *pradhans* translated a rural system of governance into an urban form of informal leadership. The structure of leadership was amorphous – there were no clear duties and responsibilities defined for these *pradhans*; rather they were called upon ad hoc by the residents during property or marital disputes.

The rural form of *panchayati* governance then achieved a significant urban transmogrification in the camp. The *panchayat* continued to take decisions on day-to-day disputes and crises, but unlike the rural context, they were dealing with 'urban' issues (which included housing, crime, basic services) and hence their solutions relied upon a range of urban social and political networks. Further, their social status on the basis of caste or religious affiliation was not a 'given' in the city; rather they re-established their power through control over particular spaces of political visibility and social and material privilege. For example, the oldest *pradhan* built a temple next to the square on the main road and installed himself there as priest. This temple as a religious structure, and its location next to the square gave it high visibility and social status as an important building – a place where political leaders paid their first visit when then came to the camp and the first port of call of the police when they were summoned to the camp. But this temple was also a form of control over urban basic services. As a religious structure, the temple had its own water connection from the municipality – for use in its rituals. During water crises, the *pradhan* could be benevolent and decide which families in the camp to give access to this water. His 'entitlement' to this water as the priest of the temple therefore, extended his control over religious spaces to the spaces of everyday life.

Such incidences of *panchayati* leadership were common in other areas of Delhi where the primary role of such informal governance was to serve as intermediaries to mitigate risk and provide access to public services (Jha, Rao and Woolcock 2007). In such systems, squatters as 'vote banks' incredibly had more interactions with politicians and lesser access to bureaucrats, which served to keep them tied to forms of state hegemony through implicit benefits, informal deals and political connivance in circumventing the rule of law. Connections between *pradhan*s and political leadership produced a variety of inclusions and exclusions relating to who had access to land, water, electricity and police protection. Before the elections, the *pradhan* recruited party volunteers among the camp residents, who circulated party flyers and encouraged residents to go and vote for respective political parties, who would suitably reward the local *pradhan*s when they came to power. Striking in this informal model of leadership however was the exclusion and invisibility of women. It was not that women were not involved in providing support to the *panchayat*, but matters dealing with the 'outside world' were seen as the responsibility of men. In the context of uncertainty and upheaval of the settlement, women's role was seen in providing stability and permanence to the squatter home. This ideology was reinforced through the practices of later collectives in the camp.

Although from very early on, political patronage defined the structure and shape of local politics in the camp, the 'customary authority' of the *pradhan*s in the camp has receded in recent years, not least because many of these *pradhan*s have passed away. When I was conducting my research, I would see the last remaining *pradhan* sitting on the main square outside the temple every day, often with a group of men who still came to consult him on day-to-day matters. This particular scene reflects the remains of parochial power in the camp – the very visible presence of a group of men near the temple on the main square as part of a receding social and political authority. Most residents disparaged their social status in private conversations. As one young male participant described the *pradhan* 'he has been in the camp for 25–30 years, but he does no work for the *janta* [public]. Netaji [politician] comes, garlands him, he gets photographed'. But while the *pradhan* explicitly laid claims to his 'status' as a political leader, he was only presented during symbolic moments (such as during the demolition of houses with which I began this book) as the oldest male leader of the camp. Apart from this, the residents or police on their way in and out of the camp often paid their respects to one of the oldest surviving customary authority of an erstwhile local political order.

Feminist participatory activism

One morning while wandering along the narrow lanes of the camp, my research assistant and I met Abida. She stopped us to ask why we were there, because she had seen us walking along her lane before. A few brief words of exchange and we found out that she had been involved in the *Mahila Mandal* activities since the 1980s. She invited us into her house and began to talk about how much she had enjoyed her association with them. She had come of know of the *Mahila Mandal* when two women had paid her a visit in her house in the late 1980s. Abida noted wistfully that those days she used to be a shy Muslim bride who had come from the village and did not step out of the home much. She also had young children and did not have enough time, but it was her weakness for music that took her to the *Mahila Mandal* meetings.

> There was some dancing and singing there. And I enjoy music and dancing, so when that was happening I told [neighbour], that there is some music and dancing there, let's go. Then we went there and dancing was still on. We were very happy. In eight number [block] they would have meetings, like some of these congregations. [Abida]

Over the years, Abida became more involved in their activities, travelling often with other women in the camp to take part in street theatres and puppet shows across India. Later when her children became older, they too were engaged in these activities which they thoroughly enjoyed as collective events. All through this conversation, Abida's husband was sitting on one corner, and kept adding to her story. After a while, I turned towards him and asked what he thought about these activities. But Abida quickly interrupted that he was always supportive, because Abida always made sure she took his permission first, and that he always knew where she was and how long she was away for.

Since the 1980s, urban development practices in Delhi and more widely in India became committed to transforming women's marginalization through participation. A variety of state sponsored slum upgradation and sites and services projects used women as key beneficiaries as well as agents of local knowledge during slum redevelopment. These were tied to the desire to bring about gendered empowerment through the 'natural' extension of women's domestic roles into the public sphere of participation and decision-making around the production of their homes and transformation of their physical environments (Chant 2003, Kabeer 1994). In many urban slums, there began a proliferation of non-governmental organizations (NGOs), community-based organizations (CBOs) or grass roots organizations (GROs) and the private sector, which collaborated directly with international development agencies in the provision of housing and urban basic services.

In the 1980s, the feminist movement in India was simultaneously mobilized by middle-class women academics and development practitioners who strived to reform the conditions which poor women were living in. They proposed that the marginalization of women was a central feature of underdevelopment and made demands on grounds of equality (John 2008). In the 1980s, feminist organizations in Delhi and across India began to work with women in slums and informal settlements in order to mobilize them into social and political action around their marginality both in the hands of the state and patriarchy (Ray 1999). The leaders of these organizations came from middle-class families and to that extent, much of their approaches were welfarist. One of their main strategies was participatory activism among slum women – through street theatres, puppet shows, folk music (Nagar 2000), as well as through informal courts (Magar 2003) and survey-based research. These feminist organizations used legal mechanisms when informal negotiations failed to deliver justice to women. While these activities in particular allowed slum women to 'institutionalize a middle-class welfare initiative into a new framework' (Magar 2003: 521) of 'working-class feminisms' (Datta 2007), they also produced a range of anxieties among women and their families around the notion of home, participation and the transgression across private and public spaces in order to achieve legitimacy as urban citizens. While for these agencies, 'participation' was an indicator of empowerment, women who actually participated did not necessarily do this to become 'empowered' in the same way that state and NGOs defined this word.

The creation of the *Mahila Mandal* (women's collective) in the camp had its roots in the presence of such a feminist NGO which was based in Delhi. This NGO was formed in 1984, a period when there was a resurgence of activism around issues related to violence against women. They worked in the camp since then, engaging its women in a model of participatory activism through street plays and theatres and raising consciousness against the injustices of their marginal location within the city, as well as the injustices of patriarchal hegemony in the forms of domestic violence and dowry in the home and family, and molestations in public places. While there were multiple differences amongst these women on the basis of caste, religion, ethnicity, and language, and subsequently multiple loyalties with different *pradhan*s, this NGO worked from a 'secular' perspective that served to highlight and mobilize women around forms of disadvantage faced as a result of their gender roles within the social and spatial context of the camp and making them aware of their rights under law. They evoked contingent relationships between women's bodies, their spaces, and their physical environment (which included housing, infrastructure and family) to highlight women's practical and strategic gendered needs.[1]

During the late 1980s, the NGO recruited a couple of women in the camp who were specifically trained in the rhetorics and practices of feminist activism. These two women went from door-to-door in the camp talking informally to other women, conducting surveys on their socio-economic conditions, and writing their 'life-stories'. Their primary task was to encourage them to attend meetings in the camp organized by the NGO. Women's motivations for joining were often around leisure and entertainment and it was a way to exchange news with neighbours. These affective forms of interaction blurred the distinctions between formal and informal communication, and were forged in places like meeting rooms which were away from the public sphere. They provided ways to articulate shared practices, experiences and memories around feminist organization. And their translation of middle-class notions of feminist consciousness into working-class practices of participatory activism encouraged women in the camp to create a resident women's collective called *Mahila Mandal*.

The links between the feminist NGO and *Mahila Mandal* were thus produced in and through informal communication but were legitimized through the NGO's location within wider state sponsorship and legitimization. Their methods were affective, using women's bodies, spaces and life stories as performative narratives through which feminist consciousness could be raised. They used dances, street theatres, and puppet shows to attract women like Abida. These shows however, were themed around issues of women's marginalization in the home and wider society – dowry, domestic violence, child marriage, spousal rape, incest and so on. They also explicitly avoided connecting these marginalizations to specific positions of difference between these women on the basis of caste, religion or ethnicity. Thus dowry, domestic violence, rape and so on were constructed only and simply as 'women's issues, which brought together a range of women from upper and lower castes as well as from different religious or linguistic groups.

The NGO held meetings in the camp with these women, which helped individual women connect their personal struggles to those of others within the shared spaces of the meeting rooms – an intermediate space which was disengaged both from power relationships in the home and from the public sphere of the camp.

---

1   Since the 1950s feminist scholars have critiqued UN development approaches in informal settlements for being gender-blind (Boserup 1970). Caroline Moser's (Moser 1989, Moser and Peake 1987) seminal work pointed out that women's practical and strategic gender needs were important areas of concern in development policies. *Practical gender needs* such as issues of adequate housing, clean water supply or sanitation were seen to arise from women's gender roles in the family. *Strategic gender needs* such as issues of safety, privacy and sexual division of labor were seen to arise from women's subordinate gender roles with respect to men.

In 2002 when I visited the camp, the meeting room was a small room belonging to Zahira, who was then one of the leaders of the *Mahila Mandal*. This room incorporated multiple activities – meetings, record keeping, discussions, and talks. It was embedded deep within the narrow lanes and except for the board announcing their name there were no visual markers of its existence. Inside the office, there was barely any furniture and everyone sat on the floor. The walls were covered with posters on domestic violence and adult literacy, letters of alphabets (for the children when it was used as a classroom) and photographs of the activities of the collective. The meeting room was a place that held memories, stressed the continuity of the collective, its welfare efforts and represented its setbacks and perseverance. It was a place where women politicized the home through discussions and dialogues on feminist issues. It was here that decisions were taken regarding the actions against domestic violence, molestation and dowry. From the gendered spaces of this meeting room, women found a shared desire to consciously enter the public sphere through these affective forms of participatory activism. Some of these women were recruited by the NGO to take part in feminist activism across the country, encouraged to participate in writing and performing plays, puppet shows, and dancing using feminist themes across different parts of India.

Such grassroots spaces of transformation are common both in urban and rural areas. We see this in Nagar's (2000) work in rural women's activism in India, where through street theatres women were able to get men concerned about the violence and violation of women's bodies. Performative narratives such as theatres presented arguments around feminist struggles to particular audiences in particular contexts. Mohan (2004) too in her work on a theatre group in rural Bengal notes how theatre and role playing led by a handful of middle-class activists were able to draw large numbers of the rural population into a performative construction of oppositional identity to the state. The themes of this performance were related to both state hegemonies around rural livelihoods, cultural identities, anti-liquor agitations, as well as patriarchal ideologies of dowry and domestic violence. Mohan notes that these oppositional political practices worked not only because of their themes but also because their 'method of theatre pushes people to construct reality and to imagine change through a practice in which people not only play scripts but also script plays' (Mohan 2004: 185). Similar performative political practices among the women in *Mahila Mandal* challenged the hegemonic models of the state and patriarchy and provided ways to understand what kinds of power differentials were at stake in society.

The effectiveness of this form of participatory activism was charted to me by participants who had been connected in a variety of ways with the work of the NGO and *Mahila Mandal*. Their varieties of involvement ranged from direct action in assisting other women by visiting them in their homes, to occasional participation in the street theatres or demonstrations. Their methods ranged from a politics of insurgency and entitlement when it came to engagements with the state, and a politics of negotiation and legal recourse when it came to engagements with the home and neighbourhood. Above all, the material and social conditions of their everyday life in the camp were seen as feminist issues that had to be addressed through feminist activism. The context of their illegality which excluded them from urban basic services was seen to be tied to women's bodies and spaces since it were women who engaged in domestic labour and faced increased difficulties in the absence of water, sanitation and electricity. As Zahira said, 'The man leaves in the morning for work, he returns only at night. But women will go to work, return home, cook, go to fetch vegetables, fetch groceries, fetch water; she has to go through these lanes at least 50 times a day'. *Mahila Mandal* therefore addressed the needs of women arising out of the structural differences in their normative gender roles from men and extended this discourse to challenge women's spatial boundaries. In this way they selectively presented their priorities 'in order to maximize the benefits to be achieved by political action' (Fincher and Panelli 2001: 129).

Women who participated in *Mahila Mandal* activities did not usually do so without the explicit permission of the male head of household. This was becoming clearer to me as I interviewed more women like Abida who had been involved in the activities of *Mahila Mandal* in the heyday of support from the feminist NGO. Men were reluctant to let women in their households join in the activities, let alone travel to other parts of India. But it was the perception that connections with NGO and *Mahila Mandal* members would give them more powers that many men reluctantly agreed to their women's participation.

Meena, one of the elderly volunteers in the *Mahila Mandal*, used the symbolic power of the *Mahila Mandal* to bargain with her husband for her participation. She said, 'I used to come home and tell him [husband] what we heard at the meeting. Then slowly he started thinking that if we don't cooperate with them and if there is a fight or some violence, then who will come to our help?' Surely enough, sometime later, Meena and her husband tried to evict their tenant who refused to leave. Meena went to the *Mahila Mandal* and requested them for help.

> When our Muslim tenant was not vacating the house, Zahira [who was Muslim] went to mediate and he said, 'Why are you not helping another Muslim but a *chamar* [lowest caste]?' Zahira said 'Traitor, you think I will help you? Don't think that Meena and her husband are alone. There are 300 people behind them.' So this is how they have helped us.

Meena recounted this incident with much pride because for her it meant that being part of the *Mahila Mandal* had allowed the equalizing of social hierarchies among the women. As low-castes, Meena and her husband had not expected Zahira to support her against another Muslim, but Zahira's unconditional help as a representative of the *Mahila Mandal* won over many doubtful men. Such an implicit agreement among *Mahila Mandal* members that feminist activism had to fight religious and caste differences, along with 'all the multifarious forms of androcentric domination' (Kapadia 2002: 19) created personal loyalties. This provided strong bonds of mutual support, cohesion and collective organization.

The politics and social action that the *Mahila Mandal* was involved in was inherently spatial, focusing on gendered disadvantages for women in their relationship to particular material and social conditions within the camp and the wider city. They related this primarily to structural differences between men and women, as well as cultural differences inscribed through the moral geographies of boundaries around women's bodies and spaces.

Women like Meena who participated in *Mahila Mandal* activities, found their involvement most productive when they were able to resist local power (from aggressive neighbours) or the police who continually harassed them for money. Those who participated began to learn about their rights under law from other *Mahila Mandal* members and began to resist police corruption. Women, who were scared of going out because of fear of molestation or cat-calls from other men, began to show equal aggression by hitting these men and 'taking revenge'. In short, most women that I spoke to, who had been involved in the *Mahila Mandal* and NGO activities in the 1980s and 1990s spoke highly of them and shared their fond memories with me. Abida finally summed up what she thought of Neeti, the leader of the *Mahila Mandal* who had knocked on her door more than 20 years back and given her the confidence to enter the public realm of feminist participatory activism.

> She is in reality a guru. Because, she is the one who has shown more to me, and others. We weren't that intelligent [confident] then, but today we have the courage to fight back in case someone is speaking rudely to us. [Abida]

Feminist activism in the camp thus facilitated three types of gendered transformations – the rise in power and social status of the women who participated in the women's collective; the increased gendered access to spaces that were traditionally denied to women in the camp; and most significantly the occasional use of a force of law to bring about gendered justice for women in the camp. These transformations were made possible due to the different ways that the NGO and the women's collective attempted to help the women in the camp in claiming their legitimate rights under law in public and private spaces. The *Mahila Mandal* advised women in the camp on a variety of legal matters around personal law, criminal law, civil law, statutory rights, and so on. They also mobilized against police harassment, helped with paperwork around filing for pensions, divorce, domestic violence, child custody, pensions and so on. Above all, they adopted a mediatory role in the camp during family disputes, and if this failed, they took recourse to law in order to protect women's legal rights.

After ten years of involvement, the NGO withdrew their formal support from the camp in 2001, but they left behind a socially conscious and literate group of working-class women who formally registered their organization and continued to maintain close connections with a variety of feminist NGOs through participatory activism. This collaboration between the NGO and *Mahila Mandal* helped to connect working-class women to civil society organizations and subsequently move away from informal structures of patronage, privilege and customary authority. The increasing presence and social power of the *Mahila Mandal* members in the camp diminished the importance of the *panchayat* as the mediator between state and camp residents. As many participants reminded me, the role of the *Panchayat* was taken over by the women's collective because this women's collective was seen more to do with 'women's issues' and hence was seen as the more 'appropriate' space of negotiation by most women.

'Once women join the *Mahila Mandal* they don't understand men'

> When I came here there was no water, so we went to the [water utility] office and put in an application. First they approved four taps and I got them installed. Still the water wasn't enough so we put in another application. Then the reply came from the office – from one tap there should be 100 families filling up. If 100 buckets are trying to fill from a tap that doesn't give enough water how can they fill it? And one family has at least four members so even if 100 families fill one bucket each, so how will one bucket be enough for the family? So we said, we fought with them in the office- the Delhi Jal Board. They still didn't listen so we went on festival days such as Diwali, Eid, we went from the organization and dug up the lines and made marches and then we got enough water. [Zahira]

In 2002, this story of the 'success' of the *Mahila Mandal* was recounted to me by Zahira. But in 2005, this same story was recounted (in different words) to me by a male participant as the success of the *panchayat*. As an erstwhile 'helper' in the *Mahila Mandal*, he insisted that the *Mahila Mandal* had not actually achieved much success in the camp – rather as men it had always been their responsibility to engage with the local authorities in order to improve living conditions in the camp. He noted that the *Mahila Mandal* was only connected with women's issues – marital disputes, dowry, domestic violence and bringing errant husbands to justice, they did not have any legitimacy as representatives of the camp. The *Mahila Mandal* was concerned with matters of the home, not with matters of the camp. The realm of the latter was for men.

It is well documented that law, police, judicial processes and the courts are generally unsympathetic to women entering public spheres through activism and insurgency. In the 1980s and 1990s as the *Mahila Mandal* members worked hard to bring about social and physical improvements in the camp, much of their dealings with the bureaucracy were channelled through the *pradhans*. This was not surprising because many of these women were working full-time for a livelihood and delegating some of the tasks to men seemed a logical sharing of their responsibilities. But this was also because officials in the municipality or statutory authorities often wanted explicitly to engage only with men. Under such circumstances enlisting men to work on their behalf was common practice among the *Mahila Mandal* leaders – it avoided direct confrontation and also speeded up bureaucratic processes.

The reader might recall that this paradox of gendered agency and social action was precisely how I introduced this book, when women from the *Mahila Mandal* purposely kept their invisibility in the public meeting on the main road in the aftermath of the demolitions. Ironically, enlisting men in 'public' negotiations of material and environmental goods served to delegate the women leaders into more 'private' matters of women's issues. Further, the participation of the women through the *Mahila Mandal* in the performative spaces of street theatres was seen to reinforce women's perceived connections with emotional and affective spaces – and situate them squarely within the home and family.

There was another reason behind the discursive rejection of the *Mahila Mandal*'s legitimacy. In the camp often violence (inflicted by men) over women's bodies was expected to be corrected in a 'sympathetic' rather than punitive way. While the injustices over women's bodies were acknowledged by all, the punitive justice system that separated women from their violent partners or families was often resisted by women themselves. Women in the camp who faced domestic violence, harassment for dowry, divorce, child custody issues and who approached the NGO and *Mahila Mandal* for help were given advice on their legal rights. Women were encouraged to speak out against injustices, to challenge hegemonic patriarchal authority and if necessary to take recourse to law in order to protect their rights. In all cases the *Mahila Mandal* would attempt to negotiate and counsel with family members, but in those cases where negotiation failed, they would use the law to bring family members to justice. Nevertheless *Mahila Mandal*'s use of law within the home was seen to destabilize the prescribed location of women within the home and as reproducers of the family (I will discuss this in further detail in Chapter 7).

An inherent tension of sorts thus emerged in the camp between those whose lives had been transformed in a variety of ways through their participation in the *Mahila Mandal*, and those who perceived the *Mahila Mandal* as dealing with women's issues which were tangential to the everyday struggles faced by the residents in the camp. 'Women's problems' were seen to have less to do with the material struggles around water, electricity, housing, sanitation and so on and more with matters between husband and wife. Thus many women resisted joining in the activities (saying they had no domestic conflicts) and many others also left after a short association. Despite the many ways that the women worked with different public bodies to improve the physical environment of the camp, they were described by many participants as a collective which put women's individual needs first. In the traditional gender roles subscribed to women in the camp, this began to be seen at odds with women's normative roles as mothers, daughters and wives – their 'freedom from ego' (Chakrabarty 1992: 335) and the ability to serve and be subservient voluntarily. As a male participant noted,

I think they have not functioned properly. They use women and leave them. They ask the women to gather, conduct meetings, put up banners, take photographs. They have broken some homes, through divorce. Once women join the *Mahila Mandal* they don't understand men. They want to take revenge, threaten men that they will put them behind bars. [Ramprasad]

Residents' welfare association

In 2003, the Delhi municipality decided to connect all squatter settlements to mains electric supply. Before that, these settlements had tapped electricity from the main lines. The provision of electricity however was to be done through private subcontractors, which allowed the municipality to avoid financial risks and yet accumulate economic gains from the use of services. Overnight, each house in the camp was installed with an electric meter and overnight they realized that they were paying for overpriced electricity.

The meter contractors came here and in collaboration with the political leaders, they decided to put meters here. We were getting electricity for free, so we were not happy to have the meters put here. Now the electricity charges that generally there is 200–250 rupees, but these show 2500 [rupees] including the electricity and wire charges. 1700–1800 [rupees] like this. So we all got together and went to the police station. So, the SHO [Station House Officer] said who is your *Pradhan*? Elect a leader, *a male leader* [my emphasis] who will talk to us. All of you are talking; 200, 250, 400 of you have come. Elect one person. We said there is no such person, we are all together. He said first elect and then come and talk to me. We said okay give us your permission and we will elect. SHO sahib gave us permission, we came here had a meeting and elected a leader. [Moinullah]

This event recounted to me by Moinullah, one of the elected leaders of the camp, speaks of a particular intersection between the politics of illegality and the politics of gendered social action. On the one hand, this is a moment of political and social transformation, whereby the illegal urban condition of the squatters produces a need for democratic representation in order to counter the injustices of exclusion from urban infrastructure. Here Moinullah speaks of their entitlement to urban basic services, the denial of which was possible through a maintaining violence of law. On the other hand, a democratization of participation in the camp set forth by this incident also initiates concerns around 'appropriate' gendered representation. While the state promotes gendered participation in the public sphere through NGOs, ironically the police as an agent of the state normalized gendered ideologies within spaces of participation. Thus the camp's gendered exclusions were not just a 'home-grown' struggle over space and social power; rather a process intimately linked to the spaces of illegality, overseen and produced by the founding and maintaining violence of law.

Earlier the cops also knew that there were too many self-styled *Pradhan*s – BJP,
Congress, Lok Janshakti Party workers kept on claiming they were *Pradhan*s,
but this doesn't add any weight to this post. Some local political workers tried to
create problems … as they realized that once an elected *Pradhan* is there their
vote politics will get affected. So they complained to their leaders and tried to
stop these elections. We knew there was risk of untoward incidents also, but
with lot of patience we carried the process forward. I still have the rules and
regulations and other material which I read out to members and they put their
stamp of approval on it. We held meetings continuously for two months. We
also started with a membership drive, created awareness among people about
benefits related to this. I think this the first *jhuggi* camp in Delhi where such an
elected *Pradhan* is there. We gave animals as election symbols to candidates.
This was done to make people realize that political parties treat poor people as
animals. [Kanhaiya]

Kanhaiya's enthusiastic recounting of the achievement of democracy in the
camp reflects a continuous contestation between political patronage and political
representation at local levels. Kanhaiya and other candidates who stood for the
election took this process very seriously; the rules and regulations were drafted
on stamp paper to give them legal validity, and each candidate had to define his or
her agenda for the election. Candidates like Kanhaiya went from door to door in
the camp trying to convince people to cast their votes. Their agendas were related
to a variety of everyday difficulties faced by people in the camp, primarily around
the electricity bills as well as water and sanitation, but were also more gendered
agendas such as providing help with the bureaucracy of widow pensions in the
camp.

Overall 16 candidates stood for the elections and 1200 people from the camp
voted in these – approximately 25 percent turnout. The elections were held during
the day in the market square from eight in the morning till five in the evening.
22 police officers were on duty in the polling booth, and the entire event was
videotaped. At the end of the day, the votes were counted and five of the male
candidates who received the highest votes were elected to the Residents' Welfare
Association. Kanhaiya felt excitement when the votes were being counted because
after half the counting, he was in the lead. When finally all the votes were counted,
he felt elated because he had won the election with the highest number of votes.
He became the first democratically elected *pradhan* in the camp along with five
other male candidates in the managing committee. These candidates then went to
the Delhi High Court and formally registered their association.

These events leading up to the election of Kanhaiya and others in the camp
show how law was present in the spaces of social organization – both as a threat
and as a resource. As a threat, law attempted to deny residents of the camp access
to electricity under the same terms as the rest of the city, and instead provided this
as an exception through the private sector. As a resource, law was present in the
ways that residents constructed the election campaign as a democratic exercise and

asserted its validity through the presence of the SHO. This evoked the authority of the state and legitimized the association through formal structures of law. The use of election manifestos for different candidates, party symbols of animals that attempted to mock the state while conforming to its rules of democratic participation, down to the videotaping of the entire process of counting, highlights the ways in which law became a performative force even though the rule of law could not validate the camp as legal. It suggests that collective organization in the camp could not have existed outside of law – rather it was in the engagement with law as performance that allowed residents in the camp to frame their struggles through democratic processes and organize a 'representative democracy'.

'Why do women drive cars?'

Significant in these democratic elections was the exclusion of one woman who had stood for these elections. Rakhi received the second highest number of votes but she was not included in the committee formed of five male members. Her exclusion from the committee was agreed upon between her husband and the other committee members to 'protect' her from the hassles of public work – a decision that received her consent. Rakhi came from one of the upper caste families in the camp; she proudly stated that her husband was a very caring and honest man – who took the popular yearly pilgrimage during the monsoons on foot to Hardwar (a holy city for Hindus at a distance of 202 kilometres from Delhi). Her husband always supported her financially, so much so that she did not have to step outside the house to work; and even if he took to the bottle once in a while, there was never any domestic violence. Rakhi therefore respected her husband's decision and said she supported it because she was aware of the many hassles of such public work, which she felt was better left in the hands of men. For Rakhi, their family occupied a position of moral authority within the camp, because often her husband would be called by other families to settle disputes or help in spiritual matters (as an upper caste man). She noted that it was enough for her to know that she had the respect of the residents of the camp as mother of her son and the wife of her husband and that her exclusion from the committee was not exclusion at all; rather the upholding of the name and honour of her family.

Part of this gendered exclusion was because in the camp, participation of women in the public sphere was largely channelled through the *Mahila Mandal*, seen to be addressing 'women's issues'. I became aware of this as I was interviewing Moinullah, one of the members of the Residents' Welfare Association (RWA), who pointed out to me that if women wanted to be 'leaders' they could join the *Mahila Mandal* because it dealt with women's issues. I suggested to him that if they worked together they might be able to exert more pressure on the state to pay attention to their living conditions in the camp, but Moinullah pointed out that they worked in different spaces and different scales – the *Mahila Mandal* on the household level within the spaces of the home and family; and the RWA on the urban scale with politicians, bureaucrats and the police (and therefore only the RWA's aims were directed at the improvement of the living conditions in the camp). He noted that it would not be advisable or appropriate for women to engage in the RWA since they dealt with the urban public sphere which was the realm of men. At this point in our conversation, he suddenly looked away from me and addressed my male research assistant sitting next to me.

> The work that men can do, why are women doing that? What is the need? What is the compulsion? Tell me, when there are plenty of men driving cars, why do women [want to] drive cars? Tell me, when the woman is the one to sit in the backseat, so why [desire] the front seat? [Moinullah]

But, even as Moinullah mapped a discursive line of separation between 'appropriate' gendered participation within public and private spheres, he simultaneously acknowledged the struggles they faced as a collective in making material changes to their living conditions in the camp. Although residents in the camp had democratized their leadership, their wider participation in the public realm was stymied in the absence of legal rights as urban citizens. Moinullah sighed, 'at the end of the day we do not have any power because we are illegal residents'.

Despite being the democratic representative body of the camp then, the RWA's legitimacy was unrealized in the absence of their legal rights to the land they occupied. While arguing for 'appropriate' gender locations within public and private spaces, the Residents' Welfare Association constructed the urban public sphere as a reflection of the gendered divisions existing in the camp. And in doing so, they forsook the possibilities of mediating with the state through NGOs – a practice that *Mahila Mandal* leaders were adept at. Ironically it was this oscillation between replication of democratic practices of the state on the one hand and reinforcement of parochial gendered ideologies on the other that became the defining feature of encounters with law within the camp. This oscillation was not just present among the leaders or residents in the camp; rather it was also embodied by the police in ways that they encouraged the creation of a democratic body within the camp. The words of the policeman asking them to elect a male leader and the male leaders' construction of the exclusion of the elected woman as 'protection' highlighted that performance of law in the camp was only a simulacra – a vague, unreal and shadowy resemblance to the very laws through which they had been labelled as illegal citizens.

Location of power

The contestations over the legitimacy of different collectives in the camp highlight the contestations over the power to divert the maintaining violence of law away from the camp. In other words, each collective was trying through its own formal and informal networks to provide access to a number of basic services in the camp.

Before the 1990s, power was identifiable and was vested in the politicians, who could manipulate the rule of law as and when they desired. This gave advantage to the *pradhans* and the *panchayat* in mediating informally with politicians. More recently, power has become fluid and is shared between the state, the urban government, judiciary, and private utility companies. As I have noted earlier in this book, this has made the amorphousness and illegibility of power more pronounced, since now power cannot be located in one institution or space. Rather the amorphousness of this power has transformed the relationships between state and residents in the camp. Instead of mediating with political leaders, different gendered collectives in the camp must find a way to mediate with these different institutions as and when they pose a threat to everyday life. This amorphousness of power has transformed the relationships between different families in the camp.

This became visible to me in a conversation that took place between two participants. Both of them were neighbours and had lived in the camp since the 1980s. To my question about what changes they had seen since they came, both agreed that while they now had access to basic services this had become increasingly expensive and unreliable.

> Ramvilas: See the thing is that in earlier days, there was no such thing as private or separate....whoever extended the [electric] wires, it was his to keep. See earlier, if we did not give the money to the minister, then he can tell us. It was his right to the money so that we could have a connection. Otherwise he would just bring his cronies and he would have the entire slum beaten up and cleared off. Then the private thing turned up but still the people that they have employed are like us. They live here, a lot of them are ruffians, and they don't do their work. They get the salary but they also ask for bribes and terrorize the people.

> Premsingh: What can they do about their work? If somebody from Delhi [government] gives them the order to disconnect an electricity connection, then they will come and do it. He is the one who gives them the salary. They don't want to come and disconnect of their own will.

> Ramvilas: Just a minute, just a minute – why is it always only us who have to suffer? There are a few select people here whose connection never fails. I will take you from home to home the next time there is a black out and show you what happens there...They are human beings and we are not? They never have an electricity failure and we have it all the time.

> Premsingh: But that's because they have a tube-well light [inverter] and that is why they don't experience a black out. Just because you don't know anything about it doesn't make it wrong. There are five people who have these tube-well connections and they pay for that. You are completely mistaken I am telling you now and here.

This conversation was revealing not simply because of the confusion among participants about the location of power, but also around the confusion regarding its location in particular bodies and households that were no longer 'outside' the camp. Indeed it was the possibility that some among themselves had been able to negotiate access to state spaces in particular ways that made it difficult for Ramvilas to accept. Premsingh on the other hand, began to argue for their 'innocence' since his son was one of these youths employed by the local electric supplier. For Premsingh, his son was simply doing his job, whereas for Ramvilas, these young men represented the amorphousness of power which could no longer be marked upon a singular body or space. This exchange then was not just about misconceptions about the location of power, it was also the discomfort and refusal to accept that power was now also located in a different form within their midst.

The ambiguities in the location of power were also central to the question of how law was encountered and experienced in the camp. It showed that while earlier, the rule of law could be superseded by the power and authority of local politicians, in more recent years, the enforceability of law within the spaces of the camp has become more ambiguous. This is not just a maintaining violence of law practiced by the state; rather law itself is being mimicked and embodied by its residents during moments of uncertainty around rights, entitlements and eligibilities towards urban basic services. In doing so, power rests more uneasily and unevenly across everyday spaces of squatter settlements. Thus one is never quite sure how the force of law will manifest in their midst. I elaborate this last point further now.

A small matter of the *chowki*

In 2003, when the camp was given electric connections, an electric substation was constructed right at the end of the main road. Each time I entered or left the camp, I would see a few men sitting inside the office there – most of them lived in the camp and they worked for the private electric subcontractor who provided the camp with electricity. Just before I began my research in 2005, the men working there decided to set up a *Chowki* (platform for Hindu communal prayer) close to the substation on the main road. This happened to be across the road from Neeti's house, who was one of the leaders of the *Mahila Mandal*. Neeti immediately objected to this arguing that they would create a commotion, that they would harass passing women, and would play music too loudly during the night. These men then went to the Residents' Welfare Association to ask for help and were supported by them on the grounds that this was about religious freedom and that it should be allowed to happen. But when the men set up the *chowki*, Neeti called the police and asked them to get it removed. The police officer who knew Neeti well, tried to reason with her, but could not convince her. Neeti was adamant that the *chowki* should not be allowed. 'This is Lakshmipuri, not a VIP colony where you can ensure that no one will make trouble' she said.

Latika, an elderly participant, who was in favour of the *chowki* being set up, described it in great detail to me one afternoon. Latika remembered that it was a tense evening because half the camp was gathered outside Neeti's house. Most of them were family, friends or kin of the men who wanted to put up the *chowki*. There were also others who came because they were shocked that Neeti was resisting the setting up of a *chowki* for prayers, when Neeti herself was devoutly Hindu and prayed everyday with her family. The police superintendent first went inside Neeti's house, while Latika and others were waiting outside. After what appeared to be a long time, the police finally came out and said to her and others gathered there, '*Seedhi ungli ghee nikal jaye to accha hai. Tedhi karenge to fayeda kya* [it is better if the butter comes out with straight fingers; what is the point of bending your fingers? – in other words, don't resist]. Four of your children are inside [in jail], they will be put away for good; so listen to what she is saying'. He spoke more directly to Latika who had been a strong proponent of the *chowki* because her son was one of those involved in its making. He said to her, '*Mataji* [mother, form of respect for elderly lady], don't be stubborn, because she [Neeti] is greater [more powerful]; and you are the ones who made her great; and you know she will get her way, you can't do anything'. Latika and others knew that he was right; if Neeti wanted she could have got the young men in the *chowki* arrested by falsely accusing them of harassing her daughter-in-law.

This incident was narrated in its different versions by various participants in the camp – in all of which, the small matter of the *chowki* was seen to have been blown out of proportions. There were a great deal of inconsistencies in the narration of this incident, but in all these stories Neeti came out as one of the most powerful members of the camp, whose word could supersede not just that of the Residents' Welfare Association, but also that of the police. Some women participants also said that in retrospect they understood why Neeti did this; because the main road was already too difficult for women to navigate through every day and it was better that another group of men were not added to their struggles. In all these different versions, the police also came out as a rational and mediatory agent rather than the other stories I had heard earlier around their corruption and harassment of the camp residents. What emerged was a form of customary and symbolic power that Neeti enjoyed, which was also highlighted by the police as something which was 'home-grown' rather than one imparted by external forces (such as politicians or police themselves).

I did not get to do a formal interview with Neeti. She was always either 'too busy' or it was 'not the right time'. Despite my many requests for a recorded interview she kept giving appointments which she did not keep. I did however get to talk informally with her a fair bit, and in all these conversations Neeti came across to me as one who was genuinely concerned about a range of feminist issues both within the home and in the public sphere. She also saw herself as an important person, one who was to be respected, and whose time was valuable. Before approaching her, like other 'postcolonial' researchers I too had situated myself in a dominant power position in relation to her; but it was clear that Neeti was the one in charge. She had friends among local politicians, NGOs, and the police, and she continuously travelled across the country campaigning for feminist issues and helping disadvantaged women.

I believe that Neeti could take a stand against others in the camp because of the position of authority she already enjoyed on account of her work. Thus contrary to what the police told the crowd gathered outside her house, she was not 'home-grown'; rather her power within the 'local' was multiplied on account of her leadership of the *Mahila Mandal* and support from a variety of feminist NGOs. And her position was more powerful than those of the democratically elected leaders of the camp who were validated by the police and political parties as the representative voice of the camp.

I would like to offer here a number of insights into why this incident should be considered as a reflection of the politics of space, law and gender. I have already mentioned how the main road was constructed as a space of aggressive and youth masculinities, a space which women usually found difficult to navigate through when they went in and out of the camp. Neeti was resisting the setting up of the *chowki* first and foremost as a 'woman'. In rejecting pleas from the other residents about its religious significance, Neeti was prioritizing 'women's issues' over that of the sustenance of cultural and religious practices in the camp. In the unreliability of procedural or judicial justice for most women (something that I will discuss in detail in Chapter 7) Neeti was assuming the role of a 'guardian' of sorts against predatory male sexuality on the main road. In doing so, she was acting upon her anxieties around the sanctity of her own home that was threatened by the location of the *chowki* across the road from her house. This was critical for Neeti because as a widow and in the absence of her son who worked in Rajasthan (a neighbouring state), she was also the head of her household 'in charge' of her daughter-in-law and two young grandchildren. Under these circumstances, the presence of the *chowki* across the road from her house was also seen as a threat to the sanctity of her family. It was not an easy task to confront the residents and the police at the same time, but she could do this because of the different ways that she had familiarized herself with the workings of law and the 'privileges' afforded to women under this law (through which Latika claimed she could falsely accuse men and get them arrested).

In resisting the *chowki* then, Neeti was prioritizing her concerns for gendered ideologies in the camp over religious and cultural practices. This is crucial to consider since Neeti herself was devoutly religious and practiced her faith regularly. Yet, she found the very terms of religious and cultural practices in the *chowki*, gendered and exclusionary and potentially dangerous for other women in the camp. This was also a reflection of feminist anxieties about local cultural and religious practices in everyday life, which are often used to silence concerns around male hegemonic power over women's bodies and spaces. On the other hand, this resistance which she put up on her own (but symbolically also on behalf of other women in the camp) is a reflection of how religious and gender interests evoked the law in transforming everyday spaces of the camp.

This incident is also significant because of the implicit ways that Neeti was resisting new forms of power within the camp and by extension, the marginalization inflicted upon camp residents through a violence of law. Her 'stubbornness' that the young men should not put up a *chowki* on the main road was a subversion of the image of the state vested in the electric subcontractor who had employed these young men from the camp to work for him. I have already mentioned how this had become the source of many anxieties among camp residents, which had in fact led to the creation of the Residents' Welfare Association. Neeti's resistance of these men's desire to set up a *chowki* then could also be seen as her way to refuse to cooperate with those men within the camp who were presumed to have 'switched sides'. It was her way of subverting dispersed and ambiguous forms of state power vested in the spaces of privatized electric supply and the bodies of those young men who had found their only way out of unemployment and poverty as 'linesmen' of the electric subcontractor much despised in the camp.

I suggest that in resisting the making of the *chowki*, Neeti was also asserting her role as one of the most powerful leaders of the camp, which the police also confirmed to the camp residents. It was a response to the many ways that the members of the Residents' Welfare Association and other residents attempted to delegitimize and devalue the work of the *Mahila Mandal* (as I have discussed earlier). This incident was her way of telling the residents that the Residents' Welfare Association may be the 'legitimate' democratic voice of the camp, but she was the one who knew how to work the rule of law to her favour.

Local politics, gendered organization and the force of law

Recent studies of slums abound with descriptions of the ways that residents organize themselves informally to make claims to urban basic services – water, electricity, sanitation and so on (Bayat and Denis 2000, Roy and AlSayyad 2004, Simone 2004). These informal processes are seen to work in the absence of law – as alternatives to the rights enjoyed by other ordinary urban citizens. Researchers have been quick to identify informality as a form of social agency of the poor, through which the redistribution of goods and opportunities are achieved. But informality is also always pitted as an oppositional relationship between the state and the citizen. Bayat (1997) for example, notes that one of the goals of informality is to achieve autonomy from the state and its modern institutions, functioning outside the boundaries of the state and bureaucratic institutions. In such accounts, scholars make a moral division – between state on one side and subaltern citizens on the other.

The struggles for legitimacy between different collectives in the camp show that this is not the case. In seizing opportunities through informal networks, the urban poor do not necessarily work outside of law or against the state. On the contrary, their social organization and agencies are a careful manipulation of law, in so far as this would allow the seamless functioning of everyday life. More crucially, the performance of law during events that attempt to mimic the state at a local level produces a fraught terrain of local politics that includes rumour, gossip, manipulation and direct confrontation between different collectives. Understanding the internal divisions and subjective differences that constitute this local politics, allows us to get a deeper insight into how the violence of law acquires meaning and salience within everyday spaces of squatter settlements.

In writing about the violence of law, Veena Das asks whether we could make a distinction between state 'processes of establishing legitimacy [which] differ between the inaugural moment, which is, in some ways, extraordinary and the time of continuity when the state is experienced in the everyday life of the community?' (Das 2004: 180) We could ask a similar question about the different gendered collectives that emerged in the camp – could we make a distinction between their founding moment which was brought about by a particular relationship with a rule of law (whether formal or informal) and their continuing endeavours to establish their legitimacy and shape the everyday spaces within the camp? From this perspective, any attempts to transform the material quality of spaces in the camp would provoke these collectives to re-establish their legitimacy as the 'voice' of residents in the camp. The small matter of the *chowki* then becomes central to struggles for power and legitimacy of the different collectives. It suggests that while the rule of law and its enforceability is continually evoked within everyday spaces of the camp, encounters with law in everyday life is often experienced through a manipulation of law. To do this however, requires a sound understanding of the formal and informal workings of institutions of the state such as the police. Ironically this reinforces forms of power validated and legitimized by the state – it means that those with support from state sponsored NGOs are able to better manipulate the rule of law to their advantage as against those democratically elected by those in the camp. And it might mean that women as 'legitimate' beneficiaries of state-based 'empowerment' projects can exercise more control over the shaping of everyday spaces than those attempting to do this through democratic representation.

The above observation brings me to the question of how the gendered body becomes the terrain of mediation between law and everyday life. A crucial feature of this is the state attempt to 'empower' women through participation. As 'participation' is increasingly formalized, slum women have become the primary recruits at both ends of the development process – knowledge production and aid delivery. It means that slum women are increasingly trained and recruited by NGOs as researchers of their own conditions in order to generate data for aid delivery to those worthy of development. In doing so slum women learn about the importance of particular types of information about themselves and understand the significance of this information in the development process.

Although NGO approaches have been widely critiqued as not recognizing the heterogeneity of women's identities and experiences, in the context of the camp these approaches have produced women as 'legitimate' beneficiaries of state development. Women in their new roles as 'participants' have begun to realize the significance of their location within grassroots social organizing, which has transformed their social power and status within local contexts. This new role has produced among women an enhanced consciousness about the workings of law, regulations, procedures and bureaucracies through which material resources can be accessed and control over particular spaces of everyday life can be maintained. These women have developed a heightened sense of understanding of their role within law, an understanding that NGOs are now the main channels through which they can link up with the state aid and ultimately stake claims to legitimacy and urban citizenship. Women in the camp have therefore become aware of the possibilities of their 'inclusion' through legitimate urban institutions and their ability to access a variety of urban institutions with whom they bargain for services, and are advantageously located compared to other 'non-participating' women. The politics of women's organization and struggles to access power and authority over everyday spaces resonates with what Chatterjee (2004) notes as the exercise of democracy by those formally included in state based models of 'participation'.

The gendered body therefore becomes critical at the juncture when claims to legitimacy of social organization are rooted in the 'appropriateness' of particular bodies across public and private spaces. The founding and functioning of these collectives in the camp suggest that despite the presence of active spaces of participation for the residents, the terms of entry and participation were limited by normative gender boundaries between public and private, which were reinforced by the police as the image of the law. Participation in and legitimacy of the different collectives in the camp were subsequently mediated through the presence of 'appropriate' gendered bodies within the home, neighbourhood and the city. Although these were attempts at maximizing the impacts of their social organization, they indirectly sustained a continuum of gendered power from the home to the urban public sphere.

Yet the events around the *chowki* force us to consider what sorts of agents can women be in the urban public realm? I suggest that despite the delegitimization of women's presence in democratic organization in the camp, the 'small matter of the *chowki'* underlined the real location of symbolic and moral power in the camp. This was a double irony – while the power of the *Mahila Mandal* leaders could be taken as an indication of the 'success' of grassroots feminist politics in the camp, it could also equally mean that participation through state sponsored NGOs can supersede the authority of local, more democratic forms of power, and indirectly reinforce state authority. On the other hand, while the exclusionary gendered nature of democratic organization in the camp was sanctioned by the police, its 'real' powers were limited in the absence of any legitimate rights to the land which the community it represented occupied. And it shows that while the police are constructed as a threat to their material homes by other residents, they can be used as a resource by those familiar with legal processes to pursue their own moral projects and shape the nature of spaces of the camp. While the rule of law for residents in the camp was experienced as violence over their homes, for the

Mahila Mandal leaders, this rule of law was also a productive space, from where power and authority over different spaces in the camp could be manoeuvred.

In charting out an anatomy of political society in Mumbai, Hansen notes that understanding the 'political' means looking at public spaces – 'from central squares to street corners in the slums' (Hansen 2001: 232) since these spaces lie at the heart of political society where state, 'community' and society become visible and effective. In this regard Hansen is sceptical of Chatterjee's distinction between state/civil society and political society since he sees them as making distinctions between state as a space of legality and political society as a space of informality. For Hansen, we must examine the mundane forms of politics 'not by seeing them as a reflection of something else already grounded in community, caste, or class; rather, we must study the political as it is formed and given life through acts of representation' (Hansen 2001: 232). This political he concludes is a permanent performance.

The contested politics of legitimacy of the Residents' Welfare Association in the camp suggest that the 'political' is indeed a performance – of law and of state forms of democracy. Yet it is not so easy for me to conclude that this political takes shape only in public spaces or that we need only to look at public spaces to understand how political society is conceived and executed in the camp. Indeed much of the contestations between the different collectives took shape in/over access to public spaces in the camp. However the public and private were in reality two ends of a continuum that were connected through the gendered body. By this, I mean that the contestations over legitimacy which drew upon the appropriateness of the gendered body in particular spaces and places of social action, produced gender relations in the public realm as a reflection of gendered social power in the private realm. It is not enough therefore to look only at the 'political' in street corners of slums; rather to investigate how entry into the public realm of participation by women is possible only by the insertion of the state (through NGOs) into the space of the home. It is not that the state and community are visible only in public spaces; rather it was the performance of law as a reflection of state authority and legitimacy that brought both the public and private into the realm of the political in the camp.

Here I find myself agreeing with Hansen (2001) that political society cannot be so distinctly separated from state/civil society although I come upon this conclusion via a different route than that of Hansen. Hansen examines political society in Mumbai as that brought about through the state's right-wing political party Shiv Sena who creates permanent networks through informal brokerage outside of law. I suggest however that even in 'illegal' settlements (seen as existing outside civil society), law (as a reflection of state legitimacy) is drawn into the realm of the political through repetition, performance and simulacra. The differences among the different collectives in encountering this law – whether through informal mediation, affective and performative body politics, performance of democratic processes through an image of law, determined how the gendered body mediated the relationships between law and everyday life.

Finally, I find it the hardest to agree with Hansen that politics should not be seen as a reflection of subjective difference; rather as representation. I find it difficult to separate subjective differences from acts of representation or performance. In particular, if we think of performance of law as a form of politics, it is impossible to think of how legal subjecthood imparted by this law can remain distanciated from subaltern claims to rights and entitlements – an issue I discussed in Chapter 1. Subjective differences during acts of representation are crucial to understanding how the founding and maintaining violence of law continues to insert law into the rhythms of everyday life – a topic I will discuss in more detail in the next chapter.

Chapter 6
Contested Boundaries of Infrastructure

On 15 August 2005, the day of Indian independence, the *Mahila Mandal* mobilized a handful of women to break a part of the boundary wall that separated the camp from the urban forest. This was not the first time that they had attempted to break it – they had engaged with the guards on a couple of other occasions. This particular day though was symbolic as the day of Indian independence. As the women from the *Mahila Mandal* came together and shouted anti-government slogans, they were watched by other residents and encouraged as they made their way to the rear of the camp towards the wall. They had axes and shovels – tools to break the wall. They managed to break a part of that wall, which resulted in their arrests by the police. The wall had only been partially damaged and the women were released after a few days.

This boundary wall was constructed by the municipality through a legal order from the courts as a result of Public Interest Litigation (PIL) brought forth by an NGO concerned about the 'soiling' of the urban forest. Before it had been built, camp residents had regularly used the urban forest as a place for defecation, but the boundary wall was erected by the Municipality to prevent this practice. The wall now separated camp residents from the forest and from their place of sanitation. Defecation in the forest was now 'illegal' practice and was regularly enforced through armed guards posted along the wall who assaulted residents who attempted to scale the wall into the forest.

The boundary wall is the site of a contested politics of illegality, class and gender. It was built by the municipality to keep away those 'illegally' accessing it for reasons other than 'civic enjoyment'. For the *Mahila Mandal*, the wall with its varieties of dangers and exclusions stood for the marginal position of women in the camp and in the city, and hence one that had to be addressed through feminist participatory activism. They argued that in the absence of legitimate places of sanitation it were women who were disproportionately affected in the camp, and thus breaking the wall was an assertion of their entitlement from the state for basic urban services. The wall thus became a metaphor for feminist struggles; it represented their peripheral status within the city and the camp; and was a physical reminder of the ways that the city separated them from itself. Above all, the wall produced a new consciousness of their 'illegal' status in the city, which they argued had gendered consequences.

Such everyday forms of resistance have been discussed by many scholars as symbolic gendered acts that challenge state hegemonies through the divisions that are imposed on public and private among poor women (Nagar 2000, Secor 2004, Silvey 2003, Staeheli 1996). This gendered 'resistance' however was not valorized in the camp; indeed many men and women participants described this as an act of 'vandalism'. Many blamed the *Mahila Mandal* women for drawing the attention of authorities towards the camp, fearing this would increase police harassment. The leaders of the Residents' Welfare Association claimed that this damaged much of the 'relationships' that they had built up with the politicians, police, statutory authorities and utility companies. Some participants (both men and women) felt that instead of this 'vandalism', the residents should have put pressure through NGOs, support organizations and politicians to have the wall removed.

> The organization [*Mahila Mandal*] here had around six, seven of our sisters and daughters arrested on 15th August. The road into the jungle had been closed – it was a Supreme Court order. So this organization incited simple women to create a drama, abuse the police, create trouble, they continued this for months after that, the police too got their backs up one day, they served orders on 5–6 people. After that, neither the *Mahila Mandal* nor anyone else came to their help – no one came to their aid and as for the women who got jailed, because they were in jail for a week they don't even think of associating with the organization any more … 80 percent houses have been ruined through this organization, not mended -- history is witness, you can see for yourself. [Jabbar]

> The first thing is that 85 percent of these women work as household help – washing vessels, sweeping, scrubbing. So they are poor women, they were earning their living. These people [women leaders] incited them to do something illegal. They should have thought instead that there is no advantage in this leadership. If there is some big thing to be done, it is ok. Demolishing walls, hitting someone, challenging government work, without understanding the implications, what kind of activity is that? [Lalkishore]

These condemnations of feminist activism are consistent with some of the arguments I presented in the previous chapter. Clearly the political action was gendered, and in its gendering, the women had transgressed the boundaries between private and public. As if activism was not enough, incarceration was seen as the most public violation of women's bodies by the State. The *Mahila Mandal* leaders brought together a dispersed group of women to assert their rights to sanitation in front of the State, yet this 'transgression' into the public realm of political activism produced their delegitimization within the camp. The women's 'resistance' was 'in your face' and disorganized, it was symbolic in intent, but it was seen as opportunistic and selfish in putting 'vulnerable' women in the camp in trouble with the law. In many ways this was seen as a 'pollution' of women's bodies and gendered bodily codes, as they came in contact with the police and a 'masculinist' public realm of incarceration. Those critiquing the *Mahila Mandal* activism, trivialized the act of breaking the wall as 'creating drama', which linked gendered insurgence to certain perceived qualities of women's personalities as emotional, irrational, and attention-seeking.

In this chapter, I examine those spaces of infrastructure where struggles are faced everyday by those who are excluded from legitimate spaces of water or sanitation. I see the anxieties which some participants expressed around the legitimacy of *Mahila Mandal*'s actions as related to the anxieties over what really constitutes a viable and legitimate form of urban politics in a context of illegality. I suggest that as the courts and the middle-classes criminalized the use of the forest for defecation, participants turned their attention to localized gender differences in order to transform their relationships with illegality. The everyday spaces of water and sanitation in the camp worked through a range of contested boundaries that shaped their transgressions across real and imagined boundaries of legal/illegal, public/private, and inside/outside. They provide us with possibilities to rethink the relationships of squatters with the city, with each other, and with the force of law. These boundaries were also material and social in that they demarcated access to resources through physical barriers, and transformed social power relationships during control over the spaces of water and sanitation. These boundaries produced both marginalizing as well as productive possibilities in everyday life. Anxieties over the transgression of boundaries shaped a powerful internalization of discourses between dirt and purity, order and disorder, morality and immorality, and a range of other subjective positionalities that are often placed along a local social hierarchy.

Law and the 'impure' body

Discourses of 'dirt' and 'purity' have been critical to the drawing of social and spatial boundaries around particular people or social groups, and classifying them into hierarchies of social status (Douglas 1966). While in the west, these translated into spatial boundaries particularly between the working and middle-classes in industrial cities of Manchester and London, discourses of health and hygiene were translated in the 19th century colonial world through racialized categories. In much of colonial Africa and Asia, cities such as Cairo, Lagos, Delhi, and Kolkata, the discourses of dirt and filth rested on the bodies and spaces of the native population, which ensured the separation of the 'masses' from the colonial rulers and the creation of large urban slums within historic neighbourhoods. For example, in Johannesburg's inner-city slums, the 'African slum problem' was constructed through a 'reassertion of a popular white discourse connecting 'race' with disease, criminality, and drunkenness' (Parnell 2003: 613).

In Indian cities, the racialization of dirt and disease has intersected with the particularly unique spaces of caste. Caste had existed in India as a fragmented and fluid body of classification till the British mapped this through elaborate and detailed classificatory systems in the nineteenth century (Gooptu 2001). This not only made caste political, but in this context, the absence of sanitation infrastructure in the non-white neighbourhoods, and the role of the lowest castes in shifting dirt and waste out of the colonial city, mapped their bodies and spaces as 'untouchable'

(Prashad 2001). Thus the categorization of caste along clearly defined occupations by the British and the symbolic associations of dirt and filth with low-caste bodies, resulted in clear demarcations in public spaces of the bodies of 'untouchables' from upper caste Hindus, and (sometimes) from Sikhs and Muslims. Defilement and impurity operated at symbolic, material, and regulatory levels where everyday practices around cleanliness began to be entrenched in the connections between low-caste bodies who performed 'menial' tasks and the 'filth' seen to be associated with the spaces they inhabited or moved through.

The 'problem' of dirt and defilement by squatters has been noted by postcolonial scholars as the characteristic feature of modernity and colonization in India (Chakrabarty 2002, Kaviraj 1997). It resonates with notions of dirt as 'matter out of place' (Douglas 1966: 36) where squatters are seen as the source of urban disease and crime – their location within the city in these settlements understood as the material and symbolic association with disorder, one which urban development strives to clean up. Absence of infrastructure in slums and squatter settlements means that water and waste flow through the places that are very visible locations of everyday life – homes, streets, roads, and public land. While the lack of water leads to reduction in hygiene levels on squatter bodies, open defecation on the other hand, is seen to defile urban public places. Such ideas of impure bodies and spaces can be traced back to early nineteenth century social reform ideas in the West, where sanitizing the city was seen as the route to improving the lives of slum dwellers while protecting other urban citizens from the ill-health and immoral effects of living in close proximity to slums. For example, in England, the Public Health Acts of the 19th century facilitated the state to become a significantly important player in intervening in initiatives for sanitation and waste disposal in order to stop the spread of disease to other parts of the city (Chaplin 1999). And these ideas of the hygienic city were also related to the individualization of the self through particular spaces like hospitals, prisons and the bed (Joyce 2003). Thus, bodily sense and respecting bodily privacy were connected to the discourses of hygiene in wider urban spaces (Illich 1986).

In post-independence India, notions of impurity that are historically associated with the bodies of lower castes have usually overlapped with the 'filth' associated with bodies of squatters in urban India. This is owed to a large degree to the presence of modern technologies of water supply and sanitation within middle-class homes, which makes public defecation and lack of sanitation among squatters anomalous and pathological. Defecating in the open reflects the practices of a rural peasant – a subject whose bodily acts spread filth in urban spaces, and is hence undesirable. Such moral geographies of dirt and filth often take violent forms as Baviskar (2003) highlights through the murder of a squatter who had transgressed onto public land used for leisure by the urban middle-class in Delhi. 'Illegality' of squatter settlements in this context is critical since it shapes how basic services are accessed by the squatters and how material 'dirt' of squatters is produced by the very conditions which they struggle against.

Related to this, are the discourses on health and sanitation associated with the squatter home, through various studies pointing to the increases of diseases, particularly among the most vulnerable population groups of women, children and elderly. The availability of modern technologies of disease prevention and treatment to the middle-classes make them relatively immune to the problems of epidemics or contagion in a way not possible in the colonial period. But in slums, the lack of water and sanitation gives rise to water-borne diseases such as malaria, cholera, diarrhoea, dysentery; the small unventilated room where cooking is done often leads to respiratory diseases like asthma, bronchitis and even lung cancer. Women as the primary persons responsible for food preparation are thus seen by development practitioners as more susceptible to a variety of these diseases. These two related issues construct squatter settlements as not just places of nuisance, but also as gendered sites of biopolitical interventions.

In Delhi and other colonial cities, such 'biopolitics' were the cornerstone of slum clearance programs of the British Raj (Legg 2007). In Singapore, Yeoh (2003) notes that not just bodies but also particular buildings and places such as prisons, hospitals, cemeteries and abattoirs, were constructed as the dirt of cities and hence removed to the fringes of the city. But unlike colonial cities, the middle-classes are no longer as susceptible to epidemic outbreaks or public health risks. In fact most epidemics that have occurred in Indian cities since the 1980s have disproportionately affected the urban poor. For example, the cholera/gastroenteritis epidemic in Delhi in 1988 infected those living in informal settlements. Similarly the plague outbreak in Surat in 1994 also affected those living in areas with low levels of sanitation facilities and waste disposal. Yet middle-class concerns over health have proliferated the discourses and practices of urban development and have manifested as interventions around water and sanitation in urban slums.

Postcolonial scholars have suggested that rubbish brings into view the boundaries that divide the home from the outside. This is because in traditional Indian society the throwing of rubbish outside the home does not necessarily mean the defilement of public space; rather of transferring dirt onto a negative space of that which is not inside (Chakrabarty 2002, Kaviraj 1997). This notion of the outside as a negation of the inside is seen to mark the difference from a modern sensibility towards public space for civic enjoyment (in the Habermasian sense). For Chakrabarty, the modernist understanding of rubbish is that of an 'observer who does not inhabit the conceptual or theoretical framework of the actor whom he or she observes' (Chakrabarty 2002: 69). This observer position is not necessarily 'Western' but 'modernist', since Western concepts of dirt and impurity were also practiced and reinforced by urban middle-classes who then attempted to sanitize their cities and urban spaces at the turn of the nineteenth century urban India (Gooptu 2001).

The force of law on the other hand attempts to turn the 'outside' into civic spaces – 'benign, regulated places, clean and healthy, incapable of producing either disease or disorder' (Chakrabarty 2002: 77). As Ghertner (2008) notes, a reinterpretation of nuisance laws among the judiciary in recent years has tied the 'illegality' of slums to aesthetic and sanitary qualities of cities. Ghertner asserts that the interpretation of slums as 'illegal' is tied to the effectiveness of evidence presented to the courts of the slums as 'nuisance'. For him, this reinterpretation of what legally constitutes nuisance, has led to the reconstruction of the meaning of 'public interest' and the imposition of middle-class private interests over public spaces. I interpret this as a direct transposition of the social and historical construction of the boundaries between home and outside (as articulated by postcolonial scholars) onto a legalistic framework, maintained and validated through an interpretive force of law. Taking this approach means examining how the violence of law transforms the subjective criteria of dirt in public places to objective markers of 'nuisance' and 'disorder' in public places.

In the camp, dirt and nuisance was localized among participants to produce different kinds of politics of inside/outside and public/private. This politics involved not just modernist or class-based notions of dirt, but also internalized notions of gendered, caste and religious impurity. Thus while using the postcolonial notion of 'dirt' and its legal manifestation in 'nuisance' as the broader framework of my analysis in this chapter; I also depart from it in the following ways.

I do not suggest here that squatters' refusal to conform to the 'modernist agenda of order and sanitization' should be seen as the 'refusal to become citizens of an ideal, bourgeois order' (Chakrabarty 2002: 77). Rather I suggest that the relocation of certain bodily practices (such as defecation) from private to public places should be understood as the only option of survival within a context of illegality. In other words, the 'illegal' condition that denies squatters the right to private spaces of water and sanitation pushes them to access these through practices that are also constructed as 'illegal' by the state. Thus the public defecation of squatters is not a resistance against a bourgeois order, but a mundane politics of everyday survival. And their exclusion from private access to water and sanitation available to the 'legal city' produces their own physical and symbolic dirt and nuisance which is different from but related to middle-class notions of dirt and disorder.

In this chapter, I see the everyday struggles in accessing water and sanitation as fragmented by the socially differentiated meanings of dirt and defilement across positionalities of caste, religion, ethnicity and gender. Much of these meanings invoke internalized and embodied associations with purity and morality during access to spaces of water and sanitation. Because water supply and waste disposal are highly dispersed and fragmented in the camp, struggles to access water and sanitation also emerge from squatters' illegal status and hence lead to consciousness of legal subjecthoods and entitlements. These struggles reinforce the differences and boundaries between legal/illegal, centre/periphery, city/slum among squatters. The question of what constitutes dirt shifts continuously during access to water and sanitation and works through a range of dualities that are evoked in parallel to the modern/anti-modern dualisms that postcolonial scholars highlight. The politics of dirt and defilement used by different squatters to access water and sanitation construct an identity that is internally fragmented and fraught with tensions, yet significant in the ways that it is called upon repeatedly to stake their entitlements from the state through a modernist discourse. Thus the politicization, contestation, and resistances that take shape over exclusion from urban basic services show how modernist notions of 'dirt' also infiltrate subaltern positionality in the context of illegality.

A note on Delhi's basic services

The provision of urban basic services usually follow a different spatial logics than those of other more 'legitimate' parts of the city because the illegality of the urban poor absolves the state from private connections. For example in Delhi, during 1985–99, 503 pay-per-use toilet complexes were constructed, and during 1985–90, 917 water hydrants and 601 hand pumps were provided. However, these were shared amenities provided at 'neighbourhood' scales, not as private amenities at household scales as is common in the planned city. Water had to be drawn from public standpipes, from where it had to be physically carried to individual homes; toilet complexes were located in specific public areas within slums where residents had to queue to use facilities – decisions that had huge impacts on gendered relationships within the family and community. Yet ironically over the years, the standards required for these provisions have fallen (Banerji 2005) – while the earlier schemes provided one water tap for every 50 residents, and one toilet for 20–50 residents, since 1995 these schemes provided one water tap for every 150 residents and one toilet every 50 residents. As a recent report highlights, the actual provisions are in fact close to one tap per 250–300 residents (Anthony and Maheswaran 2001).

A survey of Delhi's slums conducted over a decade ago by the Indian Social Institute (Anthony and Maheswaran 2001) found that only 56 percent of slum dwellers received tap water, while only 21 percent had any access to toilet facilities. A more recent report in 2004 by the Municipal Corporation of Delhi (MCD) found that just over 21 percent of JJ clusters have piped water supply (as against 98 percent in regularized-unauthorized colonies) and only nine percent have access to sewer facilities (as against 80 percent in regularized-unauthorized colonies) (Ministry of Urban Development 1991). Interestingly, JJ clusters in South Delhi, while receiving relatively higher service provisions than those in other zones also reported some of the highest incidents of 'difficulties' while collecting water, which included fights, spending long time in queues, walking long distances, and even 'pleasing' someone in order to have access to water (Ministry of Urban Development 1991).

The challenges of infrastructural technologies in dealing with physical and technological issues like topographic variations, water shortage, low water table, and lack of water purification systems have made the spaces of infrastructure extremely uneven and dispersed across squatter settlements in the city. Currently, there are 1,600 unauthorized colonies and 1,100 slums still waiting for municipal water connections in Delhi. While most residents in the city face acute water shortages in summer months it is still possible for many middle-class households to install booster pumps or store large supplies of water in underground or rooftop tanks. In Delhi, two-fifths of the urban poor use contaminated groundwater extracted through tube wells, 85 percent of households have no water purification methods and are often subject to water-borne diseases. Two-thirds of Delhi's population receives only five percent of the 3,600 million litres of water that is officially supplied, while only 21 percent of unauthorized colonies (which includes squatter settlements) are covered with piped water supply. Estimates (Shaban and Sharma 2007) suggest that the consumption of water ranges from 313 litres per day for the affluent, to 16 litres per day for slum dwellers, with the average consumption in Delhi slums at 82 litres per day.

These statistics reflect the terms under which squatters in Delhi negotiate their access to those places where water and sanitation are available. Behind these statistics hide the very real struggles of those denied water and sanitation through a violence of law.

Boundary 'wars' in the urban forest

The camp has a sanitation crisis. There are no sewer lines, no waste disposal facilities, no cleaners and no place to defecate. The open drains running along the lanes repeatedly contaminate water supply lines and propagate diseases. Public toilets provided for the residents are not enough, they do not function, and they charge for use. Much of the defecation takes place in the forest where animals are also reared. There is contamination with water, with food, and with faeces. As one participant put it – 'we are living in the midst of shit'.

That is the story told by most participants in the camp. The camp's status as a *jhuggi jhopri* colony cuts it off from those sewage lines that are part of the 'legal' city. The physical layout of the camp makes this provision also technologically challenging and expensive. While neighbouring resettlement colonies were planned along orthogonal grids, which allowed for economical layouts of water and sanitation services, the camp has the most intricate system of winding lanes, alleyways and topographical undulations which would make it extremely difficult for a sanitary engineer to devise a solution.

Certain areas of Delhi have been historically better connected to urban infrastructure while others have been denied these as a result of their location outside the dedicated development zones of the masterplans. Invariably, most squatter settlements fall under this latter category – located along railway tracks, canals, forests, under bridges, and 'leftover' places in the city, squatter settlements have been largely 'zoned out' from the provision of essential services. This is reinforced by their 'illegal' status – repeatedly reiterated by the state and municipality as the reason for their lack of services. The lack of formal and legal connection to water and sanitation lines means that much of the practices around water occur in public places – roads, urban forests, railway tracks, and canals where water is collected and bodily waste is disposed. This is quite unlike other middle-class and planned low-income colonies, where water and sanitation practices are largely 'private', enacted in bathrooms, washrooms, or kitchens. Squatter settlements on the other hand, are marked by the absence of such private spaces for water and sanitation. 'Public' places in so far as they accommodate different bodies and bodily activities in full view of each other, then become sites of contestations around improvised (and often illegal) access to water and sanitation.

Since the late 1970s, the urban forest had served as the place of defecation for the squatters, while separating the camp from the middle-class colonies on the other side. It had managed to maintain this separation because the city had turned its back to the forest. For decades, the forest provided much needed spaces to the camp for disposing their rubbish, their bodily wastes, and also keeping their distance from these wastes. Some of the houses on its peripheries even constructed private toilets which drained into the forest land. Lower caste squatters reared pigs in the forest. For many years it was as if the camp was forgotten by the 'legal' city because it remained hidden within its backyards – between the forest and resettlement colonies. The urban forest then constituted an important boundary between the legal and the illegal city; it contained the squatters within, while at the same time marking the separation between their bodies, their faeces, and the rest of the city.

In 2003, an NGO interested in the conservation of the urban forest, filed a contempt petition against the Delhi Development Authority (DDA) and the Forestry Department in the Supreme Court. This alleged that large-scale tree-felling and illegal encroachments had taken place in the forest despite the 1991 directive which gave the forest protected status as the only natural aquifer and reservoir in South Delhi. The Supreme Court upheld the petition and issued contempt notices to the DDA Vice-Chairman, the Delhi Government, and Forestry Department officials. In the aftermath of the Supreme Court ruling, the municipality constructed a wall separating the camp from the urban forest, which was policed during the day. New walking and jogging tracks were cleared in the forest, and it is now frequented by walkers, joggers, and picnickers from the middle-class colonies.

Cases like this are common across Delhi and in other metropolitan cities where public defilement is increasingly controlled through legal orders initiated by the middle-classes and legitimized by the judiciary (Verma 2002). I have discussed in Chapter 2 how in Delhi such divisions are constantly reinforced through a legal-urban order that ties middle-class constructions of dirt and disorder to an objective and brutal interpretation of law and property rights. Further, Ghertner has argued that the reinterpretation of nuisance laws in recent years by the judiciary has shaped a 'more subtle production of a new aesthetic ordering of "the public" and its "proper" uses' (Ghertner 2008: 2) leading to the expulsion of those populations that do not conform to the aesthetic norms of Indian cities. Such processes of demarcation and exclusion of the urban poor from public spaces is explained by Chakrabarty.

> What speaks is the language of modernity, of civic consciousness and public
> health, even of certain ideas of beauty related to the management of public space
> and interests, an order of aesthetics from which the ideals of public health and
> hygiene cannot be separated. (Chakrabarty 2002: 66)

For the squatters, the urban forest was the only place where they could maintain a
safe distance between themselves and their faeces, for the middle-classes, it was a
place of leisure, its meaningful location as the green 'lung' of South Delhi violated
by the very visible acts of public defecation. The location of the forest between
these conflicting interests juxtaposed this between two parallel purposes – fit
bodies of the middle-class and impure bodies of squatters. It outlined a threat and
presented a danger – of the transgression and dissolution of social and physical
boundaries between middle-classes and urban poor, between legal and illegal
citizens and by extension between the legal and illegal city.

'Is this your father's property?'

The forest was also always a contested gendered space. The gendered aspect
of defecation has been repeatedly explored in the context of urban governance
(McFarlane 2008) and more significantly within feminist critiques of development
(Moser 1989). The private acts of defecating has gendered consequences in ways
that the most intimate parts of the female body get exposed to the male 'gaze'.
Violence over and violation of women's bodies during defecation in public places
makes the gender question increasingly significant for squatters. For the women
in the camp, daily struggles with defecation reminded them of a fracturing of the
home and the gendered body between private and public space, but for men in
these families, violations of women's bodies were often perceived through the
notions of morality, family honour, and masculinity.

My purpose here is not to re-examine this widely accepted understanding of
gendered bodily violations during defecating on open land – arguments which
even the *Mahila Mandal* used to frame their political action of breaking the
boundary wall. Instead, I present here another interpretation of these contestations
which were internalized and embodied during the violation of women's bodies.
This interpretation complicates postcolonial arguments around class based
constructions of hygiene and aesthetics in public spaces. I want to illustrate here
how this bodily violation is framed by women in ways that discursively reinforce
the marginalizations imposed through a force of law.

> When I used to stay that side, I went to the jungle for toilet, there were three
> men there. I was going and they were coming. And they were trying to touch my
> chest, and I turned myself as I passed them – I was lucky I didn't fall into the
> drain. Now, they went off and I was thinking, wait a minute, you will come here
> again. This is the way to the jungle. So I kept waiting there for them. When they

came ... I hit them with a stick. I was so angry. I said, 'Is this jungle your father's property? Has he bought up this place that women can't pass through here?' Then some other men came to my help and they beat them up too. [Sunita]

I met Sunita through the *Mahila Mandal* meetings. She was always a very articulate member and a dedicated worker. She was also the daughter of Neeti, one of the main leaders of the collective. Sunita was married with two young daughters, but she lived with her mother because her husband and in-laws lived in a small Rajasthani village where it was difficult to find employment. Living with her mother Sunita was able to participate in some of the activism work with different NGOs from time-to-time. Sunita's work and relationship with of the key figures of the camp already placed her in a position of heightened feminist consciousness of the many violations over women's bodies. Her reaction therefore reflected her confidence in dealing with a difficult situation, but also unsurprising considering that most women who worked with the *Mahila Mandal* cited similar reprisals over errant men.

What struck me in Sunita's narrative was not just how she articulated her 'reprisal', but how she constructed the notion of public space and her entitlement over it. In her story of the reprisal, she constructed the forest as the 'public' because it was not privately owned by any private individual or organization. Such a discursive construction of urban space was used by Sunita to assert her right over places in and around the camp, and to draw symbolic boundaries around

Figure 6.1   Urban forest behind the boundary wall. Photo: Author 2002

their bodies. But this description of the 'public' was erroneous because despite its discursive power in controlling predatory men within the camp, it did not afford those like Sunita and others in the camp the legal right to use public land for defecation. Sunita's construction of public land thus presents a paradox – in framing her rights to this land, Sunita implicitly invoked the logics of 'propertied citizenship' (Roy 2003b) to deny these men any greater privileges than herself to this land. In her view if the land was not privately owned it was to be shared by all. And in so doing, Sunita reinforced the notion of public property through which squatters have been made illegal urban citizens.[1]

When participants described the incidents around the wall, they often expressed an ambivalent attitude towards its causes. While it was the only place where they could defecate and hence a space to which free access was desirable, the forest was also a space of unimaginable dangers. This was not least because women's bodies were often violated, as we saw in the case of Sunita earlier, but also because these violations were carried out by those among their midst. Further, these violations were not just limited to women; rather they extended to young children, who often played along the fringes of the forest -the only available open space in the camp. Many families were fearful of letting their children play there because stories of abduction and rape of minors were common. Occasionally there would also be stories of murder. In these stories, no one could say for sure that the perpetrators lived in the camp, but there was a general agreement that the perpetrators were on 'this side' of the urban forest. Another speculation was that the perpetrators came from other parts of Delhi but that socially they too belonged to similar slum environments. In other words, even if the perpetrators were not geographically in Lakshmipuri, it was commonly agreed that they came from similar social backgrounds as them.

'Mistakes made by poor people'

The notion of 'dirt' then was inherently embedded in the notion of the forest through a logic of fear, violence over and violation of bodies. This dirt was material because of its associations with defecation and because participants wanted to keep a distance between their faeces in the forest and their homes. But there was another aspect of this dirt which was more subjective and which became more apparent as participants attempted to find reasons behind their exclusion from the forest.

For a long time, the low-caste residents who lived towards the back of the camp had reared pigs as a cheap source of meat. These animals were usually seen

1   I say this because although this land is not privately owned by individuals, it is owned by the Delhi Development Authority and the Forestry Department. And therefore Sunita's argument is counterproductive, because her logics of ownership rights reinforce precisely the 'illegality' of their entry into the urban forest, because it was owned by the state institutions.

feeding on the rubbish strewn around the back of the camp particularly where it opened up into the forest. Since this was also a place where the residents regularly went to defecate, it was commonly believed that these pigs fed on the faeces of the residents and were therefore 'dirty' animals.

Associations with the 'impurity' of particular animals can be found in other contexts – for example in Cape Town, McKenzie (2003) reveals how the presence of stray dogs in the public sphere was constructed by the middle-classes as 'disorder' and as the presence of an urban underclass. In India, pigs have culturally stood for dirt and filth among many social groups. Pigs are generally understood to feed on rubbish, but pigs are also associated with forms of taboo within religious and cultural practices – the eating of pigs is prohibited in Islam, and animal meat is generally prohibited for upper caste Hindus in North India, since it is seen to lead to the impurity of caste bodies. Pigs then became associated with the dirt and filth of the forest and consequently of particular cultural practices of low-caste groups. In the context of the camp, the connections between the impurity of particular animals and humans were drawn on caste and religious lines.

> Some mistakes have been committed by the poor people also. Like they kept some stray animals – like some used to keep pigs – the *bhangis* [low castes] and all here. It's because of this reason that the government closed the jungle. [Shazina]

Shazina's narrative suggests how conflicts with middle-class interests in public land were understood through social differences within the camp located within a caste based hierarchy by both Hindu and Muslim participants. Her argument resonated with the case of solid waste management in urban Pakistan where Beall (2006) found that caste-like social hierarchies existed among Muslim and Christian cleaners. While Muslim participants did not necessarily see themselves within any hierarchy in the Hindu caste system, they attempted repeatedly to distance themselves from and assert themselves as symbolically and morally 'purer' than low-caste residents. This was a particular kind of spatiality that saw the conflation of a rule of law, bourgeois aesthetics and 'unsanitary' practices of lower-castes. In this construction, Muslim participants presented themselves as 'victims' of the transgression of impure bodies of the *bhangis* and their animals across symbolic and material boundaries. The criminalization of the sanitary practices of squatters by the judiciary was understood as the dangers of transgression of 'impure' animals and bodies across internal and external boundaries of the camp. For Shazina, who was Muslim, it reworked the connections between sanitation and illegality to a validation and justification of entrenched social hierarchies within the camp.

This spatialization and internalization of dirt in participants' narratives suggest how encounters with law internalize notions of dirt among squatters in particular spaces. If class-based interests produced a legal-urban order of aestheticized urban public spaces, then these were far from straightforwardly received by squatters.

Participants repeatedly transposed anxieties over sanitation across local social differences, across gendered bodies and spaces, and consequently produced reworked versions of earlier social hierarchies and differences within the camp.

Legalizing from below

In discussing how people encounter the state at the margins, Das (2004) notes that far from being an abstract representation of authority, the state works in everyday life through 'signature' – present in its writing technologies which give it a ghostly presence in everyday life. Das calls this the 'magical quality' of the state because of the way it works through obscurity and power, but also notes that this 'magic' has very real consequences. The forces mobilized for the performance of this 'magic' places its subjects in a position of vulnerability during its mimicry. It is this vulnerability during mimicry that I turn to next.

I am not examining states' writing technologies here, although the idioms through which worthiness to development schemes of the state are constructed remains relevant. I am more interested here in understanding how a violence of the boundaries of legal/illegal during access to water and sanitation has been presented as the argument for 'legalization from below' – as a form of mimicry of state procedures and rituals. Development scholars and practitioners have given resounding praise to the efforts of poor slum women in Mumbai who are constructing, maintaining and managing toilet complexes on their own in slums. Indeed it is now argued that instead of tenure legalization, women can be empowered through their participation in community infrastructure projects in slums and squatter settlements (Gulyani and Bassett 2007). Other scholars go so far as to suggest that legalization and legitimacy should begin from sanitation and not from land tenure (Burra, Patel and Kerr 2003, Wegelin-Schuringa and Kodo 1997).

The mimicry of the state works most potently during moments when exclusions from the spaces of sanitation are transformed through a politics of legitimization. The most enthusiastic endorsement of this transformation has come from Mumbai NGOs who have been organizing slum women to design and manage their community toilets (Burra, Patel and Kerr 2003). Appadurai's optimistic portrayal of the work of these slum women which created 'recognition from below' (Appadurai 2001: 37) has received support from other NGOs who are similarly working in urban slums in other cities to deliver basic services. The public toilets in Mumbai are as Appadurai notes, a way for slum women to show the authorities that they can do it better, by setting precedents and creating new 'legal' solutions on their own terms. While maintaining distance from one's faeces has become one of the signifiers of class status in urban areas, Appadurai notes that public toilets built and managed by the slum women have transgressed class divisions and generated new models of democracy from below.

The toilet festivals organized by the Alliance in many cities of India are a brilliant effort to re-situate this private act of humiliation and suffering as a scene of technical innovation, collective celebration and carnivalesque play with officials from the state, the World Bank and middle-class officialdom in general. The toilet festivals feature the exhibition and inauguration not of models but of functioning public toilets, designed by and for the poor, incorporating complex systems of collective payment and maintenance with optimal conditions of safety and cleanliness. These facilities are currently small-scale and have not yet been built in anything like the large numbers required for India's slum populations. But they represent another performance of competence and innovation, in which the 'politics of shit' is (to mix metaphors), turned on its head, and humiliation and victimization are transformed into exercises in technical initiative and self dignification. (Appadurai 2001: 37)

Appadurai's observations are seductive to say the least. Indeed they suggest that women's participation through NGOs can do what the UN has been suggesting all along – it can empower low-income communities, it can deliver services through state sponsored NGOs, and it can improve the lives of the urban poor. It crucially also illustrates how law becomes a resource for the poor in terms of transforming their relationships with illegality through mimicry of state responsibilities in providing community sanitation facilities. But I see this mimicry as placing its actors and their links to local power in a position of vulnerability.

I remain sceptical about valorizing women's participation in community infrastructure and its celebration through 'toilet festivals' in Mumbai's slums, since I find that community managed infrastructure often becomes the only route to sanitation when all others are closed. Paradoxically, while the state excludes its 'illegal' citizens from formal access to sanitation, it simultaneously celebrates it when these subjects organize their own arrangements through NGO support. NGOs in Mumbai advocate what Roy calls an 'infrastructure of populist mediation, one that deploys, in quite effective ways, technologies of governing such as strategies of enumeration and exhibition' (Roy 2009: 66). I agree that these institutions are able to create through gendered participation, a politics of legitimization from within the gaps of development plans and government policies. However, the claims of 'governmentality from below' through the participation of women run the risk of mobilizing a traditionalist discourse, where women's cultural responsibility over domestic sanitation is extended to the public realm of slum neighbourhoods. This positionality in fact reinforces entrenched systems of gendered power within families and communities. Community infrastructure projects then, seem to have shifted the 'problem' of the slum from 'legitimization through tenure' to 'legitimization through sanitation'. And it is in the gaps between state provided sanitation and community managed toilets that women's 'appropriate' role in this process becomes apparent.

My scepticism is related to the ways in which examples of 'successful' community infrastructure in Mumbai has been politicized to provide solutions

for the 'sanitation crisis' (Davis 2006) in the South. These examples are used
to promote a 'willingness to pay' discourse (Bakker 2005, Dutta, Chander and
Srivastava 2005), through which water and sanitation is made economically viable
for utility companies. This assumes that squatters are not only agreeable to paying
for water albeit within the specifics of local contexts (McFarlane 2008), but also
that this can be made affordable to them through improvements in efficiency in the
technology and management of infrastructure. This produces within local contexts,
forms of mimicry of state responsibilities in providing adequate sanitation, through
support from state-sponsored actors. This mimicry also produces public toilets
as market commodities – which squatters are truly hard-pressed to pay for. For
example, a recent report (NIUA 2003) in Delhi found that although large amounts
of money have been invested in toilet complexes in squatter settlements, nearly 60
percent of the urban poor continue to defecate in the open.

I find that the everyday practice of defecating on public land and punitive
measures taken by the state against this practice produces a fractured and disjointed
politics, which is often confused about the question of legitimacy and entitlements.
This confusion is part of the illegibility of the state which oscillates between the
rational and magical (as Das calls it) nature of the force of law. But in attempting
to mimic the state while encountering illegality, I find that it also produces a
number of vulnerabilities in localized gender relationships not recognized or
detailed in these accounts. First by reinforcing women's association with domestic
responsibilities of sanitation, it weakens any attempts at transforming gender
inequalities at a local level. Second, it produces sanitation as a commodity rather
than a right. Consequently it reinforces the notion of squatter settlements as 'spaces
of exception' where special laws, regulations and processes have to be set in place
in order to provide those basic services, which are otherwise taken as given in the
legal city. Therefore, while constructing and managing their toilets might provide
slum dwellers with a 'legitimacy from below', we should ask what are the politics
of its marketization to slum dwellers through gendered participation; and what
politics of gender are evoked when these toilets become the symbols of legitimacy
and urban citizenship?

Public toilets as state spaces

In the late 1990s a toilet complex was built on the north-western corner of the
camp through a partnership between the municipality and an NGO. But it had
remained largely unused – it did not have enough toilets, it was only open during
the day and it charged residents for each use. When I visited the camp, the toilet
complex sat incongruously among the loose bricks, plastic containers, and bamboo
poles strewn around it. Although it was a single storey block, architecturally it
looked much more formal in its surroundings. Embedded within the narrow lanes
of the camp, it was also the only structure in the camp built by the state and hence
ironically the only structure which was legitimate.

Figure 6.2   Toilet complex inside the camp. Photo: Author 2005

Toilet complexes such as the one in the camp stand both inside and outside the law. For the state and for development agencies, toilet complexes can be seen as places where the 'sanitation crisis' has been solved– their presence within squatter settlements would also ensure that public spaces such as the urban forest would remain 'public'. As a structure built in an 'illegal' squatter settlement it was a 'space of exception' in that its presence was made possible through a violence of law that excluded squatters from access to private spaces of sanitation. The presence of the public toilet therefore was shaped by a threat of sanitation outside of law – as a space provided on account of development schemes put together to deal with sanitation 'problems' in slums. It was a space of sovereignty, through which power was exerted on the bodily practices of 'illegal' citizens living inside the camp. Its presence assured the residents of their legitimacy in terms of tacit recognition of their rights to sanitation, while on the other hand, its communal facilities reminded them of their 'exceptional' location vis-à-vis the legal city. Above all, the toilet complex was always a temporal space to be dismantled once the illegal city was demolished.

A recent study by the National Institute of Urban Affairs in Delhi, found that the municipality has provided 376 public toilet complexes in approximately one third of its total low-income settlements (NIUA 2003). Of these 237 were permanent and the rest was prefabricated or mobile units. These toilet complexes are usually built through public-private partnerships with NGOs holding contracts for their management and charging for their use. As a result they are usually found to be in very poor maintenance, they have inadequate number of shower and water-closet spaces, and restricted opening hours, which result in increased length of queues, and anxieties over costs of use. The toilet complex in the camp was similarly rejected by participants as a state space, which turned a basic human right into a commodity and mapped encounters with law on the squatter body.

> The government made a [toilet] complex there and wanted to take money from the poor. Those who can't feed themselves, how can they pay for latrine? Suppose someone has diarrhoea, then how many times he has to go to the toilet? All the money that we save for food, we will pay for latrine? Look at government politics, how to kill the poor. [Sunita]

Toilets complexes that charge for use effectively marginalize and exclude squatters from those spaces that are enjoyed by the legal city as 'normal'. They push squatters further to the margins of illegality and law through a discourse and practice of 'exception' housed in the structure of the toilet complex. Pay-per-use toilets in the camp became the sites of control by sovereign power and hence necessary sites for the establishment of boundaries between legal/illegal, city/slum and centre/periphery.

The toilet complex was also an affective space for participants where law was continually encountered from the recesses of hunger and illness. The power exerted through law was in the everyday routines of the body, in transforming normal biological processes into a schedule restricted by its opening hours. Participants were therefore forced to make do, rather than attempt new forms of 'legitimacies from below'. With the restrictions in the use of the public toilets, creative solutions were improvised – reflected in comments like 'ask us where we do not [defecate]'. Those with larger homes constructed make-shift water closets within their homes, which were connected to the open drains running through the lanes. Others with smaller homes relied on a system of night soil sacks, which were collected every morning by sweepers hired by them. Many residents however could not always gather the resources required to add a private privy, most did not even have the room. Even those who used the public toilets found themselves desperate outside its opening hours.

In the camp, amidst haphazard, confused and uncoordinated efforts to find a place, any place to relieve oneself, the forest across the boundary wall, continued to serve as an 'illegal' place of defecation. But it was also a place of danger, patrolled by sentries who had orders to stop them from entering the forest. Since its closure however, ladders propped up against the boundary wall – at night, residents of the camp climbed these to go across the wall to defecate. They put bricks on the other side to act as steps and every night there were injuries as residents attempted to put their foot on bricks on the other side that the sentries had removed during the day. These everyday difficulties were articulated to me by the leader of the Residents' Welfare Association.

> Now, some people have put up ladders there. If they [police] get to know, they will beat them up. *Chowkidar* [sentries] are on duty – with guns. By chance, in darkness or daylight [if people go] the police often pick up and beat people. [Moinullah]

Climbing this wall was inherently dangerous as it meant the transgression of material and social boundaries that separated the middle-classes from the poor. It also meant that one had to be fit and agile – a reason why most confrontations with the sentries took place with the young men in the camp. It was not possible for women, young children, and the elderly to scale these walls without injuring themselves – an argument also used by the *Mahila Mandal* to frame their activism. Although the construction of this wall was perceived to be a result of miscalculations around its use by low-caste residents, it stood as a metaphor for the lines that separated them from the legal city, and subsequently their entitlements to defecate in the same way as other 'legal' urban citizens. These exclusions were perceived by participants as a violence of law that infiltrated upon the biological processes of their bodies.

These struggles to 'illegally' defecate in the forest despite the construction of the boundary wall were remarkably inconsistent with participants' denunciation of the *Mahila Mandal* action to break the wall as 'illegal'. But these inconsistencies themselves suggest the approach towards law that participants were taking in the camp. In this approach, it was not that law was inconsequential, but that illegality was only perceived as a threat and source of anxiety when it failed to achieve desirable outcomes and led to their falling 'out of favour' with state institutions. The *Mahila Mandal* action was denounced for these very reasons, because their action invited the force of law to discipline the 'unruly' bodies of women in the camp.

Gendered labours along the main road

If the forest delineated the boundary between the legal and illegal city, the main road to the camp traced the lines that separated legal and illegal slums. I have discussed in the previous chapter how the main road was a gendered space where the movement and location of gendered bodies were marked by the normative rules of 'appropriate' or 'out of place' gender performances. There I mentioned through the incident of the *chowki* how these gendered codes produced the main road as a site of contestation over the legitimacy of gendered social organization. I will now re-examine the main road through its location within the gendered spaces of water collection.

To understand the spatially coded practices on the main road, I borrow from Chakrabarty's (2002) skilful unpacking of the notion of a 'bazaar', a place that is both the outside and public; a place that serves multiple purposes of – a border (between the camp and resettlement colonies), an 'outside' (of the home and the camp), economic spaces (as the market), movement (in and out of the camp), as well as a place of 'infrastructure' (for water collection). Thus in contrast to the enclosed 'inside' of the home, the main road can be seen as a deeply ambiguous place where a variety of bodies and practices get 'mixed'. As Chakrabarty notes of the bazaar

> It is exposed and therefore malevolent. It is not subject to a single set of (enclosing) rules and regulations defining a community. It is where miscegenation occurs. All that do not belong to the inside lie there cheek by jowl, in an unasserted collection, violating rules of mixing; from feces to prostitutes. It is in other words a place against which one needs protection. (Chakrabarty 2002: 73–4)

In this analysis above, Chakrabarty was not making any commentary on the bazaar's gendered codes, so it is not clear how this postcolonial moment is experienced across subjective positionalities. But we can conclude that if the bazaar is a place of 'miscegenation', the protection that one would need from this would be largely mapped onto women's bodies. As a place where women are 'out of place' or 'in place' for legitimate reasons, the gendering of Chakrabarty's bazaar is consistent with the gendered codes mapped onto the main road in the camp. Women could not be seen there in the same way as men, and if they were, they became connected to the ambiguous (and dangerous) mixing of the public sphere. And it is the mixing of bodies during the access to water in the public sphere that anxieties over purity and dirt became apparent.

I have already mentioned that the condition of illegality within which the squatters were placed meant that they were excluded from the water connections that were provided to the rest of the city. Instead they had to rely on a variety of schemes that made water available as a community facility along municipality roads. Thus, unlike middle-class neighbourhoods, where water came into private taps inside the house, the collection of water in the camp was carried out on the main road. This posed a variety of anxieties around the 'mixing' of gendered bodies.

Exclusions from the legal spaces of urban water produced a higher degree of connections between the gendered body and the 'public' space of the main road, through the tenuous labours of residents transporting water from the road to their homes. These connections were the outcome of policy regulations that determined the installation of municipal pipes in 'unauthorized' colonies only along recognized municipal roads, and at grossly inadequate levels. Spatial differentiations around dirt, disorder, and impurity were thus shaped from the very conditions of illegality that produced the need to access the main road for water.

The main road was also a boundary between legal and illegal slums. It produced self-perceptions among squatters of their own disorder and impurity in relation to the 'legal' resettlement colonies across this border. It generated discourses around dirt that were closer to the modernist notions of hygiene, and were related to the lack of water for cleansing, which produced physical dirt on bodies and spaces of squatters. When water was collected along with other 'impure' bodies on the main road, the spatial separation between these bodies and water was threatened. This meant that the mixing of bodies produced 'defilement' in and of water, which was not necessarily associated with the material impurities of water; rather with doubts on the symbolic purity of this water. The main road, as a public place, then also became a contested place of infrastructure, which was ambiguously located simultaneously between modernist and subjective notions of dirt and filth.

Much of the development literature on infrastructure, has focused either on women's gendered relationships with water (Lahiri-Dutt 2006, Sultana 2011) or on regulatory problems associated with the state's control over the use of infrastructure (Gandy 2005, Page 2005). This literature however, has not examined how the notion of boundaries and bodies are transformed when water is accessed in 'illegal' settlements. The practices of filling water on the main road, which were part of everyday struggles in the camp, were marked by the anxieties that squatters faced over their transgressions across the notion of private/public and inside/outside. The differences in notions of dirt, disorder and impurity among those who came to collect this water on the main road imposed a spatial morality within its spaces, which was produced in a context of illegality. These notions of dirt on the main road were a set of relational, material, and symbolic classification systems that existed in parallel to the state and middle-class notions of 'dirt' in public places. These were used to construct a system of meanings and spatial ordering among the squatters themselves, to determine access to particular spaces of water and to reinterpret existing social hierarchies through their everyday struggles over access to infrastructure outside the legal city.

Tenuous labours of water collection

One afternoon, I was sitting inside the home of one participant Nasir who began describing their struggles with water. Till then, I had only heard of these struggles, but had not seen the jostling, rushing or fighting that went along with the arrival of municipal water in the taps. This was mainly because most of my interviews were carried out in participants' homes and the water taps were on the main road. So although I always heard about it when water arrived, I had not been able to make my way to the main road during this important event. That day as I was talking to Nasir however, his young son came running with urgency in his voice – the water had come to the taps and Nasir was needed immediately. Following close behind was my research assistant, who wanted my camera so he could take pictures of this event. Nasir did not like his young unmarried daughters to bring water from the main road, and his wife was poorly, so he began to make his way to the main road. I followed.

Every two to three days, the municipal standpipes on the main road started to hiss. The little boys playing around these pipes knew what that meant and ran inside the camp to inform their families. The shopkeepers also watched out for the hissing sound – for it meant that water was about to come out of these pipes, as soon as the air inside the pipes was pushed out. These shopkeepers informed their families, and they informed their neighbours and all rushed out of their homes towards the main road. Within minutes, the standpipes were surrounded by containers of all shapes, colours, and sizes – but none were too large since they became heavy once filled and had to be physically carried to their homes. In the apparent chaotic collection of containers around the pipes, there was a system of queuing – the containers acting to stand in for their owners till the water started flowing out. This water came for a few hours every two or three days, at no regular timings, and at no regular intervals. The main road during these moments entered a moment of suspension of its economic activities to turn itself over to the spaces and practices around the collection and transportation of water to individual homes.

But water did not come in all the standpipes at the same time. Those on the lower end of the main road received this earlier than others. This municipality

Figure 6.3   Queue on the main road around the standpipe. Photo: Author 2005

water was also the only source of drinking water but residents from the higher ends of the slopes often did not get water at all. Those residents living near water pipes were invariably the first few residents filling up the most number of containers from these standpipes, since they were close to these standpipes.

While illegality determines the context of communal water supply to the camp, topographies and physical locations within the camp shaped the unequal control over this water by some residents. Those living on the higher slopes were often denied water. The topography, irregularities, and water pressures in the standpipes close to their homes made them reliant on a system of 'favours' from those closer to other standpipes. Favours could mean a range of things – from friendships or familial relationships between households, to taking 'pity', to making a payment in cash or kind for filling water from a pipe that is not one's usual filling place. Taking favours invariably meant that one was always last in the queue, spending a large part of the day on the main road, waiting till the last trickle of water from the standpipes dried out.

I do not need to reiterate that filling water is a gendered and performative act. But the necessity of filling water on the main road produced a doubly contested public space – where women's visibility was validated through her gendered role of collecting water but, since this visibility often came at the cost of bodily violations and violence, her gendered performances during this moment had to be enacted through specific bodily codes that related to caste or ethnic practices. For married Rajasthani women in the camp, the traditional sari covering one's head was an expected form of dignified attire in public places. The sari did not need to be strictly adhered to by other married women – *Punjabi* or *Jat* women for example wore *salwar kameez* as part of their everyday attire, although they too often covered their head with a veil. Young pre-adolescent girls often wore dresses while young unmarried women also wore *salwar kameez*, but they were not usually expected to cover their heads. While young women were usually fit enough to carry water, their physical agility was largely determined by these bodily codes that required them to avoid eye contact with men and their attire which often restricted their movements during filling water.

One participant, Rajnarayan had a busy job as a driver in the nearby middle-class colony. He went to work early in the morning and came home later – in short he had no time for filling water which came at all odd hours of the day. His wife was usually responsible for filling water, but as a Rajasthani, she followed strict codes of veiling in public places. She always wore a sari, and draped its end over her head. During the filling of water she would have to hold the end of this sari with her teeth so that it did not fall off her head. Rajnarayan explained that this was because she had moved into the camp after their marriage, so she was the de-facto daughter-in-law of the entire neighbourhood, and hence had to follow the same gendered bodily codes, which she would normally do in front of her in-laws back in their village in Rajasthan. One day however, Rajnarayan came home to find that it were these bodily codes which had been the cause of not having enough water at home.

One day she [wife] was filling water somewhere outside [main road] – there was a fight among ladies. That woman was wearing salwar-suit, my wife had on a sari. Now in the tussle, while trying to keep her clothes in place, my wife got beaten. When I came home in the evening, she started crying, said such and such thing happened. I said, I am a Rajasthani, let me rebel first. I told her to wear salwar-suits, no problem. I will handle whoever says anything about it – otherwise, wearing saris makes it difficult – not to fight, for everything. [Rajnarayan]

Rajnarayan's account highlighted an aspect of the spatiality of gendered bodies during their transgressions across public and private spaces. His insistence over his wife's bodily codes in public spaces as akin to being in the presence of in-laws spoke of the extension of the marital home to the wider space of the camp. Such an extension was intended to address the anxieties that Rajnarayan also felt about his wife gong to the main road to bring water. I will speak of these anxieties in more detail in the next chapter, but at this point I would just like to highlight that Rajnarayan did not ask his wife to switch to *salwar kameez* in haste. He thought long and hard about its consequences and in terms of the trade-offs decided that it was better that his wife wore *salwar kameez*, but only during the collection of water.

Rajnarayan's account is suggestive of the transforming relationships between gender, space, and the body during the collection of water on the main road. This transformation is connected to the shifting set of relationships between public spaces of water and private spaces of gender relationships at home. Struggles over water provided possibilities not just for transgressing the cultural codes over women's bodies and spaces, but also involved men in this transformation. Rajnarayan's ethnic position as a *Rajasthani*, while shaping traditional views about women's bodily demeanour and attire, persuaded him to encourage the transgression of ethnically gendered codes over his wife's body. Since most economically active men were not engaged in water collection, the transformation of these bodily codes in their households was critical for them to continue with their employment. While women's gender performances on the main road were tied to particular gendered dynamics of power within the family, gender transformations on the main road were as much material and social as they were temporal – they were sanctioned only for specific spatial practices and at certain times, and they were part of the economic trade-offs made within families and households.

'Privileges' of the male child

Transporting water is largely reliant on the corporality of gendered bodies – these bodies which transport water are culturally and socially expected to be women, but they also have to be physically fit and able in order to do so. The agility of young male children however has largely been left out in feminist literature on water considering how the transportation of water relies not just on gender roles, but also gendered 'privilege' in the access to water. Like Nasir's son, young male children in the camp were culturally sanctioned and available (unlike economically active men) to scour the camp for news and updates about water. They were usually the first ones to know where and when the water was flowing and how long the queues were around these outlets. Male children were also physically fit – a necessary bodily requirement to fill and transport the water to individual homes. Households with male children therefore had an 'advantage' because family honour was not vested in the bodies of male children – and this was particularly salient in households where young married or unmarried women were not sanctioned to step outside on the main road to jostle with other bodies for water. This shaped gender negotiations within households, where members had to decide who amongst them, was temporally available, culturally sanctioned, and bodily fit to collect water from the main road.

While standpipes and tube wells remained the main sources of water for residents of the camp, the increased scarcity of water during summer months saw the water tanker make its appearance on the main road during this period. Its presence meant two things for the residents – first that previous spatial privileges of those close to the standpipes were reordered. This was a new source of water

Figure 6.4   Filling water from the tanker. Photo: Author 2005

with a new set of negotiations. Residents knew that they could not wait in queues to fill from the tap – there were too many of them and each had too many containers. So the young boys were hoisted over the tank – they dropped in a number of pipes through the wider opening on top of the tank and their family members standing below would then fill their containers through these pipes.

But this privilege also came at a social cost. In conditions of poverty, male children often held the social capital for the family's future. Usually they were expected to live with the extended family; even those who moved elsewhere regularly sent remittances to their parents and extended family. Under such circumstances, the education of male children was related to the future well-being of the family. Yet, the everyday needs around water, made it necessary for the household to set aside its long-term aspirations in favour of the immediate ones around water. Sending children to collect water from public places thus produced the future marginalization of particular social groups by excluding their children from education. As Nasir lamented, 'This son of mine, instead of giving him knowledge, I have given him the job of filling water. Fill water, son, otherwise where will we go? That is why he is behind in everything [in school]'.

Thus privilege vested in the male child was a paradox. On the one hand, it was able to provide particular households with increased access to water, yet on

Figure 6.5   Private standpipes in the lanes. Photo: Author 2005

the other hand this access also ensured the subsequent lack of social capital and potential unemployment when they became young men. But families were eager to make use of these privileges if it made access to material resources such as water (which were hard to come by in the camp) was made possible. In such cases, the bodies of the male children were not just corporally beneficial in accessing water; they were also symbolic in restricting access of other families to this water.

This aspect of the symbolic construction of male privilege became pronounced when water was accessed 'illegally' by the residents. By 'illegal' I mean that these residents tapped water from the mains supply on the main road to bring this to their respective lanes, which were closer to their homes. This provided them with a modicum of regularity over the storage and use of water. Residents in these lanes pooled in their money to install a variety of water outlets here – water taps, boreholes and tube wells. This 'illegal' and improvised access to water was sustained through bribes to water board officials who came to inspect from time to time.

During such access, the symbolic power of the male body was utilized in a different way to maintain control over the spaces of water. I was informed of this by Shazina, who with her two neighbours had pooled in money to channel the water supply from the main road to their lane. While filling water from this tap was part of the informal 'deal' between them, her neighbour dishonoured his agreement with her, using his sons as a form of symbolic threat to deny Shazina her access to water.

> We were putting a water tap, so I said ok, it's like this – let us split it into three parts – one is the neighbour, one me, the other you. ... that man [neighbour] didn't let us fill water even for a month – started saying how dare you fill water from my tap? What can you do? I have my girls to think of. He had many sons, six, seven sons. He was very arrogant about that, he was obscene. [Shazina]

Control over spaces of water was related to exchanges between informal and illegal modes of accessing water. The presence of male children was a source of symbolic danger during the exercise of this control – it was used to make or break deals and agreements around informal access to water. In this case, it was not that he had actually harmed Shazina or any of her daughters, but it was always the perceived capacity to carry out a harmful future act that made many households powerful in the camp. Young adult sons (interpreted as predatory masculinity capable of doing harm to young unmarried girls) were used to assert control over others and over the spaces of water. Control over spaces of water was therefore ambiguous, symbolic, and gendered, and did not follow any 'rules' of fair dealing.

Mixing and subjective 'dirt'

Let me come back again to the issues of mixing of gendered bodies during the collection of water. I have already discussed how this mixing and the anxieties over mixing seem to be pertinent both on the main road and within the lanes. Thus far however, I have discussed this mixing in terms of gendered anxieties, privilege or disadvantage. But such mixing also evoked other subjective positionalities that were specific to particular conditions of illegality. As I have already noted, this was related to the ways that squatters were coerced to negotiate around public access to water, not experienced by the rest of the city or even in the resettlement colonies across the main road. This occurred because accessing water in the public places of squatter settlements increased the interactions between bodies in ways that were not seen in the planned city.

The anxieties over the mixing of bodies became particularly salient during the filling of water from the tanker. The tanker brought residents in contact with each other in much more intense ways than the filling of water from standpipes. Water was not filled one at a time as in standpipes, but simultaneously and collectively from the tanker. Under such circumstances, spatial separations between high/low-caste and Muslims/low-caste could not be maintained around the water tanker. This erosion of spatial separations between different bodies during water collection was then transposed onto the symbolic qualities of water. As Shanaz explained,

> How can it [tanker water] be [drinkable]? People like *bhangi*, *chamar* [lowest castes] also come and fill the water and it is immoral to drink that water. We cannot drink that water then – they are lower caste … We are Muslims so we would like to keep away from the *bhangi's* at least. [Shanaz]

Shanaz's narrative was ironic because the physical qualities of the tanker water made it unsuitable for drinking anyway. Her narrative however suggested how the 'purity' of water was connected not to the absence of pathogens, but to the symbolic and moral geographies of caste bodies associated with this water. While Shanaz herself was Muslim, her internalization of a Hindu caste-based hierarchy through which the symbolic qualities of water were determined, resonates with Beall's observations in urban Pakistan where, 'despite the vigorous denial of caste as anathema to an inclusive Islam, the stigma of *Churha* identity endures as a "thought world" as pervasive as the moral order suggested by the Victorian sanitation movement and development thinking' (Beall 2006: 93). Similarly for Shanaz, this water entered an 'immoral' space of dirt and filth during its presence on the main road and its association with low-caste bodies. The main road then as the site of water collection was produced as a site of beliefs around dirt and pollution among squatters saw the modernist visions of 'dirt' and entrenched local social hierarchies run parallel in the spaces of water on the main road. The spaces of infrastructure in the context of illegality then became the site not only of everyday struggles around water, but also of the anxieties over the maintenance of moral geographies of 'purity' that had little to do with water.

What emerged from these stories was a localization and internalization of the spaces of exception into moral geographies inscribed upon bodily practices. Such internalization of social differences during the struggles over water is consistent with the discussion earlier in this chapter when class-based exclusions of squatters from the urban forest was internalized through pig rearing practices of lower castes. While communal facilities were the only option to address urban basic services in 'illegal' settlements, it was at the same time productive of a diversity of social power relations that reworked older social hierarchies through new embodied everyday practices. These embodied everyday practices attempted to rework the sharing of public spaces in uneven and unequal ways.

Reworking the 'inside' and 'outside'

One participant, Madanlal who lived on the main road narrated his positive interactions with his neighbours along the main road and in the resettlement colonies which gave him access to water when needed. I asked whether he knew anyone in the camp apart from those who lived on/across the main road, and he replied that he never went 'inside'. Madanlal, then began to describe how he preferred to interact only with those living 'outside'. 'Was there a difference then between inside and outside the camp?' I asked.

> There is a lot of difference, because here [main road] there is no *jhuggi* in front. There [inside] one *jhuggi* is in front of the other, one door faces the other, in between there is drain. If one throws water and it goes into the other house, she will shout saying why have you thrown water into my house? That is why the environment inside is not good. [Madanlal]

Madanlal went onto explain how he considered those people inside undesirable as friends because they made their children defecate in the open drains that ran through the narrow lanes and threw their household waste into these drains. He complained that such practices led to the clogging of the drains, stagnant water and subsequently the spread of diseases. He added, 'that is why we are always suffering from diarrhoea and dysentery, because people inside are not aware of how to keep their houses clean, how to keep their neighbourhood clean'.

The smaller homes inside the camp were at a particular disadvantage when it came to everyday practices around water and waste. They did not have extra floors or rooms or roof spaces and were forced to keep their water containers on the lanes. Using this water to wash dishes or clothes required physical space, and for the smaller homes, this happened increasingly on the lanes. Practices around such uses of water in the lanes triggered a new set of contestations among neighbours around notions of dirt, disorder, and filth. Water thrown in the lanes was invariably waste water emanating from individual homes. It led to conflicts between neighbours over the transgression of household filth across the boundaries of this home. These conflicts produced an internalization of the modernist discourses of 'dirt' among participants, which in turn produced new meanings of 'inside' and 'outside' in the camp.

A range of scholarship notes how Victorian ideas of health and disease have lived on in development discourses around infrastructure (Beall 2006, Beihler 2009, Craddock 1995, Illich 1986). Such discourses refer in particular to stagnant water as the breeding grounds of diseases such as malaria, cholera, hepatitis, dysentery, typhoid, and diarrhoea. With a series of WHO reports highlighting the impacts these have on women, children and elderly, the Indian government has defined slums as the battleground against waterborne diseases. From time to time education campaigns are organized in the camp by NGOs to spread awareness of diseases, to educate in terms of safe drinking water, disposal of waste and faeces and so on. Participants like Madanlal recognized these more obvious connections of dirt to modern notions of health and hygiene. This perception of dirt was no less symbolic than the material evidence of dirt, both of which were present simultaneously within his narrative. They formed a source of moral panic and symbolic dangers within particular spaces like the 'inside', which were enough to justify his disassociation from those spaces and the families therein.

Madanlal's narrative thus presented a different notion of the 'inside' and 'outside' than those offered by postcolonial scholars – this notion reflected how the squatters themselves align with modernist discourses of dirt and disorder, and engender their connections to women's domestic practices and gendered interactions. These divisions between the outside and inside did not relate to the boundaries of the home (although it arose from references to domestic practices of water use), but to the boundaries of the camp itself. The notion of dirt, disorder and filth was related to the use of water and the throwing of waste in similar ways to the 'modernist gaze' (Chakrabarty 2002). But this was also an inversion of the purity and sanctity of the 'inside', to present a boundary not related to the home, but rather to the physical and symbolic boundaries associated with the camp. The 'outside' in Madanlal's narrative reflected the zone where the camp was seen to have materially and socially 'modernized' in terms of order and purity.

Thus water collection, storage, and use were shaped by various social and material relationships between households, neighbours, families, social groups, state, utility companies, and local authorities in particular spaces of the camp. The places where water was collected, stored, and used were sites of transformation and transgression of social power and gender relationships and the establishment of new modes of social control during encounters with illegality. As sites of uneven power relationships, these places delineated a set of spatializations around access to, storage, and use of water, which connected squatters and their bodies to dirt and filth in ambiguous ways. Above all, it showed how the notions of public/private and dirt/purity were imagined and reworked by the squatters themselves during their violent exclusions from the legal city.

Returning to the boundary wall

The violence of law in everyday life becomes publicly visible during access to spaces of water and sanitation in squatter settlements. The contestations over their access show that illegality is not just structural or symbolic – it is also embodied, corporeal and material. Bodily encounters with the law along the boundary wall of the camp challenge the most basic notions of normality taken for granted in the legal city. The tenuous labours of collecting and transporting water from the main road to squatter homes bring to the fore how illegality is tied to the corporeal aspect of bodies. It is these moments that are subject to an interpretive violence of law, or the maintaining force of law, which consequently ensures the presence of the state within the bodies of squatters. While Agamben (2005) notes that sovereignty is exercised not just over bodies, but over life and death, I would like to suggest that sovereign rule becomes most powerful when it reduces everyday life to a collection of bodily functions – eating, drinking, washing, cleaning and defecating. This is not the explicit torture and bodily harm as Agamben (2005) proposes; rather the control and regulation of mundane and everyday activities. Examining the struggles to fulfil these bodily functions highlights how the violence of law is exercised in the most 'ordinary' spaces of everyday life.

The issue of the boundary wall points not only to how law is encountered during bodily practices of defecation, but also how squatters themselves construct legality as the only legitimate relationship between state and citizen. I was told how young men tried to scale the wall and often broke their limbs, how they were often caught by the sentries and taken to the police station where they had to pay bribes to the police to be freed, about the women who were now forced to use the public toilets but faced harassment from local men as they stood in the long queues, of the elderly and disabled residents who could neither scale the wall nor had the resilience to queue for toilets and so were resigned to using night soil sacks. These stories were everyday realities of the exclusion of squatters from spaces of urban infrastructure, but these stories were also narrated to me with a sense of finality. It was surprising because apart from the insurgent action of the *Mahila Mandal* which was criticized, the Residents' Welfare Association had not pursued the authorities to provide them with better toilet facilities. I found that participants' acceptance of the boundary wall was related to their sense of transience, because they were convinced that Delhi had no place for *jhuggis* (see Chapter 4), and that moving to resettlement colonies was their only hope. It was this notion of temporality that I believe produced an acceptance of much of the exclusions that they faced – in other words, they were able to cope with these difficulties in their everyday life, because they also believed that these would not last for very long.

Could one argue then that violence of law is most insidious within the sites of everyday when it convinces its subjects that illegality is temporary? I am reminded here of Zizek, who notes that 'any given field of symbolically structured meaning in a way always presupposes and precedes itself. Once we are within a field of meaning it is by definition impossible to adopt an external attitude towards it', and therefore the 'hidden chasm of this vicious circle appears only at its purest under the guise of tautology: "law is law", "God is God"' (Zizek 1991: 203). Zizek invokes this tautology as the very basis of a 'mystical authority of law'. By this he refers to the ways that the violence of law is sustained through its concealment, even from its own subjects who then see law as authentic. While in this book, I have argued that squatters do not accept the neutrality of law or its interpretation, there is always an invocation of an originary (authentic) legal framework of justice (in the constitution), corrupted by political interests. It is this evocation that constructs law as the only route to relocating oneself from the illegal to the legal city.

In charting colonial biopolitics in Delhi, Legg notes that governmental finances played an important role in the separation of 'health from disease, order and disorder, boulevards and galis, white and brown' (Legg 2007: 209). Legg argues that these divisions were acknowledged and defended by the colonial government, through the creation of physical barriers like gates, walls and fences. Most crucially he notes that colonial governmentalities brought about forms of resistance with people taking up 'categories of political society and articulating them in languages of petition, protest and democratic rights' (Legg 2007: 209). For him, the negotiation of difference based on an abstract category of race in colonial Delhi is one which initiates modes of resistance. As I have already mentioned in this chapter, Appadurai too evokes this notion of resistance through 'deep democracies' in slums. Appadurai bases his argument on the ways that slum women with the help of NGOs construct and manage their own toilets to create what he calls 'legitimacies from below' (Appadurai 2001). Such forms of politics that are usually the extensions of political society, posit an oppositional stance to the state in collective organization. They suggest that resistance is the only form of politics that one can enact against the violence marginalizations experienced in everyday life.

I find that models of resistance are not helpful in understanding the fragmented and contested nature of political action in the camp. I find that the camp as a space of exception is established when its peripheral location in terms of water and sanitation becomes an essential component of its distinctiveness from the legal city. This distinctiveness produces in turn a range of responses that include 'bargaining and negotiation, deception and manipulation, subversion and resistance as well as more intangible, cognitive processes of reflection and analysis' (Kabeer 1999: 438). Instead of collective resistance, I find that the violence of law which excludes squatters from water and sanitation in the public sphere are transposed across local social differences of gender, caste, religion and generation. This transposition produces reworked versions of the boundaries between inside/outside, public/ private and legal/illegal, which then transform the material and symbolic nature of everyday spaces.

These boundaries are as much material as they are symbolic and social, maintained through their continuous policing not just by the state but also by squatters in order to make sense of their encounters with law. This produces other forms of local violence that excludes residents on the basis of gender, caste and religion from the spaces of water and sanitation along the forest and main road. In the context of the local then, the violence of law works both within and outside the body reconstituting them through different symbolic and moral codes of inclusion and exclusion within the camp.

Instead of resistance, the sites of cleavage (both public and private) during access to water and sanitation show how law and subjectivity are related in everyday life. Why for example did the *Mahila Mandal* and RWA react to the issue of the wall in different ways? Why did the *Mahila Mandal* not share the support and backing of the other residents in the breaking of the wall? As Hansen (2001) argues in the context of Mumbai, I find that political society in the camp cannot be taken as distinct from state/civil society but tied intimately to both. Further, as I have argued in the previous chapter, often gender relations in the public realm are a reflection of gendered social power in the private realm, which makes it harder to categorize resistance as shared by the community as a whole. Often 'resistance' is atomized, disorganized and contested. In the context of the camp they were not thought through and indeed served to divide rather than organize people around rights to water and sanitation.[2] Relationships with illegality are key to understanding these politics since exclusions that are sanctioned by violent judicial interpretations, produce a variety of anxieties around what constitutes valid and legitimate forms of political action, and the 'appropriate' agents to enact this action.

These anxieties around the legitimacy of feminist activism were also related to the perception that their everyday struggles were not going to last for very long. Participants feared that resistant action might jeopardize their chances of resettlement in the 'legal' city. Recall the words of Rajkumar in chapter four who noted that the 'crooked lanes' of the camp will not be spared during the Commonwealth Games 2010, one can get a sense of how convinced residents were about the imminent demolition of their houses. And in fact, their lack of access to spaces of sanitation produced a stronger desire to be part of the legal city. Their hesitancies around political action for access to water and defecation revealed their sense of transience and anxiety about their future. They found subversive rather than resistant models to cope with their present even as they waited for the inevitable. I turn to this notion of subversion in the next chapter.

---

2   Having said that, the RWA came into being because of collective concerns over provision and billing of electricity. However, the democratic elections in the camp that were a direct result of these concerns did not radically transform the power of its members on ground.

Chapter 7
Legitimate Domesticities

> I told them [feminist NGO] about my home, and how my father misbehaved and when I was sent to my aunt's place, how her husband misbehaved. They asked me to file a case. They sympathized with me and gave me courage. Then, my parents bribed him [*pradhan*] and he started applying to different places saying that they abducted our girl and are forcing her to convert to Punjabi religion [Sikhism]. They [police] arrested Sunita *didi* [elder sister; used as a form of respect] and beat her up. I went to the *Mahila Mandal*, they told me to call [the police] whenever someone harassed me. [In the police station] a lady police said, 'I will beat you up; you are acting smart; your parents are thinking well for you; do whatever they wish'. Another lady police asked, 'why do you wish to stay with her [Sunita]; does she have your pictures?' I had taken a legal notice from a lawyer; the lady police threw the notice on my face and said, 'take it away, even if you go to the court no one will sympathize'. [Shazia]

Shazia, a victim of incest left her parents' home to live with one of her neighbours Sunita who had two children, and was separated from her husband. Shazia was a quiet young woman, deeply troubled by her experiences at home and by her continued harassment from her family. She lived in fear of being attacked, and spoke many times of ending her life during the interview. She had worked as a beautician before, but her parents had convinced her employer to fire her, and had taken all her savings. With no employment and no savings, Shazia was reliant on Sunita who accommodated her in the small room that she rented with her children. Sunita on the other hand was disliked across the camp particularly because she violated its gendered spatial codes – she was often seen walking outside after dark, talking to young men, and was also rumoured to be a police informer (but her beating in the hands of the police tells us otherwise). Sunita did not really care what people said about them, or that both she and Shazia were often verbally abused by Shazia's family, but she was adamant that Shazia should stay with her because her return to her home and family was unthinkable after what Shazia had been through.

Shazia might be seen as a woman who was conscious of her legal rights, which made her take recourse to law to assert her independence from her family. She contacted the police, a feminist NGO, and the women's collective in the camp. She also used the services of a lawyer to claim her legal rights as an adult to live independently. Shazia's case however illustrates that agency, independence and recourse to law often came at huge personal costs to women. The use of law to seek separation from the family did not necessarily promote well-being and freedom in the way that feminist scholars would like to see. Remarkably, Shazia did not even attempt to seek legal redress for violations over her body; rather she was simply seeking separation from her family. I will come back to the reasons why this might be the case later in this chapter, but at this point I want to note that the procedural justice experienced by Shazia at the hands of the police and her moral disciplining in the camp was a reminder of how normative ideologies of the home and family were able to supersede a rule of law that attempted to 'protect' squatter women. Shazia's case clearly shows that we need to examine how law is silenced and obfuscated within the most intimate spaces of everyday life even as squatters attempt to become part of the legal city. Crucially, it suggests how violence is present not just in the founding or maintaining moment of law but also in the very absence of law from the intimate spaces of home and family.

I became aware of Sunita and Shazia through stories from other residents in the camp. We were repeatedly given their example as a 'problem' which the *Mahila Mandal* or the feminist NGOs had not been able to resolve successfully, and subsequently as an example of the further evidence of the 'immoralities' of the legal processes through which the *Mahila Mandal* sought justice. By this, it was meant that the rule of law had not been able to return Shazia to her 'rightful' place within her family home; rather using this law, the *Mahila Mandal* and the NGO had separated her from her family. In fact one of the members of the Residents' Welfare Association who approached the NGO to request them to return Shazia to her family, complained about their inability to see the 'immorality' of the rights that Shazia had asserted under law. He asked – 'we understand the law, but if someone has become a prostitute, would you let them be? Just because she is an adult?'

These attitudes towards Shazia indicate the ways that the rule of law is rejected within personal spaces of home and family by making claims to the morality and indestructibility of the home even when the family itself poses a threat to women's bodies. But it also indicates how the state and the family were connected through gender ideologies around women's legitimate location in particular spaces even as the 'woman question' itself became the marker of modernity and development for the state. The hegemony of family perpetuated by the police in Shazia's case suggests how the moral geographies of the family were able to traumatize Shazia's personal life not only within the spaces of the home but also within the neighbourhood and city. Above all, it raises the continuing dilemmas between the legal idea of gender equality enforced by the state and the cultural constructions of gender roles within the home and family that are practiced in the camp.

The squatter home is one of the most politicized and pathologized spaces in development discourse, but for squatters it is the space of mundane everyday domesticities. In earlier chapters, I examined this home from the perspective of urban development, collective organization and infrastructure – issues that are hotly debated in development policies. In this chapter, I focus on particular aspects of home and family which are crucial to everyday life in the squatter home yet remain less visible in public policy and debate. I examine issues that are salient in Shazia's case – the oppositional construction between morality and a rule of law, family and state, city and slum within this home. Lived experiences of the single-room squatter dwelling are an important part of these oppositions because they connect to wider discourses and practices around morality, parochialism and development.

I write this chapter with some trepidation. Of all the spaces discussed in this book, the spaces of moral authority in the home and family seem to present the most difficult ethical challenges around interpretation of participant narratives. Like Goldstein (2003), who was writing about the black humour ensconced in the stories of rape in a Rio shantytown, I too am aware how participants' narratives around domestic violence, incest, rape and adultery can be seen precisely as the indicators of moral 'degeneration' and arguments for their resettlement. But like Goldstein, I also suggest that these narratives have to be understood in a context where violence is experienced and negotiated as a mundane aspect of everyday life. It is therefore important to interrogate even the most absurdly misogynist narratives around women's bodies and spaces in order to understand on what basis these are produced and on what grounds these are sustained. I argue that particularly violent ways of normalizing the home and family may originate among the squatters because this forms their only way to subvert a rule of law that seeks to marginalize them in all other aspects of urban life. Subversion is not always a conscious effort; rather a coping tactics in a context where the home is under threat and a resultant struggle ensues to sustain the indestructibility of the family.

I call this chapter 'legitimate domesticities' for a few reasons. In the impending threat of demolition, everyday or ordinary domestic life remains both an aspiration and an organizing principle of the family and household in the camp. Yet as Shazia's story shows, only particular types of domestic arrangements are considered moral and hence legitimate, even when these take the most violent forms. On the one hand, the squatter home is continually monitored by the state through the number of development policies and programmes that establish a legitimate domestic life both socially and materially. On the other hand, patriarchal authority within the family and beyond controls who is or is not a legitimate member of this domestic life. Thus the notion of legitimate domesticities oscillates between morality and rule of law, between subjective agencies and state prescribed forms of home and family.

In taking this approach, I find that anxieties over the material annihilation of a home through the demolition drive of the state, leads to a resultant anxiety over its future sustenance, anxieties over loss of patriarchal authority over this home and subsequently anxieties over a loss of masculinity. Consequently, this leads to a moral discourse of the family within the home, which attempts to endure beyond its material annihilation. As Nikolas Rose (1987) suggests, the connections between law and family produces the home as the site of concrete, contingent and local instances of power and marginalization. Normalized as a mundane aspect of household relationships, violence over women's bodies in the home becomes a culturally sanctioned method of maintaining the moral authority of the family and disciplining its 'unruly' members. Such discipline is not just enacted over gendered bodies – these are also bodies that are placed with reference to intra-household hierarchies – wives are subservient to husbands, children are subservient to parents, sisters are subservient to brothers, younger siblings are subservient to older siblings, daughters-in-law are subservient to mothers-in-law and so on. But I also find that the notion of family becomes more productive when it is extended to protect minorities in the camp during communal violence in the city. Domesticity became central to the ways that squatters constructed a gendered urban citizenship and belonging through conviviality and neighbourliness. The home and patriarchal family thus also became ways to conceive of alternative forms of home and legitimacy in the city.

Home and the outside

> If a girl was to be raped, if she, for example, were my daughter, and I am asked what is to be done to the rapist, I will straightaway say hang him. But the law will not accept what I say. So there are two standards. If there are ladies, women, they are equivalent to a sister, a daughter, and if there has been injustice to them, then hanging is the right thing. [Moinullah]

Moinullah, a participant was articulating an unfairness of law while he justified the reasons why women should stay in their 'rightful' places within the home. Living in Delhi meant that participants like Moinullah were never too far away from news of urban violence, particularly violence over women's bodies. Although fear of crime was a concern, this fear was largely interpreted as violence over women's bodies rather than communal violence or terrorism. Such concerns served to justify gendered separation between public and private spaces and the control over women's bodily presence in public places. Such anxieties were related to cultural values and norms that constructed family honour and masculinity through the purity of women's bodies. Consequently, loss of family honour was related to a loss of masculinity where its men were constructed as inadequate, and consequently this led to a belief that men were stripped of their authority and power as head of households. This justified a retreat from the city as the place of marginalizing citizenships into the home as the 'protective' space of the family. Thus, even as participants recognized that the city marginalized them through law, they sought to highlight the importance of and strict adherence to a set of laws in women's bodies in public spaces.

Male participants like Moinullah took this ambiguous position towards law. On the one hand men often lamented the leniency of judgment passed on those who sought to violate the bodies of women in public spaces. On the other hand, they criticized the law that sought to protect women from violence at home. This ambiguity also constitutes the condition of everyday encounters with law and illegality in the city. It is consistent with Caldiera's (2000) observation that working-classes are usually the strongest proponents of violent punishments even though they are the most disadvantaged through the rule of law. As Caldiera suggests, the 'model of the family, the institution in charge of disciplining people and preventing their contamination by evil, is applied directly to the public sphere (Caldiera 2000: 364). This was indeed important in Moinullah's case. Women's gendered roles within the family as 'sisters, mothers, daughters' were extended to the public realm to highlight the immorality of violence over their bodies in public spaces. Yet as Shazia's case clearly shows, the violence perpetuated by the family upon women in the domestic sphere was seen as 'ordinary' and removed from the nature of violence perpetuated within the public sphere.

I approach these ambiguities towards law through the anxieties of transgression across the threshold between private and public domains, articulated as the divisions between *ghar* and *bahir* (home and outside world) (Chatterjee 1989). Chatterjee suggests that during the nationalist struggle for Indian independence, the home was taken as the gendered domain of the inner spiritual self, which was pure and authentic, while the outside world dominated by the colonizers was seen as a masculine realm of fear and danger for women. Women thus became the protectors of the 'authentic' Indian home from the intrusion of the outside (Chatterjee 1989). In this context Chakrabarty observes that 'freedom' meant not just the end of colonial rule, but also for women, a 'freedom from ego, the ability to serve and obey voluntarily' (Chakrabarty 1992: 335). Chakrabarty argues that while the discourse on modern domesticity in colonial Bengal had inserted western notions of 'private' and 'public' into middle-class Bengali lives in the 19th century, these were also reworked in two significant ways during the nationalist struggle – first by opposing the 'new' patriarchy of the colonizers through a redefined version of the 'old' patriarchy of the Indian extended family; and second by investing the Indian woman with a 'sacred authority' over home and domesticity.

These postcolonial scholars were analyzing the cultural conditions that produced the Bengali home at the turn of the 19th century. Apart from being historically and geographically specific to Bengal, their observations were also related to the Indian middle-classes who were familiar with western ideas of privacy and the public sphere. But these observations on the colonial Bengali home are also useful in understanding everyday encounters with the law in Delhi's squatter homes in a number of ways. First, the anxieties and uncertainties around the sanctity of home in colonial Bengal were produced during a moment of hegemonic authority of the colonizers. Although not quite the same, the violence of illegality in Delhi's squatter settlements also produces a set of uncertainties around the sustenance of the squatter home. Second, the construction of the selfless Indian woman who protected the home from the 'dangers' of the outside during colonial rule provides us with ways to think about the processes by which the intrusion of the state (as law) is resisted through a gendering and valorization of the squatter home as women's realm. If 'illegality' can be seen to produce a new threat to the sanctity of home and to women, we can then direct analysis of the reworking of gender within the squatter home and outside at a time of extreme uncertainties over the sustenance of this home. We can then explore how private and public subjectivities are simultaneously transformed and internalized among squatters in everyday life.

My approach in this chapter is to look for the processes through which the locations of gendered bodies are normalized within spaces of the home and outside and how this normalization then reinforces the violence of law. Unlike middle-class homes, the squatter home is not hidden from outside view. Rather it is the potential of the squatter home to be laid bare of all its material and social elements for scrutiny by the state that produces particular embodied performances that attempts to compensate for its porosity. 'Justice' in the home then is not related to 'law'; rather to the various ways that the moral authority and validity of the family and of gendered locations can be maintained *despite* the intervention of law. The location and materiality of the body becomes critical to the enactment of justice through its gendered performances within the home and outside. As Shazia's case suggests, the body often becomes the terrain of violence, violation and incursion in attempts to sustain family authority during encounters with law.

However, Shazia's case also shows that such interventions over the body did not go unchallenged or uninterrupted. Das discusses in the context of violence, how women took the 'noxious signs of violation and reoccupied them with the work of domestication, ritualization and renarration' (Das 2004: 59). For Das, to be vulnerable is not the same as being a victim, which points to the need to pay attention to the gaps between 'a norm and its actualization' (Das 2004: 63). Das sees violence not as an interruption in everyday life but as incorporated into the ordinary. In aligning myself with this approach in this chapter, I am making an argument different from a politics of resistance. I am suggesting that the challenge to family authority came from within, through subjective experiments with life and death. These 'experiments' provides us ways to think about squatters' corporeal encounters with law, not as the control over their bodies by the state, but as the annihilation of gendered bodies despite their protection by law.

Anxieties over loss of masculinity

Delhi recently has seen a large scale rise in male unemployment. This has almost exclusively also hit the manufacturing and industrial sector. As I discussed in Chapter 4, the *Almitra Patel* ruling, which framed the 'problem of slums' as one of pollution and sanitation produced a climate where the public petitioner subsequently called upon the judiciary to intervene in a range of urban 'problems'- air pollution, pollution of the Yamuna river, cleaning up of parks, streets, public land, and so on (Veron 2006).

The most damaging of these litigations was in 2000, when the Supreme Court, fed up with years of inaction on a 1996 court order to close 168 polluting factories, threatened to bring contempt charges against top bureaucrats. When finally forced to act, the Delhi municipality provoked chaos through indiscriminate enforcement of the court's orders. Instead of shutting down polluters, they sealed all factories.

By March 2001, the deadline set by the Supreme Court; Delhi was 'cleaned' of all industries (Navlakha 2000, Veron 2006). 50,000 workers lost their jobs with the enforcement of this court order. They were mostly from slums and squatter settlements across Delhi. The factories that were closed were not just large industrial units but also smaller home-based factories that employed a variety of skilled and semi-skilled labour.

The Delhi employment data reflects how these closures had gendered effects on men in low-paid casual or informal work. Unemployment rate of males increased by four percentage points in Delhi from 1993–94 till 2004–05 as against falling unemployment in other cities like Mumbai (from over five percent to three percent) or Chennai (from over five percent to three percent) during the same period (Sharma and Krishna 2007). In fact during 2004–05, the chronic unemployment rate among males in metropolitan cities was recorded to be the highest in Kolkata (over five percent) followed by Delhi (almost five percent) The data indicates that the trends exhibited by male unemployment in Delhi were clearly higher than those of other cities and in India as a whole. Although this data did not differentiate between types of employment, the wider connections between the removal of factories and unemployment were evident among my participants.

In 2002 when I visited the camp for the first time, I became aware of a rising unemployment among the men. In most families however, the women were economically active, which often called to question the normalized male gendered identity as 'breadwinners'. The men were going through a sense of redundancy within the public domain as workers and within the home as head of households.

> There is no employment for the poor person who used to work in factories. They have closed down all the factories. So there is too much unemployment in Delhi. There are many people in our lane whose factories have closed and they are roaming around now looking for jobs. Some are just sitting at home. If they get a job then it will be better. People are very stressed because of this. [Shalu]

That there are direct links between male unemployment and domestic violence is something that most scholars agree upon. Although domestic violence is not restricted to working-class households, male unemployment in the camp was seen as the biggest contributor to anxieties among men about 'unruly' women who left the sanctity of the home to feed the family.

> If women work, men will be unemployed. The man will earn, support his entire family, the woman's expense is on herself, it doesn't help the family … if in a hundred rupees she can spend on lipstick etc … then after getting into service [employment] she will need at least a thousand rupees a month, sometimes for a haircut. The son will not even cut his hair; he won't spend on powder, colour and all the rest of it. [Rajaram]

Rajaram's perspective was part of a much wider construction of masculinity, femininity and gender roles that is both historic and ideological – it was repeated to me by other male participants often as a justification of the right to deny women to step outside the home. While women's economic contribution in the home was rejected as an individualistic and consumerist strategy, the reality of course was quite different. In a context where women were often the primary or only earners even in male-headed households, instances of women spending their money grooming themselves was neither visible to me nor plausible as a story. In fact in many households, the men often proclaimed proudly that they spent their earnings on alcohol or that they took money from their wives to sustain their addiction, because their wife's earnings were rightfully theirs. These men were unemployed and their construction of masculinities was part of the wider cycles of unemployment in Delhi that had led to many working-class men losing their jobs in factories. Women as domestic help, as beauticians and as seamstresses were part of different employment bases and were therefore still employed.

Domesticating women's labour

Among my participants, Shazia forms one end of the spectrum of women whose lives were violently controlled by the norms of family. Another participant Rajni forms another end of this spectrum. I met Rajni in 2005, on the last day of my fieldwork in the camp, when I came across a group of women talking to each other. We smiled at each other, I introduced myself and requested interviews with them and was invited to step into Rajni's house.

Rajni came into the camp after her marriage in the mid-eighties. Her husband put together some money and bought a house which they then expanded and rented out to another couple on the first floor. Rajni however was frequently abused by her husband, who would publicly beat her, dragging her by her hair across the lane in front of their house. He would also punch her in the face, which made her lose a few of her teeth when she was pushed into the open drain. But Rajni stayed with her husband for 10 years and had two children during that time. In the early 2000s, she began an affair with their tenant upstairs who was married but who Rajni claimed was ill-treated by his wife. If anything, this affair served to intensify the domestic violence she faced from her husband. In 2001, Rajni decided in a bold move to divorce her husband. Although he continued to harass her, Rajni kept the house to herself, trained as a beautician in one of the well-known salons in the city and began to earn a living for herself and her two children.

When I first met Rajni, I was pleasantly surprised at her outspokenness and her straightforwardness in describing the details of her affair with a married man and how that helped her 'escape' from her own violent relationship. Over the years, I have kept in touch with Rajni, as our family beautician who comes regularly to visit my friends and family who live in the middle-class colonies across the urban forest and gives them salon treatments at home.

Rajni and Shazia are just two of the many women, who come from the slums in the city to the middle-class colonies to provide beauty treatments to the middle-class women in the comfort of their homes. Despite popular belief, most young women from slums prefer not to work as domestic help, rather in more service sector work as beauticians or *mehendi* (henna) artists. These vocations are seen as more 'honourable' than washing dishes, or sweeping the floor, or worse still, cleaning bathrooms. Cleaning professions are seen ideally as the job of the lower-castes, or those freshly arrived from rural areas, who do not have any other skills. Although domestic work allows the repetition of gendered work typically done by women in their own households, doing this in other middle-class households are often constructed as the lowest priority for many young women who attempt to place themselves at a higher social position than their parents who they believe struggled a lot more as first generation immigrants in the city. Young women in urban slums and squatter settlements who have grown up in the city now prefer to accrue vocational training in sectors where they can be in more direct contact with middle-class women, and this often takes the shape of providing services towards the aestheticization of middle-class women's bodies. Similar to what Secor (2003) finds in Istanbul, spatially and socially differentiated work was critical to how my female participants constructed their identities as 'good' or 'bad' women. Work as beauticians became a way to construct their relation with the city, to differentiate themselves from older women in the camp who worked as domestic help, and link themselves to other gendered bodies marked by power, aesthetics and social class in the city.

In almost all cases beautician work is unregulated, much as informal work has tended to be. Thus these women do not show up in any data on employment or household economics. In fact most often women like Shazia are sent out to work in beauty parlours or to middle-class homes as a way to supplement household incomes. Their salaries are often paid by their employers to their parents or husbands and in many cases (Shazia being one example) parents or husbands also have control over whether and under what terms these women are given employment. But sending these women out from their homes, create a variety of anxieties for their family around their sexuality and gendered interactions in the city. Thus in many cases husbands or parents remain suspicious of the gendered performances of the women in their families outside the home. These suspicions manifest in regular domestic violence where beating wives becomes a way of asserting authority in the home over which the men are increasingly seen to have lost control.

Another way to look at Shazia's transgression then was not only that she had left the space of her home, but that she had entered the economic spaces of the city. Whilst her entry into paid employment had been encouraged by her family on account of her contribution to the family income, her leaving of the family home brought her family to punish her by convincing her employer to fire her. Such stories of 'punishment' were common. Even when families were struggling to make ends meet, it was common for family members to attempt to regulate women's paid employment in the city. This was particularly heightened in beautician work, which raised anxieties around the moral 'corruption' of these women.

One participant Razia Begum went through a particularly difficult period to prove her morality. Razia had taken a job (with her husband's consent) with a local photographer who was also her neighbour. Her husband trusted this neighbour as an employer because he knew this person, but very soon this employer began to blackmail Razia with compromising photographs of Razia with his customers. Razia claimed that he had digitally retouched her photographs and that these were false threats to extort money from her. But for a long time Razia could not tell her husband for fear of being doubted. When she finally did tell him, his reaction was as she had expected – she faced regular beatings both in the home and in the lane in front of her neighbours. Finally Razia could not take it anymore and left for her parents' house. But she missed her three young children who she had left behind in the camp, and sent her mother to see how they were doing. When her mother met her husband, she reasoned with him, who went to bring Razia back from her village. When she returned, both she and her husband launched a complaint with the police about this neighbour who had given the family so much grief and suffering. The neighbour was also beaten by her husband and his friends for taking advantage of a married woman. Razia claimed that after this incident, the domestic violence decreased; she was also back with her children, but did not ever leave home unless accompanied by her husband. When she spoke to me, Razia was convinced that she would not go out to work in Delhi as long as her husband could support their family.

Razia was one of the many cases where women found it hard to convince their partners of their fidelity and gendered conformity outside the spaces of the home. When faced with male attention, women often attempted to hide this from their partners and families which increased the cycle of suspicions if their partners got to find out. But such gendered performances by the women were also class-biased. For example, most of these women would not consider their conversation with my male research assistant to have jeopardized the trust of their families or partners in any way. Indeed, many of them even confided in my assistant about their harassment from 'perverts' in the buses or on the streets, adding that these incidents could not be shared with their husbands who would instead be suspicious of them. My research assistant on the other hand was seen as embodying 'middle-class' values of understanding and sympathy, as well as being markedly different from those men who harassed them. His entry in their homes was not seen to raise suspicions among their partners for these very reasons, since his visit was 'legitimate' which placed him outside the circle of undesirable male advances faced by women in the camp. My male research assistant's class and 'official' position therefore constructed him as sympathetic and 'safe' male figure whom my female participants could confide in and whom their partners could trust with 'gentlemanly' performances within the home.

Women's entry into the public realm was undesirable by most families yet became necessary for the family in a context where male unemployment was rampant. The transgressions of this home during women's employment were understood as the violence of law that oversaw male unemployment. Gendered transgressions of the threshold separating home and outside became the source of anxieties around the breakdown of the normative home and family. This was asserted at various moments of everyday life through violence over the gendered body.

Thus while the state's rule of law was seen to exclude them from the legal city, it was seen simultaneously to encourage women's 'corruption' at the cost of family. And the state rule of law was rejected in the upholding of this normative family and home since this law was itself seen as immoral and discriminatory. This affected the 'support' that women received from their families towards their employment and how they attempted even during this employment to maintain 'appropriate' bodily boundaries.

'After all our position is lower'

The anxieties over women's entry into public spaces were not only part of a normative discourse circulating among men in the camp but also sustained through the quiet acquiescence of those women who I interviewed.

> After all our position is lower than that of men isn't it? I have got so much experience [education]; but still, I can't go beyond it; without him [husband] I have no place here. I mean, I have seen this in many places; without a man, there is no [legitimacy]; people look down upon you; they think wrong things about you, if I ever say 'my man drinks'; I have seen this, I have experienced it – when I used to be overly worried and wanted to work somewhere; then people look at you from a wrong point of view. Men look at you thinking of how they can take advantage of the situation, because your home is broken. [Kiran]

This was narrated to me by Kiran, a middle-aged woman with two college going sons and an alcoholic husband. Kiran was a teacher in the local school in the camp. She had been the primary earner in the family for many years, while her husband spent most of his income on alcohol every evening. Kiran was well-known in the camp. When she went out with her husband, she (and not him) would be greeted by her students and their parents. But while this would disturb her husband, Kiran calmed him by reiterating his authority in the home, stating that he would always be head of household, and she would always be 'behind' him, even if she was well respected outside.

My incredulity at this comment was clarified by Kiran as the necessary condition of a 'lower-class' society, where women's legitimacy and identity was solely on account of her attachment to a patriarch – either a husband or father or son. In other words, a male figure was necessary as a symbolic 'protector' in the spaces that Kiran had access to, both in the camp and in the city. Outside this relationship, all men were seen as predators. Thus although Kiran's husband was often excessively violent towards her under influence of alcohol, his role as a symbolic head and as male authority in the family served to legitimize Kiran's stepping outside the house, in ways that Shazia's leaving the home had not been.

Kiran however, constructed her approach not as subordination; rather as a reworking of modern values with 'Indian cultural traditions'. Modernity for her meant education and awareness, not individualism or independence from the family.

> Modern can mean, see, being educated, to understand things; not just going out, roaming about with boys, all sorts of things, watching films, this and that; that is not modern. Certain traditions remain with us. Such as respecting elders in the house; to go along with what he [husband] says, not to speak over him; [not flaunt] my own education, 'yes, I am literate, this and that'; and at appropriate moments I do speak up, 'it should be this way, not that'. I do know some things.

How do we understand this construction of gendered hierarchy within the home and outside which is perpetuated by women themselves? How do we interpret narratives of Kiran and those like her who advocate women's legitimacy through their location within a patriarchal family even as their economic contributions which sustain the home are disregarded by the same family?

Let me go back again to Chatterjee's (1989) insights into the inside/outside dichotomies produced during India's struggle for independence. For the nationalist middle-classes 'outside' was a treacherous domain of British imperialist power and of oppressive masculinities, which were bent on humiliating Indian women and defiling the 'honour' of the Indian nation. The inside was a sanctified space – the realm of women, of family values and of 'authentic' Indian culture. The 'outside' represented the West which was important to impart modernity and democracy, but which was unable to touch the inner identity of superior cultural traditions (Chatterjee 1989) of the Indian family. In Kiran's narrative, in a similar move, home was protected from the corrupting effects of modernity and the West even as modernity was required to impart education to Indian women.

Sunder Rajan further notes that within the home, the woman question has been reinforced through 'modernization-without-westernization' (Rajan 1993: 133) – a notion reflected in Kiran's narrative where she clearly delineates between modernity as education and awareness and tradition as respect towards the home, family and elders. Within this home, female individualization was acceptable in so far as it functioned for the social good of the family; women's transgression into the 'outside' was acceptable, so long as it did not disturb the hierarchical order of patriarchal authority within the family. Thus women's entry into the outside world was legitimized so long as these spaces were constructed as extensions of the private realm of gendered domesticities where women's bodies were seen to be legitimately located – thus Kiran's education and public respect was not to be 'flaunted' but always presented as a less significant aspect of her primary gender identity as a wife and a mother.

The tensions that participants like Kiran saw between western modernity and Indian 'culture' was based on a range of essentialisms that were surprisingly similar to the nationalist ideologies of the middle-classes that Chatterjee articulates. As he notes, the nationalists also advocated female individualization and education and hence transgressions across the boundaries of the home were constructed as an aspect of domesticity and social good (Chatterjee 1989). But Kiran's narrative also referred to another system of differences – between middle- and 'lower-classes' in urban Delhi – the former seen as succumbed to the 'corrupting' influences of the West, while the latter attempting to retain Indian 'traditions' within domestic spaces. The justifications presented by my male participants to deny women the right to economic activity were also part of these sets of differences when the moral corruption of middle-class women by western values, was placed in opposition to the traditional values retained by women of 'lower-classes'.

Despite this lowering of her position to patriarchal authority in the family, Kiran was by no means outside the domain of household decision-making. Kiran's strategy towards getting her way with her husband supports Kabeer's argument about the 'less measurable manifestations of agency such as negotiation, deception and manipulation' (Kabeer 1999: 435). Her power within the family was secure in that she negotiated possibilities in the present within existing social and symbolic orders. Her transgressions of home and the world were made possible through a negotiatory agency that served to uphold the sanctity of the home and male authority while sustaining her employment outside the boundaries of home. Women like Kiran and others often explicitly articulated their 'lower' position within the home in order to receive consent and cooperation of male family members, and their 'lower' class status within society in order to morally validate this approach. Readers might recall a similar argument presented by Radha in Chapter 1 where she demanded her entitlements from the state on account of her inferior position as low-caste. Narratives of one's lower class or caste as I have noted earlier, were not necessarily the perception of one's access to social power in everyday life; rather they were historical and contextual statements through which claims to particular spaces were asserted. Thus Kiran's argument of being lower-class could also be interpreted as an argument for her entry into employment on account of the failure of her husband to perform his normative role as 'provider', which was expected of working-class men. Men often had to reluctantly give their consent to these transgressions of normative gender roles but in entering the public sphere, women constructed this as part of their domestic role and gendered identity of social production (and reproduction) within the home. In this arrangement, the moral authority of the home and family was maintained by its members who felt committed to abide by the 'rules' of domesticity, and regulated their lives and that of others by its terms (Rose 1987).

Internalizing the 'pathology' of the squatter home

Despite male anxieties over women's entry into the public realm and paid work, the home itself was full of dangers for these women (as aptly illustrated by Shazia's story earlier). Stories of young girls being molested by their neighbours, young boys raped by older boys, fathers raping their daughters, sexual relationships between siblings, as well as other stories of extra-marital affairs, inter-caste or inter-community liaisons and pre-marital sex were common themes among participants' narratives. There were many women such as Rajni who I introduced earlier, who used her affair as a strategy to escape from her violent relationship. For most women, despite the construction of the home as a place of safety, sanctity and morality, these were far from the reality of their everyday lives.

The material condition of the single-room dwelling was an important aspect of the construction, perception and experience of these dangers within the home. Participants repeatedly referred to the narrow lanes, the small houses and the congested environment as part of their problems and everyday struggles. The material qualities of their domestic space were seen to make their homes insecure and 'public' in so far as the physical envelope of their home did not contain audible conversations or restrict visual access into the interior. Neighbours could hear the intimacies between partners and the one room shared between extended families were often seen to produce 'hidden desires' among other family members and neighbours – desires that were seen as immoral and illegitimate. Gendered sexualities were often constructed as part of this problem – men were seen as impotent and alcoholics, while women's unfulfilled sexual desires were seen to push them from the home to the outside world. And this condition was seen to be produced from their marginalized economic spaces and illegitimate status in the city.

> This is mainly because of poverty. This is because of shortage of space. If there are separate and big rooms, there is privacy. At times the wives feel like having sex but the husbands have become very weak due to continuous drinking. It leads to attraction towards others; or where domestic fights are frequent, spouses get attracted to other persons. [Ramkishore]

Independent social workers in the camp reinforced this 'problem' of domestic intimacies in another way – arguing that women should resist being compliant partners to their husband's virile masculinities. They counselled women to exercise control over their husbands' desires, because such desires were seen not only to increase the number of children, but also passed onto children who were witness to intimacies between parents within these single rooms, and were in danger of enacting these with siblings and other family members. Such 'uncontrolled sexualities' were mapped along a continuum from the home to the city, where children turned to family members to fulfil their sexual curiosities, and women turned towards neighbours and the wider city to satisfy their sexual desires beyond the marital relationship. Thus although women and children were situated squarely within the home, they could not be taken to be 'safe' even within the home.

> One thing is that there is a shortage of space; this is the biggest problem ... because the discussions the husband and wife need to have, in order to run the family, these they are unable to have, you can't do anything in front of the children. Then when they don't have these conversations, what happens is that when crises come in the family, their balance doesn't work. I have one room. If I had two, perhaps I would not have remained worried about my husband for 25 years; I would have covered it in 10 years. If I had a separate room, I would have found ways to run the family. So this is the biggest problem and five or 10 percent of people live in first [middle] class [colonies]. The rest of the country – 80 percent lives like this. Meaning family relationships cannot be built. This too makes our country backward. [Sharda]

This direct link between the family and the nation was made by one of my female participants who sought to connect the material conditions of this home with development, family values with the future of the nation, and most importantly, morality with middle-class lifestyles. Through these narratives, participants internalized some of the very discourses circulated by the state and middle-classes that marginalized them. Illicit intimacies and a general degeneration of family values were seen as the consequences of the lack of physical space within the house. Privacy, as the key to ensuring bodily personal space for family members became the key marker of morality and control over unruly sexualities. In so doing, participants reinforced state discourses of pathology vested in the one-room dwelling unit.

Much of these arguments will be familiar to readers as harking back to Victorian moral arguments for slum clearance. The demolition of one-room tenements to remove overcrowding and to allow sunlight and ventilation in buildings has been widely documented as the social engineering approaches of British urban planners during the nineteenth century. Gillian Rose notes how slum spaces in London's east end 'articulated bourgeois fears and fantasies of social and sexual confusion' (Rose 1997: 282). She notes that in 1933 an ex-nurse wrote a 'whole book devoted to the possibilities for adultery and incest in the convoluted spaces of East End slums' and that the area's chaotic overcrowding was described as 'degrading, demoralizing, destructive of physical, mental and moral health, completely ruinous of human well-being and happiness' (Rose 1997: 282). As I have already mentioned in earlier chapters, In India such discourses of the moral degeneration of residents of slums were prevalent during the colonial era (Gooptu 2001) and later appropriated in postcolonial discourses around slum demolition and resettlement.

The squatter home, brutally pathologized in development discourses has often been forced open with its contents laid bare for scrutiny by the state and its agents. In this process, a discursive construction of its overcrowding, hygiene concerns, and misogynous social relationships has been monitored and doctored through a set of development programmes and initiatives by the state. I want to suggest however, that participants' narratives of the moral degeneration of the one-room dwelling were in fact attempts to use law and development as resources to chart an alternative future within the city. Participants were aware that discourses of immorality were often instrumental in the removal of slums, and that slum clearance was also related to the development and progress of a modern nation. In joining their voices with the nineteenth century town planners, participants were mapping a politics of entitlement to decent housing. In this politics, the state as the source of law, citizenship and justice was seen as responsible for this material social condition in the camp. Through a violence of law, formulated and enacted by the state, participants saw themselves as illegitimated and informalized into living in 'inhuman' conditions – conditions which many said were worse than how they kept their animals in the villages.

In their mapping of morality, home and family then, were mappings of entitlements from the state for 'decent' living conditions, for privacy and for legalization. Their articulations of the connections between family and modernity can be interpreted as arguments for removal and resettlement into better accommodation by the state. By connecting their 'moral decline' with that of the modern state, they were placing the responsibility of their condition squarely on the state and hence demanding that the state provide appropriate solutions in the form of larger spaces and more privacy for family members. Thus the internalization of the moral pathologies of a single-room squatter home was also related to the desire to become legal citizens of Delhi.

Intimacies, violence and justice in the home

I began this book with the notion that the violence of law is encountered through the corporeality and performance of gendered bodies. While the control of bodies by sovereign power has been well charted in a growing body of Foucauldian analysis, I am more concerned here in how a state based violence of law is related to the violence perpetuated by family within the squatter home. If feminist geography describes the home as a place 'where aggressive forms of misogynous masculinity are often exercised with impunity' (Duncan 1996: 131), then how does violence within the home become ordinary and everyday through specific performative acts of the gendered body? How is conflict in familial relationships shaped from within the gaps of founding and maintaining violence of law?

In discussing communal violence during the partition in India, Das suggests that certain forms of violence experienced and witnessed by participants betray the very purpose of the body itself and hence become unsayable in everyday life. She notes that 'there is a deep moral energy in the refusal to represent some violations of the human body, for these violations are seen as being "against nature", as defining the limits of life itself' (Das 2004: 90). She relates the impossibility of verbalizing violence to the impossibility of working on the memories of this violence within the frame of everyday life. Das was referring to acts of witnessing and remembering violence as spectacular and exceptional forms of bodily violations. Yet certain violations of the body and violence over it are also precisely about its normalization as a part of everyday life. I am referring here to forms of domestic violence that are denied the label of 'violence'; rather articulated as normal and ordinary. In such instances, it is not that those witnessing or perpetuating or experiencing this violence are unable to talk about this; on the contrary they are able to verbalize this violence through the rhetoric of a 'moral' and 'legitimate' form of domesticity.

When I posed questions to participants around domestic conflict, I was reminded time and again of violence as legitimate. I was told that there was a family hierarchy where each member had to be respectful to those above them, that this was only in cases when a husband suspected his wife of infidelity or if the wife went against the husband's wishes. I persisted with follow-up questions – would they then consider violence towards their husbands if they were suspicious of their husband's infidelity? Exasperated, one female participant replied.

> When husband and wife quarrel, these big [middle-class] people come and ask why they are fighting; it is not good to quarrel. They show that there is a fault. Where there are four vessels, there will be between the vessels [bangs two vessels together] see, isn't there a noise? You are educated, no? You won't understand. [Beena]

I consider this narrative as a defining research moment because it highlights the challenges of feminist activism and political action, which often relies upon law to 'protect' women from domestic violence. In this case, the label of domestic violence is taken as an imposition of 'western norms' and middle-class values that are at odds with 'traditional' forms of domesticity. And I was silenced as the voice of the educated middle-class who sought to question the 'mundane' conflicts of their everyday life as 'extraordinary', as 'wrong'. Her identifying me as an 'educated' person resonates with a 'speech act', through which the simultaneous assertion and acceptance of male authority within the home, and the location of this home along class divides, is maintained. The metaphor she used was also distinctly material and gendered, as the use of cooking vessels associated with domesticity and women's gendered roles within the family, and in so doing violence and conflict was also delegated to the everyday, ordinary spaces of domesticity. Further, in excluding my views from her social world, she was rejecting middle-class approaches towards women's empowerment through legal recourses.

This moment prompted me to consider domestic violence in the squatter home as produced from the fear of uncertainty (Appadurai 2006). Discussing large-scale ethnocidal violence in the 1990s, Appadurai suggests that these are mobilized from connections between globalization and uncertainties over incompleteness of identities. This creates 'intolerable levels of anxiety about the relationship of many individuals to state-provided goods – ranging from housing and health to safety and sanitation – since these entitlements are frequently tied to who "you" are and thus who "they" are' (Appadurai 2006: 6). For Appadurai, the violence over bodies that accompanies genocide is produced by a 'surplus of rage' associated with this uncertainty and incompleteness in the differences between minority and majority cultural spaces.

Goldstein (2003) suggests that in a context of violence, the body often offers the only oppositional space. In her study of the Rio slums for example, religious belonging through strict regimes over bodily performance – demeanour, behaviour, attire and speech; formed the only way that women could shield themselves from the violence that affected them. Such body politics were also evident in Ghannam's (2002) study in Cairo where she found that bodily negotiations of religious identity became the only way to deal with the stigma of public housing, the loss of established community networks and the diversity of population in their new location. In Mumbai slums on the other hand, Chatterji and Mehta found that violence during communal riots produced the experience of 'particular dramatic moments when subjectivity is authored and translated' (Chatterji and Mehta 2007: 22). These studies however were all explored at a moment when violence over bodies occurs in public spaces and results in a continuous sense of anxiety and fear of its return.

Within squatter homes however, violence can be seen to relate to the fear of uncertainties around a home in the city. The anxiety that is produced as a result is precisely about their relationship to state provided legal housing and urban services. Justifications of misogynist practices are supported by women through the anxiety over the incompleteness of this home in terms of its legitimacy. While structurally and materially this home was not permanent, the violence over bodies was justified as attempts to sustain the symbolic home of the family. The violence actually seen as illegitimate was the violence enacted upon them by the state through the 'forced opening of the home to the outside' (Chatterji and Mehta 2007: 77), Disciplining of its 'unruly' members by the family then was constructed as a legitimate form of domesticity.

Thus the squatter home was constructed in relational opposition to a rule of law, which attempted to regulate every aspect of private life through values of liberal democracy and gender equality, but at the same time also attempted to 'legally' erase their homes and everyday lives in the city. The world outside the home was often a place of daily humiliation and marginalization; it was also a place where the rule of law was enforced to their disadvantage. Law had marked them as illegal encroachers and pickpockets; they faced regular harassment from different arms of the state – police, municipality and public utility companies. Law was then generally seen as the domain of the powerful – the urban elite and middle-classes. For participants, the rule of law was neither emancipatory nor protective; instead it was seen to be 'invading' the home and inscribing itself upon women's bodies.

The rule of law was therefore challenged to pursue moral and ideological projects of the home and family within the city because this law was seen to marginalize and criminalize squatters and deny them of their very rights to the city. In this context, procedural justice and equality through law could not be relied upon to deliver moral values that were seen to be the basis of producing the affective emotional ties that bound family members to each other during violence, tragedies and crises. Under these circumstances, modernity and law did not form part of their spaces of everyday reference and engagement. It was not surprising then that the 'gender equalizing' approach of personal law within the home was largely resisted as a corrupting modernizing influence of (western) middle-class origin. The uncertainties of their future in the city and anxieties over the 'incompleteness' of home and family produced a normalization of violence even in its extreme forms.

> Some kill themselves with suicide, some just shock themselves to death with electricity; some do this, some do that. It is a state of mind. If you have no money, then it does come into the mind sometimes that all that is left is to commit suicide by hanging. And once you hang yourself, then it is over. There is nothing left of the family. The whole family is ruined. [Beena]

The same notion that presents women as the markers of family honour and femininity also construct women who take their lives as those who have 'failed' to perform their gendered roles and enacted the ultimate betrayal towards their families. The family in this case is not blamed for its failure to 'protect' these women – rather it is the family which is portrayed as the victim of these women's 'betrayals'. As I persisted in asking for reasons behind these suicides, participants squarely put blame on the intolerance of 'modern' women towards poverty, or on women's demands for consumer items (such as cosmetics or new clothes) which could not be satisfied by their unemployed husbands, or conflicts with their partners or in-laws which led them to suicide. Sometimes these suicides would turn out to be foul play and the police would arrest the husband or family members on suspicion. In one such incident, it was rumoured that the woman's parents paid bail for the husband and in-laws who were charged with murdering her. In doing so, the final violence over the body was enacted, a betrayal of those women who even in death were made to uphold their family 'honour'.

As I write this, I am presented with many ethical dilemmas. How can one accept these tragic events as part of everyday domesticities? How is it possible to examine these as anything other than the violence of masculine power and patriarchal authority? Is it possible to resist the theorization of such tragic loss of lives as the inadequacies of rule of law? I say this because apportioning the violence within the home to the failings of law and wider structural shifts in male unemployment would be to absolve its responsibility from the family and locality. On the other hand, to see this as a violent form of moral hegemony of the family would be to deny any responsibility of the state in protecting women within the home. I turn then to Fernandes and Varley (1998) to give a description of this dilemma.

> There is an intimate and albeit contradictory relationship between public policies, decisions and laws concerning the city, on the one hand, and on the other, the social attitudes, conventions and rules of everyday life contributing to the emergence of various forms of 'informal justice' in developing countries. (Fernandes and Varley 1998: 10)

I suggest that the annihilation of the body through suicides became the only possibility for 'informal justice' for women who were tied to the authority of the family. This violent body politics formed the only way to simultaneously reject 'westernized' norms of equality and patriarchal authority for more 'traditional' forms of dissent that were affective, emotional and corporeal. I suggest that this type of dissent formed the 'weapons of the weak' (Scott 1985) – a calculated and not a 'natural' consequence, since beneath the surface of compliance and agreeability there were undercurrents of ideological and symbolic resistance. While violence on and violations of women's bodies within the home and the neighbourhood were quietly normalized as the mundaneness of family life, culture and tradition; threats of self-harm from women were commonplace as strategies to resist the authority of their husbands and in-laws. These threats were within the context of a state law that automatically rushed to incarcerate male family members for accidental death of women within seven years of marriage. These 'speech acts' around self-harm became the only routes for women to construct subversive rather than resistant positions against the moral authority and hegemony of their families. It constructed the annihilation of the body as a form of dissent against family authority and an indication of the rejection of law for conflict resolution within the home. 'Justice' in the home was not desired through western liberal notions of gender equality; rather through a parallel notion of women's abject and corporal rejection of family authority. This explains why Shazia was attempting to break away from her family by asserting her independence as an adult, not to seek justice for her bodily violations through law. She was in fact attempting to seek redress from her family through her absence from home.

'Justice' achieved through such affective methods was not limited to women. Stories circulating around parallel notions of social justice pervaded different kinds of family relations. One that was quite common was the justice meted out to men who did not fulfil their normative roles as breadwinners and head of households. These men were those who had not only abused their wives but also had refused to take responsibility for their children. One male participant, whose daughter suffered this fate, had taken a substantial loan during his daughter's wedding to arrange for the wedding 'gifts'. But when she and her children were rejected by his son-in-law, he refused to approach the police to force him to pay for child custody or to return the gifts. When I asked whether he had considered approaching the *Mahila Mandal* to assist in this case, he replied,

What will the *Mahila Mandal* do? What government service does he [son-in-law] do that they will extract money from him? Suppose we take 5,000 or 10,000 [rupees] from him, he will again come and sit on our heads. As things are now, he cannot enter here, no? He cannot come and sit next to his children. When his children will not acknowledge him tomorrow, what greater punishment can there be? It is hardly necessary that the law punish him. [Sunderlal]

Since this man was seen to have failed in his gendered duties towards his family, justice was seen to have been served when his children would reject him as their father. Law was not seen as appropriate arbitrator of justice because law could not deliver affective or emotional chastisement, which were critical to family values; rather would have only been able to give his children rights to material benefits from an errant father. 'Real' justice was achieved only in the separation from one's own family – when betrayal by a father was returned by rejection from his own children.

Another story that I heard frequently was the form of justice voluntarily sought by a father who had raped his eight year old daughter. When the daughter told her mother about this, the mother asked the neighbours to help who then called the police. But before the police arrived, the father committed suicide as 'repentance' for his misdeeds. The daughter who was in her late teens when I was in the camp was seen to have been 'ruined' for marriage with anyone. That her loss of virginity was not her fault made her a 'victim' in the eyes of participants who narrated this story to me with great sympathy for her. This girl was learning a new vocation as a beautician in order to support herself; and she was also taken to pilgrimages each year by different residents of the camp, who felt that spiritual fulfilment would help her overcome some of the grief and suffering she had faced as a child. Participants however, also spoke of her father with respect, who they felt had 'done the right thing' by taking his own life, because it showed remorse and repentance, in a way that his incarceration by the rule of law would not have. Once again, justice was emotional, affective and violently corporal, rather than delivered through a force of law.

These forms of justice resonate with Caldiera's discussion of crime in Brazil. Caldiera claims that crime is perceived by people through the notion of an 'unbounded body', conceived as the 'locus of punishment, justice and example' (Caldiera 2000: 367). These conceptions are produced in a context which legitimizes interventions on the body with a disregard for individual rights. Participants in the camp argued for a similar retributive justice in terms of violations of the body in public space. Within the home however, bodily violence as justice was gendered – corporal violence was justified towards those seen as 'subordinate' in the familial hierarchy (women or young children), while affective and emotional violence was seen as more effective to punish those with patriarchal authority (men or errant fathers). Thus it was only in public spaces that the body of the molester was seen as 'unbounded and manipulable and pain and abuse are seen as instruments of moral development, knowledge and order' (Caldiera 2000: 372). Within the spaces of home the 'unbounded body' was gendered and sexualized through the logics of domestic order, family morality, and hierarchical authority.

In such parallel notions of social justice, the material and gendered spaces of the home produced particular perceptions of the connections between the family and the state. As I mentioned in Chapter 5, feminist NGOs or the *Mahila Mandal* were seen to separate women from their families instead of protecting families from the injustices of the state. Women who were continually abused by their male partners or repeatedly harassed for dowry by their in-laws were often the strongest proponents of the privacy and sanctity of the home. In our conversations, these women would admit to being raped or beaten by men in their families, and yet would repeatedly assert that these were 'private' matters that had to be dealt with affectively. Separation from the family as a result of domestic violence was 'immoral', and the use of law was seen to be violating the moral geographies of home, family and community. The insertion of law in the home struck at the heart of the 'legitimate' location of women – if families broke down, it dislocated women from their 'rightful' places in the home, and provided the state with the opportunity to emasculate men by incarcerating them.

This rejection of law in the home challenges some of the basic assumptions of feminist theory and activism – that the personal is political. It produces tensions between the discourses and practices of individual feminist rights vs. family values. Women in the camp were seen to be first and foremost carriers and protectors of heterosexual family ideologies and values. The 'true' Indian woman was defined by her capacity to transcend extreme adversity, maintain her honour, provide for her children and care for her family. Under such circumstances, law was seen as an impediment to the permanence of home and domestic life, something that all of them struggled to overcome in other everyday spaces. Maintaining the social permanence of this home in the context of its material annihilation meant the rejection of the law from all spheres of personal and family life.

'These are all family': Extending the boundaries of home

In this chapter so far, I have discussed how the squatter home occupies the spaces between morality and rule of law, development and pathology, empowerment and marginalization, misogyny and gendered subversion. These spaces shape the complex relationship between the unfolding of a violence of law in squatter settlements and the transformation of gendered relationships of power within squatter homes and neighbourhoods. In this unfolding, law begins to have meaning not only through bodily experiments with life and death, but also by re-inhabiting the city through new ways of narrating and performing the 'domestic' body.

The discussion so far in this chapter has focused on the sustenance of the family that one is born into. In other words, the hegemonic moral authority of the family in relation to the rule of law that I discussed, was in relationship to the construction of patriarchal authority. But the home and family that participants discussed often went beyond this. It related also to notions of a fictive family that was present in the immediate surroundings of their camp. This was a reworking of neighbourly relations into kinship structures in the absence of an extended family in the city.

> You have to understand that our natal or marital homes are far away. The people who are here, are our family. They are all family. These are all my sisters and these, my nieces. So it might not be official but people make bonds here, they call each other sisters, mothers, daughters, nieces, aunts, and this is where our true family is. We are not in our hometowns, so here, these are all our family. [Shabbu]

In Shabbu's narrative, the camp was domesticated through the inclusion of strangers into one's extended family. In this domestication, difference was seen as cultural and social, rather than political or structural; and therefore these differences could be reworked to construct a fictive family across religious, caste and ethnic differences. Crucially, this notion of home and family was made in the absence of a biological family, and sustained through different moments of everyday life – personal struggles, collective difficulties, violence and urban crises.

My argument here might appear contradictory to much of the discussions in Chapter 6, where I noted how difference was often internalized through the marginalizing experiences in the spaces of water and sanitation. I noted that as the city enacted different laws to spatially exclude squatters from the infrastructure enjoyed by the legal city, squatters often used gender, caste and religious differences between themselves to internalize the injustices of exclusion from the legal city. Yet, while differences were evoked to include/exclude access to infrastructure, in other aspects of everyday life and in everyday spaces, participants evoked the discourses of kinship 'bonds' and friendships. They repeatedly asserted many positive aspects of living in the camp – neighbourliness, the sharing of happiness and grief and the collective celebration of festivals irrespective of caste, religion and ethnicity. Above all, the overcoming of differences in everyday life was seen as a necessity not choice.

> Now he is a Hindu and I am a Muslim; if I have some work with him, he comes to my house and I don't offer him tea? Similarly if I go to his house and he won't offer me tea? Then tell me how will we work together? In Delhi it's nothing like that. [Salim]

In many ways residents in the camp did not decide who to live in close proximity to, yet it was precisely the spatial 'mixing' of families from different ethnicities, castes and religions that allowed residents to experience the cultural practices, festivals, and food of each other. Participants noted that their positive relationships with neighbours were on account of the ways that 'otherness' was visible within the spaces of the camp. Whereas in the villages their extended families were separated from other caste or religious groups; in the city, their interactions with individuals and families from these groups were entangled with the necessities of social and economic survival. The city imposed spatial proximity – and it produced an acceptance of this proximity. And participants insisted that such acceptance produced belonging and homeliness among those marginalized as 'illegal' citizens.

In another place, I have suggested that openness to difference in squatter settlements is 'constructed through a series of relational constructs – between the city and the left-behind village; between the city and the slum; between the wider urban public sphere and the less public neighbourhood sphere' (Datta 2012: 760). I suggest here that these constructs allowed squatters to intervene meaningfully between the rule of law and its enforcement in the camp. In other words, the construction of a fictive family in the camp which was able to respond to moments of crises through empathy, affection and humanity, was how participants negotiated home and belonging in a city that excluded them by law. Thus domestic life and family remained central to the ways that squatters constructed urban citizenship, and hence the fictive family also became the route to providing solutions during moments of crises. In this process, difference was constructed as ordinary, as part of a legitimate urban domesticity, and not the unknown and fearsome other.

In this construction of domesticity, conflict across neighbours in the streets and lanes were constructed as 'mimicry' of generational hierarchies within the home.

> The first thing is that I've never had a fight … there has never been such a difficulty and if there is any difficulty, we solve it among ourselves. The people here are such, if there is a fight, or any difficulty, we solve it among ourselves, in the neighbourhood. There are the elders, [pointing] she is one of them. If she tells me anything, points out a fault of mine, I will accept that. And there is another person whose word I will accept. She is older than me and I for instance, that woman sitting there, she is younger than me. If I say something, she will listen to me. [Shabbu]

This support provided by neighbours then, continued to operationalize the 'family' as the site of support and mediation. This construction of a wider 'family' in the camp which could be called upon to mediate during conflict, encouraged women to keep their personal struggles within the confines of a wider home in the camp and reject the intrusion of law (through NGOs or *Mahila Mandal*) into their 'private realm'. The camp as an extended space of the home, served to construct a 'family' of sorts, which provided emotional support conditional, yet productive in coping with the number of exclusions and marginalizations in everyday life.

The construction of this fictive family was however also a strategic gendered construction of local social relations in the neighbourhood sphere, which prioritized the bridging of differences across caste and religion as more critical than gender equity. While women were incorporated within this family through their involvement in festivals, rituals and conflict mediation in the neighbourhood sphere, male residents of the camp on the other hand took on the role of 'protectors' of the 'family' during violations over women's bodies or wider urban violence.

Incidents around urban violence, although rare were profoundly memorable. One powerful memory among participants was during the aftermath of the assassination of Indira Gandhi, India's Prime Minister in 1984 by her Sikh bodyguard, in whose wake thousands of Sikhs in the city were murdered. Participants insisted that communal violence had not occurred within their camp because the Hindu and Muslim men and youth made a physical barrier around the camp using campfires and guard posts. Their role was to act as vigilantes and assure outsiders that there were no Sikhs in the camp. This was the final retreat from the city, with the urban public seen as treacherous and murderous; simultaneously as the camp was seen as a safe haven. The camp also became the home for strangers who were protected from a city when the rule of law had collapsed into crime, disorder and chaos.

> It was only during the riots in '84 during the Indira Gandhi [assassination], everywhere when the *Sardars* [Sikhs] were killed, dragged, butchered, arrested, even then nothing happened here. We used to wake up all night and take turns at guarding that no outsider should enter the camp. We hid so many of them [Sikhs] and told them [outsiders] that we don't have any *Sardars* here and saved so many of them. Here, when people live in such close quarters, then they develop bonds of love and affection. They also develop sympathy for each other. [Salim]

I see these processes of domestication as 'subaltern strategies of localization' (Escobar 2001) where a constructed space of a wider home in the camp becomes the site of subversion against the outside world in both social and material ways. Yet this was also an extension of the gendered role of the family to protect its vulnerable members – its women, its children and its minority communities. This patriarchy of the family extended to a patronage and protection of minorities within the camp, because minorities were seen not as outsiders; rather as part of a wider family with whom a home in the city was shared. In this process, difference too was domesticated – in that the other became part of one's fictive family. The camp was thus domesticated through the ideology of home and family even as the state was seen to have failed in its duty to use a force of law to protect and deliver justice to its marginalized citizens.

This extension of family to the spaces of the camp was another aspect of the emotional and affective forms of justice that participants accessed within the 'home'. Such affective bonds were necessary in a city that selectively and punitively enforced the rule of law to the disadvantage and marginalization of the urban poor. These emotional and affective ties between strangers living in spatial proximity were upheld as alternative and informal routes to justice, freedom and legitimacy. Wider notions of home and family became important to maintain common territorial claims and demands for rights to legitimacy, citizenship and social justice from the state. Participants thus constructed their everyday lives in a relational engagement with law, which was seen as corrupt, discriminatory and biased against them. They questioned its liberal nature which incarcerated men if they beat their wives at home, but could not deliver justice when these women were violated outside the home, or when the state demolished squatter settlements, or when the urban public turned against minority communities. Constructing a wider family across social differences was therefore was as much about necessity as about an oppositional stance to the law which had turned its back to them. This wider notion of family in everyday life provided the means to cope with grief, violence and marginality. In a context where their construction as 'illegal urban citizens' pervaded popular imagination, solidarity and support across differences were essential aspects of survival in the city. When the state had closed all doors to the legal city, this wider notion of home and family was the only way to conceive of alternative forms of belonging and legitimacy in the city.

Yet these discourses of neighbourliness and fictive family remained fragile in a context of illegality. As discussed in Chapter 6, differences came to the forefront when wider exclusions from spaces of water and sanitation pushed residents to compete over resources and internalize the notion of dirt and disorder among themselves. Beyond infrastructure, order and peace were maintained in everyday life through the vigilance of RWA leaders who rushed to the scene of conflict as soon as it started brewing. These incidents were not frequent – they occurred once in a few years but the roots of these conflicts continued to simmer under the surface. Everyone agreed that usually these conflicts were initiated by young adults in the camp, usually under the influence of drugs or alcohol. This in itself was located across particular religious bodies since the Muslim participants claimed that Islam forbids the use of intoxicants and therefore those who started this violence were Hindu youths. More crucially, Muslim participants discussed their anxieties over the increasing militarization of Hindu youths through their connections with right-wing Hindu political parties.

> The greatest disease here is, if I am here today, as I said, I am completely clean. And I wish all people to be like this. If some mischievous person drinks and is standing there, I don't like it. And if he is harassing someone, doing something he shouldn't do and he can also see that I am not so weak that he can attack me, what does he do? He brings in a political angle – Hindu-Musalman. [Moinullah]

For Moinullah and many other residents, the 'political angle' was one which was to be feared because it presented the possibility of the camp descending into lawlessness and chaos like those witnessed in Delhi in 1984. Thus participants found different ways to explain conflict across religious difference, but situating it across more 'ordinary' territories and bodies – uncontrolled sexualities, youth cultures, alcoholism, and bullying. In so doing, they attempted to discursively construct neighbourly conflict as 'normal' by shifting its focus from caste and religious bodies to gendered bodies and generational hierarchies. The use of women's or youth bodies as 'ordinary' spaces of conflict as against the potentially 'dangerous' spaces of religious bodies served to transform the 'spectacular' nature of violence into an 'ordinary' domesticity. Yet in this very construction, gendered, caste and youth bodies became the collateral against communalism and intolerance.

Chapter 8
Visions of the Future

Here people wanted everything [land, housing, water, electricity] for free, but this is Delhi. If it is not legal there will be court rulings. [Vikas]

Each time participants asked me if I had any news of their future, I found myself turning the question around. There was a reason why I did this – I felt that since I had no news to offer, my acknowledgement of this would create further anxieties amongst them. Participants saw me as 'official' and even though they accepted that I had no formal connections to state institutions or to NGOs, they refused to believe that in my 'position', I would not be aware of any plans for their resettlement. Most residents believed that I could extract information from these institutions in a way that they could not. But my visits to the Slum Wing had not yielded any specific information about the camp; rather more general information about the strategies for removal of all JJ colonies before the Commonwealth Games. I knew that although participants kept saying that they were sure of being removed before the Games, but I also felt that in practice, this would not be the case.

So I usually replied to their questions with another question – what kind of homes did they want in the future?

Have you ever been to Begampur? Behind Malvianagar [middle-class colony in South Delhi]? There they allotted plots for the *jhuggis*. There, they have taken these things into account. There too there were *jhuggis* lying around like this. So then the minister there placed everybody in a line [plotted development] and then left lanes and roads in between. He got water installed. Then the camp was passed [regularized], and they got freedom [legal rights] to stay there. The *kuccha* [non-metalled] roads were then designed better, repaired and they are now good. They are wide roads, there are water taps on the sides; the plots were made like this. Here, there is no planning. Everybody faces everywhere – north, east, and south. [Manohar]

The precedent which Manohar drew upon to make claims to the future was one of the few examples of a regularized slum carried out by the Delhi Development Authority in the 1980s. The context of the development of Begumpur was markedly different because under the Delhi masterplan, Begumpur was an urban village and not a JJ colony like the camp. Its location in proximity to the historic Begumpur Masjid, built during the 14th century made its regularization and development important for the conservation of a heritage site. While morphologically the earlier Begumpur village might have resembled the camp, it was in fact its different classification under the masterplan which had shaped a different future for its residents. Manohar was not aware of these masterplan differentiations, but his narrative highlighted how well he was aware of the historic processes of demolition, resettlement and regularization that had shaped Delhi's neighbourhoods.

I believe that this precedent suggests how participants also conceived of resettlement – not as exclusion from the city, but as inclusion into the legal city. Part of the reasons behind using precedents was related to the geographical proximity of these precedents to the camp – Begumpur was situated on the other side of the main arterial road through which one accessed the camp, and this was reinforced by the condition of Lakshmipuri resettlement colonies across the main road. Participants like Manohar believed that there was still a legitimate future for them within the city through legal subdivisions undertaken by the state. But they were unaware that such practices were now discontinued, and the best that they could hope for was resettlement in the same location in high-density apartment blocks – a proposal put forth in the new masterplan of Delhi and reinforced by the local MP in Sunita's narrative in Chapter 4. While in 2002, the residents of the camp had expressed their opposition to this form of legalization, this is one of the trade-offs they were resigned to accept if they did not want to be relocated to the outskirts of the city.

I also believe that in the context of their illegality, Manohar's narrative was pointing to another more significant construction of the self. His description of the camp as a place with 'no planning' constructed it in opposition to 'planned order'. Manohar was intent in describing the contrasts between the 'illegal' colonies where houses 'faced everywhere', and the regularized or planned colonies where roads were wide, houses were along a straight line, and people had legal rights to stay there. In differentiating between legal/illegal through primarily morphological and material qualities of these places, Manohar was resonating the modernist logics of the urban planners and middle-classes who have also desired order and sanitization of the city since the colonial period. In demanding legalization then, Manohar was aligning himself to state and middle-class visions of modernity and development.

This brings me to my final point about participants' everyday encounters with law. In their visions of a legitimate future in the city, home was articulated through its material qualities. Home was not described as the site of memory or belonging, or possessing any of its affective or emotional qualities which were present in their descriptions of home-making in the rest of this book. Rather, in all their accounts, the future home was a 'plot', a piece of rectangular land within a legalized colony provided by the state – and this 'plot' was remarkably devoid of any description or association with the family so explicit in the narratives that I presented in Chapters 3 and 6. The resettlement colony too, was articulated primarily in its provision of planned order, facilities and services for its residents. It was narrated through the economies of space and time in their everyday lives.

I want these types of houses measured out the government. In between there should be a park in case there is a wedding or party or death. Like this is the house, this is the wall, and this is the lane. So a cutting [layout] like this and this is the lane and then in between two lanes there is the park. So in that way, if there is a lane here then a house here, and a house here, and then put a bigger road here. So put more houses and put parks close by. And then put a dispensary next to the park. So if it's close by so people don't have to go too far. Then have a hall next to the park so if it's very crowded then people can come and sit outside in the park. ... Then put latrine-bathroom in the same plot, arrange for electricity and water. Like if they install a tube well or something, so water is easily available. Make a bus depot close by so we don't have to go too far. So those kinds of facilities. It would be good for work as well, for example if I have to go out early in the morning then I can catch the bus at eight o'clock. [Zahira]

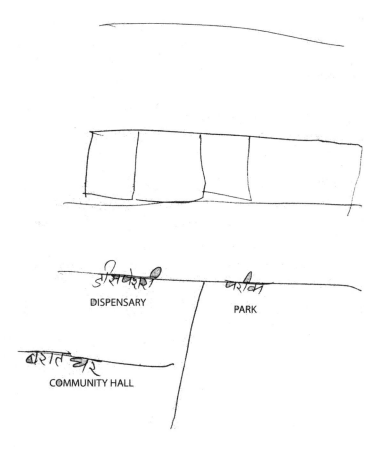

Figure 8.1   Sketch by Zahira of her future home

I suggest that this visual articulation of a home was a political response to the marginalizations in their everyday life. I introduced Zahira earlier in this book as someone who had been one of the key figures of the *Mahila Mandal*. Zahira was well aware through her work with the feminist NGO of the layouts in other resettlement colonies across Delhi. I also believe that Zahira's training by feminist NGOs in the language and rhetorics of the 'practical and strategic gendered needs' (Moser 1989) were reflected in this plan which she drew of her future home. By drawing her future home then Zahira was not only presenting her vision for a future home; but also articulating a vision of material entitlement in the aftermath of the erasure of their homes by a force of law.

And I believe that it was precisely for these reasons that the future home was devoid of any detail beyond a rectangular plot in participants' narratives. In doing so, while the participants demanded their entitlements from the state, they were also outlining the limits of state involvement in their homes. This is consistent with discussions in Chapter 7, where participants rejected the rule of law within the home, and instead sought justice through affective and corporeal body politics. They emphasized the symbolic permanence of the home through a moral authority of the family and explicitly resisted the intrusion of the state within spaces of domesticity. Through her sketch, Zahira charted her aspirations for a moment when the state rule of law would not be required inside the home – a moment when they as legitimate citizens in Delhi would face fewer hardships in their everyday lives. Her demands of a legitimate home from the state then were with regards to its material entitlements and not its symbolic or affective qualities – the latter were seen implicitly as consequences of a legal and permanent material home. In charting the outline of the 'plot' and setting it within the context of a resettlement colony then, Zahira was also drawing the lines beyond which state intervention was not desirable. She was also constructing the symbolic and material boundaries between home and outside; private and public, citizen and state at the moment when they would become 'legitimate' citizens.

Towards conclusions

The state from time to time has redrawn the boundaries of illegality through urban development, through judicial rulings, and through particular political regimes. But the outcomes are often very different across slums and middle-class colonies. In 2005, when the Delhi government under direction of the Supreme Court began to enforce its masterplan by randomly demolishing building 'violations' – buildings that had not conformed to planning regulations even in middle-class neighbourhoods and shopping areas were demolished or shut down. Mass protests from hawkers, retailers and Residents' Welfare Associations in these neighbourhoods following these demolitions led to the formulation of a Delhi Laws (Special Provisions) Bill 2006, which placed a moratorium on all demolitions till the new masterplan went through the consultation process. In

2007, along with the new masterplan, the Delhi government registered nearly 1,600 unauthorized colonies, committing to regularize and provide them with basic infrastructure services. Shortly before the Delhi Assembly elections in 2008, regularization certificates were issued to 1,266 colonies, but only 622 were cleared on the basis of reports submitted by the DDA, MCD, the Archaeological Survey of India, the Ridge department, the Forest department and the Revenue department. Of the 295 colonies in South Delhi however, only 14 were approved by the Delhi government for regularization. This did not include Lakshmipuri Camp. Yet, residents are still convinced that their wait for resettlement will not be very long. The local MP has promised them regularization and resettlement in high-rise apartments in situ. Residents of the Camp believe that will now be their inevitable future.

How do these events shed light on the relationships between law/illegality, between the planned/informal city, and between legal/illegal slums of the city? On the surface they confirm that illegality is not confined to the urban poor. Illegality in terms of building bye-laws and zoning regulations can take many forms and are part of the processes that make an ordinary city. In other words, law and illegality are part of the politics of everyday life in the city. If we dig beneath the surface however, this book has shown that the violence of law in its making and maintaining has different consequences on different social groups and spaces. In the same way that Roy (2005) highlights the role of the state in constructing and maintaining the status quo between the formal and informal city, the state is central to the ways that the illegal city is produced as a space of exception. Three important conclusions can therefore be drawn from the discussions in this book – that legal constructions of the squatter home are inseparable from the question of how the gendered body is constructed and lived in everyday spaces of squatter settlements; that encounters with law and hopes of being 'legal' are central to understanding the ambiguities around social and political action; and finally that a focus on the intimate spaces of home in the illegal city can highlight the complexities of how squatters actually relate to 'the state' and 'the law' in registers of hope, cynicism, apprehension and moral appeals for inclusion into wider society. I take up these points in more detail next.

Legal constructions of home

This book argues that the squatter home is an incomplete gendered project both for the state and its residents – legally, socially and materially. For squatters, the social construction of this home as illegal and temporary allows the state to enter the space of the inside. The mapping, surveying and enumerating of squatter settlements through practices of urban development serve to reinforce its temporality to its residents who have regular encounters with surveyors, officials and bulldozers. The material conditions of the home further challenges notions of permanence, security and privacy through its building materials and technologies, and through its 'porosity' to both social and natural elements. The social, material and gendered constructions of the home and its links with the processes (and hopes) of becoming 'legal', shape how everyday life is lived within squatter settlements.

Critiques of law found in the writings of Benjamin (1978) or Derrida (1992) are insightful about the ways that legal constructions of home are linked to the idea of justice in society. Benjamin poses the question of whether violence can be argued as moral means to a just end. For Benjamin, justice cannot be achieved through a violence of law; rather through a form of divine violence that lies outside of law and delivers divine justice. For Derrida law is an 'authorized force, a force that justifies itself or is justified in applying itself' (Derrida 1992: 925) and has no connection to justice. Derrida is highly critical of Benjamin's notion of justice linked to divine violence, which he argues absolves the perpetrators of violence of any responsibility for their actions. Rather as Derrida would argue, violence is produced from an 'interpretive force' based on the founding or justifying moment of law. Law therefore is not justice; its founding origin only defers the problem of justice. Any interpretation of law therefore could be called 'legal or legitimate in conformity with a state of law, but not justice' (Derrida 1992: 925).

Benjamin's and Derrida's insights on law and justice have immense significance for understanding the encounters with law in Lakshmipuri Camp. Constructions of the squatter home as illegal or extralegal are clearly based on an interpretive force of law. In Delhi since 2001, the legal apparatus has become an agent of often violent forms of spatial restructuring. The demolition of slums and squatter settlements has been legitimized through the authority of the state and the judiciary, but clearly they cannot be seen as just. In this context a few questions remain – what does law mean in everyday life? How are its links with justice sustained? How is justice perceived within a frame of violence in everyday life?

The encounters with law and subsequent negotiations of illegality that I describe in this book suggest that cultural and political contexts are crucial to understanding how the notion and practice of 'justice' works in highly localized, ambiguous and contradictory ways. I have argued that squatters' negotiations of illegality do not necessarily mean that they conflate rule of law with justice. Far from it, participants in the camp recognize that the rule of law often works to their disadvantage and that the middle-classes are able to ignore the law, or worse still use the law against them. Under these circumstances liberal judicial traditions are constructed as unjust and unfair even as in their everyday life, they attempt to work these to their advantage. This suggests that while law is often juridical and repressive, it is also 'the law itself which is generative of the possibilities of change – and seemingly endlessly so' (Robinson 2000: 290).

Encounters with law in the camp involve diverse performances of legal subjecthoods. Squatters do not see themselves as passive recipients of law; rather as agents who can successfully negotiate illegality through the differentiated distributions of entitlements across caste, gender, class and religious identities. Much of the claims that participants make in terms of housing, infrastructure, and resettlement are based upon 'speech acts' – assertions of entitlements from the state, focusing on specific marginalities – as urban poor, as low-castes, as women and as squatters within urban, political, and social contexts. Their politics of entitlements draw upon forms of historicized power that have produced uneven social hierarchies in wider Indian society, but rather than challenging these hierarchies, they internalize structurally defined identities to discursively construct their rights as 'lesser' subjects. Such oblique interpretations of privileges and entitlements are based on linking justice and law (inscribed in the Indian Constitution) and delinking both from the practices and agents of the contemporary state.

How has a gendered intersectional lens helped us understand the violence of law differently? A gendered analysis in this book has shown that while illegality might be a political technique of govenmentality executed through the exceptional spaces of squatter settlements, it is encountered in everyday life through performances of 'public' identity. A gendered intersectional lens has presented the gaps between the ways that the 'problem of slums' have been addressed in urban development and the 'problem of women' have been addressed in social and economic development. And it is in these gaps that squatters begin to 'read' their illegality against the relative security of resettlement; it is under this condition that resettlement becomes a desirable route to the legal city.

This lens has both direct and indirect impacts on the research process. In collecting data one must then look carefully at the links between everyday life and a force of law within everyday spaces, between the legal structure for social justice in the Indian Constitution and its interpretations and experiences in everyday life, between the notion of justice and the notion of immorality and corruption. Using this lens means seeing how court judgments become the criterion for understanding and experiencing illegality in everyday life. It shows how squatters rework their peripheral positions within the city to imagine new 'legal' futures. It also shows how the home becomes a double irony whose erasure is simultaneously desired and resisted. Desired, because the demolition of a current 'impermanent' home is seen as the only route to a 'legal' and permanent future home; and resisted, because of the many ways that the state is seen to have entered the home and taken over its sanctified and gendered spaces.

Participants were convinced that Delhi in the new millennium had no place for *jhuggis*. This conviction in their understanding was an aspect of illegality that they had internalized. This was a marked shift from how they had constructed their relationship with the city in the 1970s and 1980s – where a participant said that they had expected to receive 'everything' for free. In reality, they had never really received anything for free, since much of their everyday lives could only be sustained through bribes to various agents of the state. But since the court rulings, this desire for 'free' benefits had changed into a desire for 'legitimate' housing and basic services. This desire was shaped from knowledge of their eligibility to receive resettlement from the state on account of their prolonged inhabitation in the city. Thus when resettlement seemed to be the only possible outcome, participants in the camp had no option but to wait and hope. This hope was not utopian, rather a negotiation of the system on its own terms. And the continuous articulation of hope became a political response to their marginalization.

Gendered encounters with law

I have suggested in this book that social action in the camp involved a continuous politics of legitimization of power and authority of different collectives over different spaces. The gendered collectives that emerged in the camp suggest how they at different moments of their 'illegality' attempted to produce 'appropriate' forms of political responses. Each of these collectives drew attention to their legitimacy as the 'voice' of the residents through their customary authority, or links with NGOs or through 'mimicry' of democratic processes. These produced particular forms of collective action that were both gendered and differentiated across subjective categories of identification. One of the most dramatic moments of these politics of legitimization was in the breaking of the boundary wall, which was constructed as an act of uncontrolled gendered performance. This highlighted that mimicry and rule-following were seen as 'appropriate' approaches in addressing a violence of law, so much so that these could eliminate the need for transgression and resistance. Yet the incident of the *chowki* (see Chapter 5) challenged this understanding since even 'legitimate' representation could not locate power within the democratic collective. Rather, it highlighted that the location of power was far more complex – it was negotiated through powerful affiliations, gendered subjecthoods and knowledge of the informal workings of law.

The attempts at legitimization of their status as urban citizens through quasi-legal documents or democratic participation or feminist activism can be seen as contradictory to the simultaneous cynicism and disdain that participants express towards the law. Encounters with law were gendered not just in the ways that law structured gendered personal and public laws, but also the ways that these laws produced gendered action and performative modes of politics. I have suggested in this book that these attitudes are consistent in the context of rule of law that is seen as discriminatory and insidious at the least, and incapable of delivering justice to the urban poor at best. It is in this moment of contradiction that the violence of law is also revealed to residents in the camp – for they realize that despite their cynicism, the only way out of continuous anxiety and uncertainty is to become legitimate in the eyes of law. And it is in this context that the desire for resettlement may originate among squatters.

Can we equate the social collectives in the camp, as forms of political societies in the making? Hansen (2001) notes in the context of Mumbai that politics is a permanent performance – both by the state and by its citizens. Using the case of Hindu Radical political parties, Hansen suggests that it is no longer possible to keep a separation between civil and political society since politics infiltrates both the state and informal everyday public spectacles of processions, demonstrations and resistances. This critique of the separation of the state as a rational entity and political society tied in local forms of authority resonates with the different ways that social collectives in the camp attempted to legitimize themselves simultaneously through the state and through customary authority. I found that the work of these collectives is located along the borders of civil and political society, of formality and informality and of law and illegality depending on particular spaces and moments of encounter with the state. While law can become a resource for the feminist collective as in the case of the *chowki*, the defining moment of social action for all the collectives lay in the ambiguous construction of what it meant to be 'political' in response to a force of law. Becoming 'political' was possible in various ways – through performances of legal subjecthoods, through performances of democracy, and through the performances of gendered resistance. These performances however, were located in the more 'public' spaces of the Camp.

Intimate spaces of the illegal city

One of the important conclusions of this book is that encounters with law and subjective negotiations of illegality in public spaces can only be understood from within the intimate spaces of the home where gendered social power and patriarchal authority relate to 'the law' and 'the state' in very different ways. I have argued that from is in those intimate spaces where a large part of the desire to be 'legal' and 'legitimate' originate. As the city attempts to exclude access to everyday places through the rule of law, squatters internalize their exclusions through subjective notions of 'dirt' and 'moral purity' that reinforce entrenched social differences amongst themselves. The different anxieties over bodily transgressions related to cultural practices, domestic life, access to water and defecation, produce particular gender performances within the home that attempts to compensate for a number of exclusions in their lives. As they fear the material erasure of their homes they attempt to make this home symbolically resilient by reasserting the moral authority of the family. Since the rule of law is seen to work against them in the urban public sphere, social justice in the home rejects the rule of law by normalizing violence and subverting authority through a violent body politics. This violence engages with law through its rejection rather than mimicry.

How can we examine encounters with law through narratives of intimacy? What do these stories of marginalized intimacies tell us about the illegal city? How is the intimate made part of a 'public' politics in the city? On the surface, narratives of intimacies in the home shed light on the links between the body of the squatter and body of the nation, between family politics and state politics, and between modernity and development. More subtly however, narratives of (im)possible intimacies also suggest how the body and bodily boundaries redraw the divisions between legal/illegal, moral/immoral, and tradition/modernity; as well as how bodily explorations with violence produce the unmaking of the home. Focusing on internal divisions within the camp and the realm of the intimate encourages us avoid moral divisions between 'the state' on one side, and 'the community' on the other. These divisions run deep in South Asian scholarship because analyses of marginalizations are often focused on processes of governmentality. Examining how the politics within the home is intimately tied to the wider more public politics between the legal and illegal city also avoids the somewhat romantic tendency of conceptualizing squatters as quasi-organic entities united by their shared predicaments.

How do we then study the lives of squatters, hawkers, street peddlers and the like across the world who have been rendered as 'illegal citizens' by law? Should we begin from a position of marginality or difference? Should the body become part of the investigations into the making and unmaking of the illegal city? While the larger story of the often brutal attempts at slum clearing and resettlement of slum dwellers in the global south is well known, I have argued in this book that the relationship between gendered bodies and their 'appropriate' location in 'public' and 'private' spaces deserves focused attention during investigations of illegality and informality in urban development. Legal and cultural constructions of the squatter home are inseparable from the question of how the gendered body is lived and constructed in everyday spaces of squatter settlements. This foregrounding of questions of intimacies within private spaces and their links with the experiences (and hopes) of being 'legal' is a very different approach from asserting the differential experiences of slum women per se and provides different ways to understand marginalization, illegality and urban citizenship.

At the end of this book, a number of questions still remain unanswered. Are there ways that we can propose interventions to improve their lives? Can these go beyond the cause-effect understandings of squatters' desire to resettle that serves state/developmental goals? Can we learn from the more creative potentials of everyday life in the camp around their abilities to negotiate difference, initiate democratic processes and make a home in an exclusionary city? Will changing laws address some of these questions? How do we extend the idea of justice and citizenship from mere legality to lived experience?

Almost seven years after this study was completed, I have found that the question of illegality and its relationship with gender politics in everyday life remain pertinent in the camp even today. Since 2002, residents in the camp have been waiting for resettlement. I have argued throughout this book that this wait is very unsettling – it increases uncertainties, speculations, frustrations and leads to heightened anxieties about a secure and legitimate future. But during this time, squatters have negotiated often successfully with everyday differences as a way of home-making in the exclusionary city. Squatters have also managed to articulate a different kind of politics of entitlement from the state, which relies on an internalization of pathology and marginalization in order to stake moral claims to a 'legal' home in the future. By making these claims, squatters find within marginal spaces and places of the city, the possibility to take partial control of their everyday lives. Thus the internalization of discourses of congestion, overcrowding and 'immorality' of the one-room dwelling provides a rhetorical space from where to demand decent living conditions from the state. The desire for modernity and planned order in resettlement colonies provides a political response to their impending demolition. And the internalization of lower social status provides a political resource for staking 'legitimate' claims to rights under the Indian Constitution. I have shown that it was only by internalizing their 'uninhabitable' home that squatters claimed a 'legal' future from the state and it was by connecting the marginalizing conditions of their everyday intimacies to the 'backwardness' of the Indian nation that they also constructed their intimate spaces as central to the question of modernity and development in India. As one participant said to me,

> The problems that you see here are the same problems that the country faces. And to solve those problems, we need to address these problems first.

Bibliography

Abu-Lughod, J.L. 1971. *Cairo: 1001 Years of the City Victorious*. Princeton: Princeton University Press.

Agamben, G. 2005. *State of Exception*. Chicago: University of Chicago Press.

Ahmed–Ghosh, H. 2004. Chattels of Society: Domestic Violence in India. *Violence against Women*, 10(1), 94–118.

Ali, S. 1990. *Slums within Slums: A Study of Resettlement Colonies in Delhi*. New Delhi: Vikas Publishing House .

Ali, S. 2003. *Environmental Situation of Slums in India*. New Delhi: Uppal Publishing House.

Almitra Patel vs Union of India [F2000] 2SCC 0679 at 686 (Supreme Court of India 2000).

Anthony, A. and Maheswaran, G. 2001. *Social Segregation and Slums: The Plight of Dalits in the Slums of Delhi*. New Delhi: Indian Social Institute.

Appadurai, A. 2001. Deep Democracy: Urban Governmentality and the Horizon of Politics. *Environment and Urbanization*, 13(2), 23–43.

Appadurai, A. 2006. *Fear of Small Numbers: An Essay on the Geography of Anger*. Durham and London: Duke University Press.

Bakker, K. 2005. Archipelagos and Networks: Urbanization and Water Privatization in the South. *Geographical Journal*, 16(9), 328–41.

Banerji, M. 2005. *Provision of Basic Services to Slums and Squatter Settlements*. [Online: Institute of Social Studies Trust]. Available at: www.isst–india.org/PDF/Basic%20Services%20in%20Slums%20–%20Revised%20draft.pdf [accessed: 28 October 2008].

Baviskar, A. 2003. Between Violence and Desire: Space, Power, and Identity in the Making of Metropolitan Delhi. *International Social Science Journal*, 55, 89–100.

Baxi, U. 2005. The (Im)possibility of Constitutional Justice. In *India's Living Constitution*, edited by Z. Hasan, E. Sridharan and R. Sudarshan. Delhi: Anthem Press, 31–63.

Bayat, A. 1997. *Street Politics: Poor People's Movements in Iran*. New York: Columbia University Press.

Bayat, A. and Denis, E. 2000. Who is Afraid of Ashwaiyyat? Urban Change and Politics in Egypt. *Environment and Urbanization*, 12(2), 185–99.

Beall, J. 2006. Dealing with Dirt and the Disorder of Development: Managing Rubbish in Urban Pakistan. *Oxford Development Studies*, 34(1), 81–97.

Beihler, D. D. 2009. Flies, Manure, and Window Screens: Medical Entomology and Environmental Reform in Early-Twentieth-Century US Cities. *Journal of Historical Geography*, 1–11.

Benjamin, W. 1978. Critique of Violence. In *Reflections: Essays, Aphorisms, Autobiographical Writings* by W. Benjamin and P. Demetz, New York: Schocken Books, 277–300.

Bhan, G. 2009. 'This is no Longer the City I once knew'. Evictions, the Urban Poor and the Right to the City in Millennial Delhi. *Environment and Urbanization*, 21(1), 127–42.

Bijulal, M. 2004. *City Slum and the Marginalised: Dalits and Muslims in Delhi Slums.* New Delhi: Indian Social Institute.

Bombay Municipal Corporation vs Olga Tellis [1985] 3 SCC 545(Supreme Court 1985).

Boserup, E. 1970. *Woman's Role in Economic Development.* London: Earthscan Publications Ltd.

Bourdieu, P. 1987. Force of Law: Towards a Sociology of the Juridical Field. *Hastings Law Journal*, 38, 805–853.

Bromley, R. 2004. Power, Property and Poverty: Why De Soto's 'Mystery of Capital' cannot be solved. In *Urban Informality: Transnational Perspectives from the Middle–east, Latin America and South Asia,* edited by A. Roy and N. AlSayyad. Oxford: Lexington Books, 271–288.

Burra, S., Patel, S. and Kerr, T. 2003. Community-Designed, Built and Managed Toilet Blocks in Indian Cities. *Environment and Urbanization*, 15(2), 11–32.

Butler, J. 1999. *Gender Trouble.* London Routledge.

Caldiera, T. 2000. *City of Walls: Crime, Segregation and Citizenship in Brazil.* Berkeley: University of California Press.

Chakrabarty, D. 1992. Provincializing Europe: Postcoloniality and the Critique of History. *Cultural Studies*, 6(3), 324–45.

Chakrabarty, D. 2002. *Habitations of Modernity: Essays in the Wake of Subaltern Studies.* Chicago: University of Chicago Press.

Chameli Singh vs. State of UP [1996] 2 SCC 549(Supreme Court 1996).

Chant, S. 2003. *Female Household Headship and Feminisation of Poverty: Facts, Fiction and Forward Strategies.* New Working Paper Series, Issue 9. Gender Institute, London School of Economics and Political Science, London, UK. (Unpublished).

Chaplin, S. E. 1999. Cities Sewers and Poverty: India's politics of sanitation. *Environment and Urbanization*, 11(1), 145–58.

Chatterjee, P. 1989. Colonialism, Nationalism, and Colonialized Women: The Contest in India. *American Ethnologist*, 16(4), 622–33.

Chatterjee, P. 1993. *Nation and its Fragments: Colonial and Postcolonial Histories.* Princeton: Princeton University Press.

Chatterjee, P. 1998. Beyond the Nation? Or Within? *Social Text*, 16(39), 57–69.

Chatterjee, P. 2004. *Politics of the Governed: Reflections on Popular Politics in Most of the World.* New York: Columbia.

Chatterji, R. And Mehta, D. 2007. *Living with Violence: An Anthropology of Events and Everyday Life.* New Delhi: Routledge.

Cities Alliance. 1999. *Cities without Slums Action Plan*. [Online]. Available at: www.citiesalliance.org/citiesalliancehomepage.nsf/Attachments/Cities+With out+Slums+Action+Plan/$File/brln_ap.pdf [accessed: 9 July 2009].

Comaroff, J. and Comaroff, J. 2006. *Law and Disorder in the Postcolony.* Chicago and London: University of Chicago Press.

Craddock, S. 1995. Sewers and Scapegoats: Spatial Metaphors of Small Pox in Nineteenth Century San Francisco. *Social Science Medical*, 41(7), 957–68.

Das, V. 2004. The Signature of the State: The paradox of illegibility. In *Anthropology in the Margins of the State*, edited by V. Das and D. Poole. Oxford: James Currey, 225–52.

Das, V. and Poole, D. Eds. 2004. *Anthropology in the Margins of the State*. Oxford: James Currey.

Datta, A. 2007. 'Samudayik Shakti': Working-Class Feminism and Social Organisation in Subhash Camp, New Delhi. *Gender, Place and Culture*, 14(2), 215–31.

Datta, A. 2008. Architecture of Low-income Widow Housing: 'Spatial Opportunities' in Madipur, West Delhi. *Cultural Geographies*, 231–53.

Datta, A. 2012. Mongrel City: Cosmopolitan neighbourliness in a Delhi Squatter Settlement. *Antipode*, vol. 44(3), 745–63. .

Davis, M. 2006. *Planet of Slums*. London: Verso.

De Soto, H. 2000. *The Mystery of Capital: Why capitalism triumphs in the West and fails everywhere else*. Bantham Press: London.

De Soto, H. 1989. *The Other Path*. London: IB Tauris.

deCerteau, M. 1984. *The Practice of Everyday Life*. Berkeley: University of California Press.

Department of Urban Development. 2006. *Delhi City Development Plan under JNNURM*. [Online: Centre for Civil Society]. Available at: http://ccs.in/delhicdp.asp [accessed: 10 November 2011].

Derrida, J. 1992. Force of Law: The 'Mystical Foundation of Authority'. In *Deconstruction and the Possibility of Justice,* edited by D. Cornell, M. Rosenfeld and D.G. Carlson. London: Routledge, 3–67.

Douglas, M. 1966. *Purity and Danger: An Analysis of the Concepts of Pollution and Taboo*. New York: Praeger.

Duncan, N. 1996. Renegotiating Gender and Sexuality in Public and Private Spaces. In *Bodyspace: Destabilizing Geographies of Gender and Sexuality*, by N. Duncan. London and New York: Routledge, 127–45.

Dupont, V. 2008. Slum Demolitions in Delhi since the 1990s: An Appraisal. *Economic and Political Weekly*, July, 79–87.

Dutta, V., Chander, S. and Srivastava, L. 2005. Public Support for Water Supply Improvements: Empirical Evidence from Unplanned Settlements of Delhi, India. *The Journal of Environment and Development*, 14(4), 439–62.

Escobar, A. 2001. Culture sits in Places: Reflections on Globalism and Subaltern Strategies of Localization. *Political Geography*, 20, 139–74.

Fernandes, E. and Varley, A. 1998. *Illegal Cities: Law and Urban Change in Developing Countries*. London: Zed Books.

Fernandes, L. 2006. *India's New Middle-Class: Democratic Politics in an Era of Economic Reform*. Minneapolis, MN: University of Minnesota Press.

Future Cities and Habitat II. 1996. *Environment and Urbanization*, 8(1), 3–11.

Galanter, M. 1984. *Competing Equalities*. Berkeley, CA: University of California Press.

Galanter, M. 1988. Law: Judicial and Legal Systems of India. In *Encyclopedia of Asian History* by A. T. Embree. New York: Charles Scribner's Sons, 411–14.

Galanter, M. 2000. Fifty years on. In *Supreme but not Infallible: Essays in Honour of the Supreme Court of India,* edited by. J. Kirpal et. al. New Delhi: Oxford University Press, 57–65.

Galanter, M. and Krishnan, J. K. 2004. 'Bread For The Poor': Access to Justice and Rights of the Needy in India. *Hasings Law Journal*, 55(4), 789–834.

Gandy, M. 2005. Learning from Lagos. *New Left Review*, 33, 37–52.

Ghannam, F. 2002. *Remaking the Modern: Space, Relocation and the Politics of Identity in a Global Cairo*. Berkeley: University of California Press.

Ghertner, A. 2008. Analysis of New Legal Discourse behind Delhi's Slum Demolitions. *Economic and Political Weekly*, May, 57–66.

Ghertner, A. 2011. Rule by Aesthetics: World-Class City Making in Delhi. In *Worlding Cities: Asian Experiments and the Art of Being Global*, edited by A. Roy and A. Ong, Oxford: Blackwell, 279–306.

Ghosh, A. K. 2008. Changing Livelihood Patterns of Slum Dwellers in Delhi: From a Squatter Settlement to a Resettlement Colony. *Social Change*, 38(3), 434–57.

Gilbert, A. 2002. On the Mystery of Capital and the Myths of Hernando De Soto: What Difference Does Legal Title Make? *International Development Planning Review*, 24(1), 1–19.

Goldstein, D. M. 2003. *Laughter out of Place: Race, Class, Violence and Sexuality in a Rio Shantytown*. Berkeley: University of California Press.

Gooptu, N. 2001. *The Politics of the Urban Poor in Early Twentieth-Century India*. Cambridge: Cambridge University Press.

Government of India. 2001. *Valmiki Ambedkar Awas Yojana.* . [Online: Ministry of Urban Development] Available at: www.udarunachal.in/guidelines/vambay.pdf [accessed: 10 November 2011].

Government of India. 2010. *Rajiv Awas Yojana*. [Online: Ministry of Housing and Urban Poverty Alleviation] Available at: www.indiaenvironmentportal.org.in/files/RAYGuidelines–English.pdf [accessed: 3 December 2010].

Guloksuz, E. 2002. Negotiation of Property Rights in Urban Land in Istanbul. *International Journal of Urban and Regional Research*, 26(2), 462–76.

Gulyani, S. and Bassett, E.M. 2007. Retrieving the Baby from the Bathwater: Slum Upgrading in Sub-Saharan Africa. *Environment and Planning C*, 25, 486–515.

Gupta, A. 2006. Blurred boundaries: The Discourse of Corruption, The Culture of Politics and the Imagined State. In *The Anthropology of the State: a Reader*, edited by A. Sharma and A. Gupta. Oxford: Blackwell, 211–42.

Hansen, T. B. 2001. *Wages of Violence: Naming and Identity in Postcolonial Mumbai*. Princeton: Princeton University Press.

Hansen, T. B. and Stepputat, F. 2001. *States of Imagination: Ethnographic explorations of the postcolonial state*. Durham and London: Duke University Press.

Hasan, Z., Sridharan, E. and Sudharshan, R. Eds. 2005. *India's Living Constitution: Ideas, Practices, Controversies*. London: Anthem Press.

Holston, J. 2008. In*surgent Citizenship: Disjunctions of Democracy and Modernity in Brazil*. Princeton: Princeton University Press.

Holston, J. and Appadurai, A. 1996. Cities and Citizenship. *Public Culture*, 8, 187–204.

Hussain, N. 2003. *Jurisprudence of Emergency: Colonialism and the Rule of Law*. Ann Arbor, MI: University of Michigan Press.

Illich, I. 1986. *H₂O and the Waters of Forgetfulness*. London: Marion Boyars.

Indian Constitution. 1950.

Jagmohan. 2005. *Soul and Structure of Governance in India*. Delhi: Allied Publishers.

Jha, S., Rao, V. and Woolcock, M. 2007. Governance in the Gullies: Democratic Responsiveness and Leadership in Delhi's Slums. *World Development*, 35(2), 230–46.

John, M.E. 2008. *Women's Studies in India: A Reader*. New Delhi: Penguin.

Joyce, P. 2003. *The Rule of Freedom: Liberalism and the Modern City*. London: Verso.

Kabeer, N. 1994. *Reversed Realities: Gender Hierarchies in Development Thought*. London: Verso.

Kabeer, N. 1999. Resources, Agency, Achievements: Reflections on the Measurement of Women's Empowerment. *Development and Change*, 30(3), 435–64.

Kapadia, K. 2002. *The Violence of Development: The Politics of Identity, Gender and Social Inequalities in India*. New Delhi: Kali for Women.

Kapur, R. and Cossman, B. 1996. *Subversive Sites: Feminist Engagements with Law in India*. New Delhi: Sage.

Kaviraj, S. 1997. Filth and the Public Sphere. *Public Culture*, 10(1), 83–113.

Kaviraj, S. 2000. Modernity and Politics in India. *Daedalus*, 129(1), 137–62.

Kaviraj, S. 2005. On The Enchantment of the State: Indian Thought on the Role of the State in the Narrative of Modernity. *European Journal of Sociology*, 46(2), 263–96.

Khilnani, S. 2005. The Indian Constitution and Democracy. In *India's Living Constitution: Ideas, Practices, Controversies*, edited by Z. Hasan, E. Sridharan, and R. Sudarshan. London: Anthem Press, 64–82.

190 *The Illegal City*

Kumar, A. 2006. Condoning Unplanned Development. *Economic and Political Weekly*, 4105–8.

Kundu, A. 2004. Provision of Tenurial Security for the Urban Poor in Delhi: Recent Trends and Future Perspectives. *Habitat International*, 259–74.

Lahiri–Dutt, K. 2006. *Fluid Bonds: Views on Gender and Water*. Kolkata: Stree Publishers.

Legg, S. 2007. *Spaces of Colonialism: Delhi's Urban Governmentalities*. Oxford: Blackwell.

Linden, J. V.1997. On Popular Participation in a Culture of Patronage. *Environment and Urbanization*, 81–90.

Magar, V. 2003. Empowerment Approaches to Gender-Based Violence: Women's Courts in Delhi. *Women's Studies International Forum*, 26(6), 509–23.

McFarlane, C. 2008. Sanitation in Mumbai's Informal Settlements: State, 'Slum' and Infrastructure. *Environment and Planning A*, 40(1), 88–107.

McKenzie, K. 2003. Dogs and the Public Sphere: The Ordering of Social Space in Early Nineteenth–Century Cape Town. *South African Historical Journal*, 48, 235–251.

Mehta, P. B. 2005. The Inner Conflict of Constitutionalism: Judicial Review and the Basic Structure. In *India's Living Constitution: Ideas, Practices, Controversies,* edited by Z. Hasan, E. Sridharan, and R. Sudarshan. New Delhi: Anthem Press, 179–206.

Menon, N. 2004. *Recovering Subversion: Feminist Politics beyond the Law*. Urbana and Chicago: University of Illinois Press.

Menon–Sen, K. and Bhan, G. 2008. *Swept off the Map: Surviving Eviction and Resettlement in Delhi*. Delhi: Yoda Press.

Ministry of Urban Development.1991. *Annual Report 1990–91*. [Online] Available at: urbanindia.nic.in/moud/quickaccess/Office_Files/main.htm. [accessed: 10 October 2008]

Mohan, D. 2004. Re–imagining Community. *Journal of Contemporary Ethnography*, 33(2), 178–217.

Moser, C. 1989. Gender Planning in the Third World: Meeting Practical and Strategic Gender needs. *World Development*, 17(11), 1799–825.

Moser, C. and Peake, L. 1987. *Women, Human Settlements and Housing*. London: Tavistock Publications.

Muralidhar, D. S. 2004. ECSR: An Indian Response to the Justiciability Debate. In *Economic, Social and Cultural Rights in Practice*, by Y.P. Ghai and J. Cottrell. London: Interights, 23–32.

Nagar, R. 2000. Mujhe Jawab Do! (Answer Me!): Women's Grassroots Activism and Social Spaces in Chitrakoot, India. *Gender Place and Culture*, 7(4), 341–62.

Nandy, A. 2002. *Time Warps: The Insistent Politics of Silent and Evasive Pasts*. Delhi: Permanent Black.

Navlakha, G. 2000. Urban Pollution: Driving Workers to Desperation. *Economic and Political Weekly*, 35(12).

Neuwirth, R. 2006. *Shadow Cities: A Billion Squatters: A New Urban World*. New York: Routledge.

Nigam, A. 2002. Dislocating Delhi: A City in the 1990s. In *Sarai Reader 02: Cities of Everyday Life*, edited by R. Vasudevan, J. Bagchi, R. Sundaram, M. Narula, G. Lovink, and S. Sengupta. Delhi: Sarai. 40–46.

Nijman, J. 2008. Against the Odds: Slum Rehabilitation in Neo–Liberal Mumbai. *Cities*, 25, 73–85.

NIUA. 2003. *Evaluation of Jan Suvidha Complexes and Bastee Vikas Kendras in Delhi*. Delhi: Planning Department, Govt. of N.C.T. Delhi.

Page, B. 2005. Pay for Water and the Geography of Commodities. *Transactions of the Institute of British Geographers*, 30, 293–306.

Parnell, S. 2003. Race, Power and Urban Control: Johannesburg's Inner City Slum-yards 1910–1923. *Journal of South African Studies*, 29(3).

Patel, S., d'Cruz, C. and Burra, S. 2002. Beyond Evictions in a Global City: People–Managed Resettlement in Mumbai. *Environment and Urbanization*, 14(1), 159–72.

Perlman, J. 1976. *The Myth of Marginality: Urban Poverty and Politics in Rio de Janeiro*. Berkeley, CA: University of California Press.

Planning Commission. 1988. *National Housing and Habitat Policy 1998*. [Online: Ministry of Urban Affairs and Employment, Government of India] Available at: www.planningcommission.nic.in [accessed: 20 January 2003].

Planning Commission. 2001. *Indian Planning Experience: A Statistical Profile*. [Online: Planning Commission, Government of India] Available at: http://planningcommission.nic.in [accessed: 5 February 2003].

Planning Commission, 2002. *Report of the Committee on Problems of Slums in Delhi*. Delhi: Government of India.

Planning Commission. 2005. *National Urban Housing and Habitat Policy*. [Online: Planning Commission, Government of India] Available at: mhupa. gov.in/policies/duepa/DraftNHHP2005-9.pdf [accessed: 10 November 2011]

Planning Department. 2001. *Economic Survey of Delhi 2001–2002*. [Online: Delhi Planning Department] Available at delhiplanning.nic.in/Economic%20Survey/ Ecosur2001-02/PDF/chapter14.PDF [accessed: 20 January 2010].

Poole, D. 2004. Between Threat and Guarantee. In *Anthropology in the Margins of the State,* edited by V. Das and D. Poole. Oxford: James Currey, 35–66.

Prashad, V. 2001. The Technology of Sanitation in Colonial India. *Modern Asian Studies*, 35(1), 113–55.

Rajan, R.S. 1993. *Real and Imagined Women: Gender, Culture and Postcolonialism*. London and New York: Routledge.

Rajan, R.S. 2003. *Scandal of the State: Women, Law and Citizenship in Postcolonial India*. Durham and London: Dule University Press.

Ramanathan, U. 2005. Demolition Drive. *Economic and Political Weekly*, 3607–12

Ray, R. 1999. *Fields of protest: Women's Movements in India*. Minneapolis: University of Minnesota Press.

Roberts, B. 1979. *Cities of Peasants: The Political Economy of Urbanization in the Third World.* Beverly Hill, CA: Sage Publications.

Rose, G. 1997. Engendering the Slum: Photography in East London in the 1930s. *Gender, Place and Culture*, 4(3), 277–300.

Rose, N. 1987. Beyond the Public/Private Division: Law, Power and the Family. *Journal of Law and Society*, 14(1), 61–76.

Rosencranz, A. and Jackson, M. 2003. The Delhi Pollution Case: The Supreme Court of India and the Limits to Judicial Power. *Columbia Journal of Environmental Law*, 28, 223–54.

Roy, A. 2003a. *City Requiem, Calcutta: Gender and the Politics of Poverty.* Minnesota, Minneapolis: University of Minnesota Press.

Roy, A. 2003b. Paradigms of Propertied Citizenship: Transnational Techniques of Analysis. *Urban Affairs Review*, 38(4), 463–91.

Roy, A. 2005. Urban Informality: Towards an epistemology of planning. *Journal of the American Planning Association*, 71(2).

Roy, A. 2009. Civic Governmentality: The Politics of Inclusion in Beirut and Mumbai. *Antipode*, 41(1), 159–79.

Roy, A. and AlSayyad, N. 2004. *Urban Informality: Transnational Perspectives from the Middle–East, Latin America, and South Asia.* Minneapolis, MN: University of Minnesota Press.

Saberwal, S. 2005. Introduction. In *India's Living Constitution: Ideas, Practices, Controversies*, edited by Z. Hasan, E. Sridharan, and R. Sudarshan. London: Anthem Press, 1–30.

Sachs, W. 1999. *Development Dictionary: A Guide to Knowledge as Power.* London: Zed Books.

Santos, B.D. 1992. Law, State and Urban Struggles in Recife, Brazil. *Social and Legal Studies*, 1, 235–54.

Sanyal, B., and Mukhija, V. 2001. Institutional Pluralism and Housing Delivery: A case of unforeseen conflicts in Mumbai, India. *World Development*, 2043–57.

Scott, J.1985. *Weapons of the Weak: Everyday Forms of Peasant Resistance.* Yale, MA: Yale University Press.

Scott, J. 1998. *Seeing like a State.* New Haven and London: Yale University Press.

Secor, A. 2003. Belaboring gender: the spatial practice of work and the politics of 'making do' in Istanbul. *Environment and Planning A*, 35, 2209–27.

Secor, A. 2004. 'There is an Istanbul That Belongs to Me': Citizenship, Space and Identity in the City. *Annals of the Association of American Geographers*, 94(2), 352–68.

Shaban, A. and Sharma, R.N. 2007. Water Consumption Patterns in Domestic Households in Major Cities. *Economic and Political Weekly*, 2190–97.

Sharan, A. 2005. New Delhi: Fashioning an Urban Environment through Science and Law. In *Sarai Reader 2005: Bare Acts*, edited by M. Narula, S. Sengupta, J. Bagchi and G. Lovink. New Delhi: Sarai, 69–76.

Sharma, B.K., and Krishna, N.T. 2007. *Employment – Unemployment Situation in Million Plus Cities of India: A Critical Analysis.* [Online: Government of NCT of Delhi] Available at: www.delhi.gov.in/DoIT/DES/Publication/paper61.pdf [accessed: 01 May 2010]

Silvey, R. 2003. Spaces of protest: gendered migration, social networks, and labor activism in West Java, Indonesia. *Political Geography*, 22, 129–55.

Simone, A. 2004. *For the City Yet to Come: Changing African Life in Four Cities*. London: Duke University Press.

Slum Areas Act 1956. [Online: Helpline Law, Indian Bare Acts]. Available at: www.pon.nic.in/rti/slumcle/file2.pdf [accessed: 10 November 2011].

Srinivas, M. S.1957. Caste in Modern India. *The Journal of Asian Studies*, 16(4), 529–48.

Staeheli, L.1996. Publicity, Privacy and Women's Political Action. *Environment and Planning D*, 14, 601–19.

Sultana, F. 2011. Dying for Water, Dying from Water: Gendered Geographies of the Drinking Water Crisis in Bangladesh. In *Gendered Geographies: Interrogating Space and Place in South Asia*, edited by S. Raju. Delhi: Oxford University Press, 293–306.

Tarlo, E. 2001. Paper Truths: the Emergency and Slum Clearance through Forgotten Files. In *The Everyday State and Society in Modern India*, edited by V.B. Christopher John Fuller. London: C Hurst and Co Publishers Ltd, 68–90.

Tarlo, E. 2003. *Unsettling Memories: Narratives of Emergency in Delhi*. London: Hurst and Co.

Turner, J.1967. Barriers and Channels for Housing Development in Modernizing Countries. *American Institute of Planners*, 32, 167–81.

UN-Habitat. 2003. *Challenge of the Slums: Global Report on Human Settlements*. London: Earthscan.

United Nations Chronicle. 1988. *Global Strategy for Shelter to the Year 2000*. [Online] Available at: findarticles.com/p/articles/mi_m1309/is_n3_v25/ai_6811552 [accessed: 13 September 2007].

Varley, A. 1998. The Political Uses of Illegality: Evidence from Urban Mexico. In *Illegal Cities: Law and Urban Change in Developing Countries*, edited by E. Fernandes and A. Varley. London: Zed Books, 172–90.

Varley, A. 2002. Private or Public: Debating the Meaning of Tenure Legalisation. *International Journal of Urban and Regional Research*, 26(3), 449–61.

Verma, G.D. 2002. *Slumming India: A Chronicle of Slums and their Saviours*. Delhi: Penguin.

Veron, R. 2006. Remaking Urban Environments: The political ecology of air pollution in Delhi. *Environment and Planning A*, 38, 2093–109.

Wadhwa. K. 1988. Housing Programmes for Urban Poor: Shifting Priorities. *Economic and Political Weekly*, August 20.

Wegelin-Schuringa, M. and Kodo, T. 1997. Tenancy and Sanitation Provision in Informal Settlements in Nairobi: Revisiting the public latrine option. *Environment and Urbanization*, 9(2), 181–90.

Williams, R.V. 2006. *Postcolonial Politics and Personal Laws*. New Delhi: Oxford University Press.

Yeoh, B.S. 2003. *Contesting Space in Colonial Singapore: Power Relations and the Urban Built Environment*. Singapore: Singapore University Press.

Zizek, S. 1991. *For They Know Not What They Do: Enjoyment as a Political Factor*. London: Verso.

Index